The Big Keto Diet Cookbook for Beginners

2000+ Days Super Easy、 Low Carb & Low Sugar Keto
Recipe Book - Partner in Melting Away Unwanted Fat |
30 Day Meal Plans for Eating Better

Bojana Miletic

Table of Contents

INTRODUCTION

Welcome to the realm of The Big Keto Diet Cookbook for Beginners, where the art of low-carb cooking meets the pleasure of savoring every bite. In this cookbook, we invite you to embark on a flavorful journey that transcends dietary restrictions, turning the challenges of carb-conscious living into a celebration of culinary creativity.

The Big Keto Diet Cookbook for Beginners isn't just a cookbook; it's a passport to a world where every recipe is a chapter, every ingredient a character, and your kitchen becomes the stage for a gastronomic adventure. We believe that a ketogenic lifestyle is more than just a diet; it's a culinary odyssey that unfolds in your very own kitchen.

What to Expect:

1. Flavors That Dance on Your Palate:

Each recipe in "Keto Kitchen Chronicles" is a symphony of flavors carefully composed to delight your taste buds. From savory to sweet, we've embraced the challenge of low-carb living without compromising on taste.

2. Creative Carb Substitutes:

Say goodbye to feeling deprived. Our cookbook is a treasure trove of ingenious carb substitutes that elevate your favorite dishes while keeping them firmly within the bounds of keto goodness.

3. Simple Techniques, Extraordinary Results:

You don't need to be a culinary maestro to create keto masterpieces. "Keto Kitchen Chronicles" simplifies techniques, making every recipe accessible, whether you're a seasoned chef or a kitchen novice.

4. Balancing Act:

We understand that a successful ketogenic lifestyle is all about balance. Our recipes strike the perfect equilibrium of healthy fats, quality proteins, and low-carb vegetables, ensuring you stay on track without sacrificing enjoyment.

5. Mindful Eating, Joyful Living:

Beyond the recipes, we've woven in tips for mindful eating, encouraging you to savor every moment of your culinary journey. Because keto living isn't just about what you eat; it's about the joy you find in each flavorful bite.

Your Culinary Expedition Begins:

Prepare to be captivated by the aromatic tales, the rich narratives of each keto-friendly dish. The Big Keto Diet Cookbook for Beginners isn't just a cookbook; it's an invitation to transform your kitchen into a realm where culinary tales unfold, where every meal is a chapter, and you are the master storyteller.

Here's to the adventure that awaits within The Big Keto Diet Cookbook for Beginners – where every recipe is a revelation, every taste a triumph, and the joy of low-carb living is a journey worth savoring. Let the culinary escapade commence!

Chapter ❶
Understanding Keto Basics

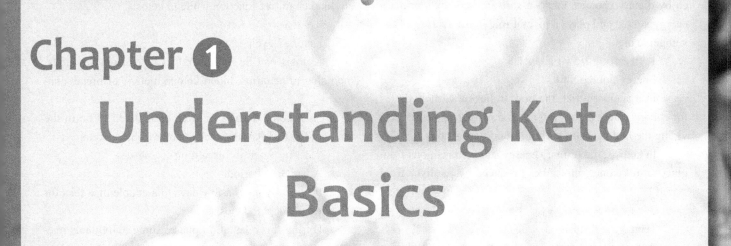

Decoding Ketosis

Ketosis: Unlocking the Power of Metabolic Transformation

At the heart of the ketogenic diet lies a fascinating metabolic state called ketosis. This natural process, driven by dietary choices, marks a shift in the body's primary energy source and plays a pivotal role in the success of the ketogenic diet.

1. Breaking Down Ketosis:

Energy Source Shift:

In a standard diet, the body relies on carbohydrates for energy. These carbs are broken down into glucose, providing the fuel needed for various bodily functions.

In ketosis, the primary energy source transitions from glucose to ketones, molecules produced by the liver from stored fat.

2. Carbohydrate Restriction:

Triggering Ketosis:

Achieving ketosis requires a significant reduction in carbohydrate intake. Typically, the daily carb intake is limited to 20-50 grams, forcing the body to seek alternative fuel sources.

The decrease in available glucose prompts the body to tap into its fat stores for energy.

3. The Role of Fats:

Fat Metabolism:

With reduced carbohydrate intake, the body turns to fats for fuel. Fatty acids, released from stored fat or dietary fats, are transported to the liver.

The liver then transforms these fatty acids into ketones through a process called ketogenesis.

4. Ketones as Energy:

Efficient Fuel Source:

Ketones, specifically beta-hydroxybutyrate (BHB), acetoacetate, and acetone, become the primary fuel for cells, including the brain.

The brain, traditionally reliant on glucose, adapts seamlessly to utilizing ketones as an energy source.

5. Benefits of Ketosis:

Weight Loss:

Ketosis promotes the breakdown of stored fat for energy, facilitating weight loss and a reduction in body fat percentage.

Stable Blood Sugar:

The low-carb nature of the ketogenic diet helps stabilize blood sugar levels, aiding individuals with insulin resistance or diabetes.

Sustained Energy:

Ketones offer a consistent and efficient energy source, reducing energy fluctuations associated with glucose spikes.

Mental Clarity:

Many individuals report improved mental clarity, focus, and cognitive function while in ketosis.

6. Measuring Ketosis:

Ketone Levels:

Ketosis can be monitored using various methods, including urine strips, blood ketone meters, or breath analyzers.

Nutritional ketosis is often considered to be in the range of 0.5 to 3.0 millimoles per liter of blood ketones.

7. Entering and Sustaining Ketosis:

Adaptation Period:

It typically takes a few days to a couple of weeks for the body to adapt to ketosis.

During this adaptation phase, some individuals may experience symptoms known as the "keto flu," including fatigue, headaches, and irritability.

Sustainability:

Once adapted, maintaining ketosis involves continued adherence to a low-carb, high-fat diet.

Regular monitoring, adjustments, and a commitment to the dietary principles of the ketogenic lifestyle are essential for sustained ketosis.

8. Individual Variability:

Bio-Individuality:

The speed at which individuals enter ketosis and the level of ketones produced can vary based on factors such as metabolism, activity level, and genetics.

Understanding one's unique response to the ketogenic diet is crucial for optimizing results.

In essence, ketosis represents a metabolic shift that empowers the body to utilize fats efficiently for energy, offering a wealth of benefits beyond weight loss. As the cornerstone of the ketogenic diet, ketosis unlocks a powerful mechanism for transforming the body's relationship with food and fuel, paving the way for sustained well-being and vitality.

Essential Ingredients

Stocking your pantry with keto-friendly staples is essential for successful and enjoyable low-carb cooking. Here's a list of must-have pantry items for keto cooking:

1. Healthy Fats and Oils:

Extra Virgin Olive Oil

Coconut Oil

Avocado Oil

Grass-Fed Butter or Ghee

MCT Oil (Medium-chain triglycerides)

2. Low-Carb Flours and Baking Ingredients:

Almond Flour

Coconut Flour

Psyllium Husk Powder

Baking Powder

Xanthan Gum

3. Sugar Substitutes:

Stevia

Erythritol

Monk Fruit Sweetener

Allulose

4. Nuts and Seeds:

Almonds

Walnuts

Pecans

Macadamia Nuts

Chia Seeds

Flaxseeds

5. Low-Carb Sweeteners:

Sugar-Free Chocolate Chips

Cocoa Powder (unsweetened)

Vanilla Extract

6. Protein Sources:

Canned Tuna or Salmon

Canned Chicken

Grass-Fed Beef Jerky

Protein Powder (whey or plant-based)

7. Low-Carb Condiments and Sauces:

Mayonnaise (sugar-free)

Mustard

Sugar-Free Ketchup

Soy Sauce or Tamari (gluten-free)

Hot Sauce

8. Canned Goods:

Coconut Milk (full-fat, unsweetened)

Tomato Paste (no added sugar)

Diced Tomatoes (no added sugar)

Chicken or Beef Broth (no added sugar)

9. Low-Carb Pasta and Rice Alternatives:

Shirataki Noodles

Zucchini Noodles (Zoodles)

Cauliflower Rice

10. Vinegars and Spices:

Apple Cider Vinegar

Balsamic Vinegar (in moderation)

Herbs and Spices (such as garlic powder, onion powder, paprika, cumin, and turmeric)

Salt (sea salt, Himalayan salt)

11. Canned Vegetables:

Canned Spinach

Canned Green Beans

Canned Artichoke Hearts

12. Coconut Products:

Unsweetened Shredded Coconut

Coconut Milk (full-fat, unsweetened)

Coconut Aminos (soy sauce alternative)

13. Nut Butters:

Almond Butter

Peanut Butter (unsweetened, if tolerated)

14. Low-Carb Snacks:

Pork Rinds

Beef Jerky (watch for added sugars)

Cheese Crisps

Dark Chocolate (85% or higher cocoa content)

15. Non-Dairy Milk Alternatives:

Almond Milk (unsweetened)

Coconut Milk (unsweetened)

Hemp Milk (unsweetened)

Having these keto-friendly pantry staples on hand will make it easier to whip up delicious and nutritious low-carb meals and snacks without compromising your dietary goals.

Cooking Methods for Success

Mastering keto kitchen techniques is key to creating flavorful and satisfying low-carb meals. Here are essential techniques for successful keto cooking:

1. Sautéing and Pan-Frying:

Use healthy fats like olive oil or butter for sautéing vegetables and proteins.

Control heat to avoid burning and achieve even cooking.

2. Grilling:

Ideal for cooking meats and low-carb vegetables.

Marinate proteins in keto-friendly herbs and oils for added flavor.

3. Roasting and Baking:

Roast vegetables to enhance their natural sweetness without added carbs.

Bake keto-friendly desserts using almond or coconut flour.

4. Broiling:

Quick and efficient for cooking meats with a high heat source from above.

Monitor closely to prevent overcooking.

5. Slow Cooking and Pressure Cooking:

Perfect for tenderizing tougher cuts of meat without added carbs.

Allows for hands-off cooking and meal prep.

6. Stir-Frying:

Quickly cook meats and low-carb veggies in a hot pan.

Use minimal oil to keep it keto-friendly.

7. Meal Prep and Batch Cooking:

Plan and prep meals in advance to stay on track.

Cook in batches to save time during the week.

8. Sous Vide Cooking:

Precise temperature control for proteins like steak or chicken.

Ensures even cooking without overcooking.

9. Making Keto-Friendly Sauces:

Utilize cream, butter, or cheese bases for rich, low-carb sauces.

Experiment with herbs, spices, and keto-friendly seasonings.

10. Creating Low-Carb Breads and Baked Goods:

Experiment with almond flour, coconut flour, and psyllium husk for keto-friendly baking.

Use eggs and baking powder for structure.

11. Making Zoodles and Veggie Noodles:

Spiralize zucchini, squash, or sweet potatoes to replace traditional pasta.

Sauté briefly for a pasta-like texture.

12. Creating Keto-Friendly Desserts:

Use almond or coconut flour as a base for cakes and cookies.

Incorporate sugar substitutes like erythritol or stevia.

13. Cauliflower Substitutes:

Make cauliflower rice as a low-carb alternative to regular rice.

Create cauliflower mash or puree as a substitute for mashed potatoes.

14. Using Coconut and Almond Flour:

Experiment with these low-carb flours for baking and breading.

Adjust liquid and binding agents accordingly.

15. Dressings and Marinades:

Create keto-friendly salad dressings using olive oil, vinegar, and herbs.

Marinate meats with keto-approved ingredients for added flavor.

16. Mindful Portion Control:

Pay attention to serving sizes to avoid unintentional overeating.

Use measuring tools to gauge portions accurately.

17. Keto-Friendly Breading:

Use crushed pork rinds, almond flour, or coconut flour for breading.

Bake or fry for a crunchy texture.

18. Using Alternative Sweeteners:

Experiment with keto-friendly sweeteners like erythritol, stevia, or monk fruit.

Adjust quantities to taste.

19. Incorporating Nutritional Yeast:

Adds a cheesy flavor to dishes without the carbs.

Ideal for creating keto-friendly cheese substitutes.

20. Testing and Adapting Recipes:

Experiment with ratios and ingredients to find what works best for your taste.

Don't be afraid to modify recipes to suit your preferences.

Mastering these keto kitchen techniques will empower you to create a diverse range of delicious and satisfying low-carb meals while adhering to the principles of the ketogenic lifestyle.

Tips on Achieving the Perfect Flavors

Achieving the perfect balance of flavors is an art in the kitchen, and it becomes even more crucial when following a specific dietary plan like the ketogenic lifestyle. Here are some tips to help you create well-balanced and flavorful keto meals:

1. Understand the Basics of Flavor Profiles:

Familiarize yourself with the basic tastes: sweet, salty, sour, bitter, and umami.

Consider the dominant flavors in your dish and aim for a harmonious combination.

2. Experiment with Herbs and Spices:

Use a variety of fresh herbs and spices to add depth and complexity.

Experiment with combinations like rosemary and thyme for savory dishes or cinnamon and nutmeg for desserts.

3. Embrace Citrus and Vinegars:

Citrus juices, such as lemon or lime, can brighten flavors.

Vinegars like apple cider or balsamic add acidity and depth.

4. Balance Richness with Acid:

If a dish is rich, balance it with acidity. For example, a squeeze of lemon on a fatty piece of meat can cut through the richness.

5. Use Quality Fats:

Incorporate high-quality fats like olive oil, avocado oil, or grass-fed butter for added richness and flavor.

6. Incorporate Umami-Rich Ingredients:

Foods like mushrooms, soy sauce, and Parmesan cheese can enhance the umami (savory) aspect of your dishes.

7. Don't Forget Salt:

Salt enhances the natural flavors of ingredients. Use it judiciously but don't be afraid to season appropriately.

8. Contrast Textures:

Combining different textures can enhance the overall dining experience. For instance, a crispy topping on a creamy casserole adds interest.

9. Build Layers of Flavor:

Develop depth by building layers of flavor. Sautéing aromatics like onions and garlic before adding other ingredients is a classic example.

10. Consider Sweetness:

In keto cooking, sweetness might come from natural sources like vegetables or a touch of sugar substitute. Use it sparingly to balance other flavors.

11. Pair Proteins with Complementary Flavors:

Consider the inherent flavors of proteins and pair them with complementary ingredients. For example, pair fish with lemon or herbs.

12. Taste as You Go:

Regularly taste your dish as you cook to adjust seasoning and flavors along the way.

13. Don't Overcrowd Flavors:

Focus on a few key flavors rather than overwhelming your palate with too many competing tastes.

14. Consider Cultural Influences:

Draw inspiration from various cuisines. Understanding the flavor profiles of different cultures can enrich your cooking.

15. Balance Macros:

In keto cooking, balance the macronutrients (fats, proteins, and carbs) to ensure a satisfying and well-rounded meal.

16. Personalize Your Meals:

Adjust recipes to suit your personal taste preferences.

If you love a particular spice, feel free to include more of it.

17. Be Mindful of Overpowering Ingredients:

Some ingredients, like garlic or chili, can easily overpower a dish. Use them in moderation.

18. Use Homemade Broths and Stocks:

Homemade broths and stocks can add a depth of flavor that store-bought versions may lack.

19. Consider Texture and Temperature:

Vary the texture of your ingredients, and consider how temperature (hot, warm, cold) can influence flavor perception.

20. Seek Feedback:

If possible, get feedback from others. They might offer valuable insights into flavor preferences.

By paying attention to these tips and developing your palate over time, you'll become adept at achieving a perfect balance of flavors in your keto cooking, making each meal a delightful and satisfying experience.

Dining Out on Keto

Dining out while following a ketogenic lifestyle can be enjoyable and keto-friendly with a bit of planning. Here are some tips to help you make smart choices and stay on track when eating out:

1. Check the Menu in Advance:

Review the restaurant's menu online before you go to identify keto-friendly options.

Look for dishes that include protein, healthy fats, and non-starchy vegetables.

2. Choose Protein-Rich Options:

Opt for protein-rich dishes such as grilled meat, fish, or poultry.

Ask for the protein to be cooked in healthy fats like olive oil or butter.

3. Embrace Non-Starchy Vegetables:

Choose low-carb vegetable sides like spinach, broccoli, cauliflower, or asparagus.

Request vegetables to be cooked without added sugars or high-carb sauces.

4. Be Wary of Hidden Carbs:

Watch out for hidden carbs in sauces, dressings, and marinades.

Ask about ingredients or request dressings and sauces on the side.

5. Customize Your Order:

Don't hesitate to customize your order to make it keto-friendly.

Ask for substitutions, like swapping potatoes for extra vegetables or a side salad.

6. Avoid Bread and Starchy Sides:

Skip the bread basket and avoid starchy sides like rice, potatoes, or pasta.

Request extra non-starchy vegetables or a side salad instead.

7. Choose Grilled, Roasted, or Baked Preparations:

Opt for dishes that are grilled, roasted, or baked rather than fried.

These cooking methods often involve less breading and healthier fats.

8. Watch Portions Sizes:

Pay attention to portion sizes to avoid overeating.

Consider sharing a larger dish or ask for a half portion if available.

9. Look for Keto-Friendly Add-Ons:

Seek out keto-friendly add-ons like avocado, bacon, or a fried egg to enhance your meal.

These additions can contribute healthy fats and extra flavor.

10. Stay Hydrated:

Drink plenty of water, especially if you're consuming more salt than usual in restaurant meals.

Avoid sugary beverages and opt for unsweetened options or sparkling water.

11. Be Mindful of Alcohol Consumption:

If you choose to have alcohol, opt for dry wines, spirits, or low-carb beer.

Be aware that alcohol can lower inhibitions, making it easier to stray from your keto plan.

12. Plan for Dessert or Skip It:

Consider whether you want to indulge in a keto-friendly dessert or skip it altogether.

Some restaurants offer sugar-free or low-carb dessert options.

13. Communicate Dietary Restrictions Clearly:

Clearly communicate your dietary needs to the server or chef.

Don't hesitate to ask questions about preparation methods and ingredients.

14. Choose Keto-Friendly Cuisines:

Some cuisines naturally offer more keto-friendly options, such as grilled meats and vegetables.

Consider restaurants that specialize in these cuisines.

15. Listen to Your Body:

Pay attention to hunger and fullness cues.

Stop eating when you're satisfied, even if there's still food on your plate.

16. Bring Keto-Friendly Snacks:

If you're unsure about the available options, bring a small snack like nuts or seeds to curb hunger.

17. Practice Moderation:

While keto allows for flexibility, be mindful of overall carb intake.

If you indulge in a higher-carb meal, get back on track with your next choices.

18. Express Gratitude for Accommodations:

Thank the staff for accommodating your dietary preferences.

Positive interactions can help create a more enjoyable dining experience.

By following these tips and making informed choices, you can enjoy dining out on keto while maintaining your commitment to a low-carb lifestyle.

Exercise and Holistic Well-Being

Incorporating exercise and embracing a holistic approach to well-being are essential components of a successful and sustainable ketogenic lifestyle. Here's a guide to understanding their importance and integrating them into your keto journey:

1. Exercise and Ketosis:

Enhances Fat Burning: Regular exercise complements the ketogenic lifestyle by increasing the body's ability to burn fat for fuel. Both keto and exercise promote fat adaptation, leading to improved endurance and performance.

Supports Weight Management: Exercise, when combined with a ketogenic diet, can contribute to weight loss and the maintenance of a healthy weight by creating a caloric deficit and preserving lean muscle mass.

2. Types of Exercise Suitable for Keto:

Aerobic Exercise (Cardio): Engage in activities like walking, running, cycling, or swimming to boost cardiovascular health and aid in fat burning.

Strength Training: Incorporate resistance training to build and maintain lean muscle mass. This can help improve metabolism and support overall strength and functionality.

Flexibility and Mobility Exercises: Include stretching and mobility exercises to enhance flexibility, prevent injuries, and promote overall well-being.

3. Holistic Well-Being Beyond Diet:

Quality Sleep: Prioritize sufficient and quality sleep to support overall health. Lack of sleep can affect hormones related to hunger and satiety, potentially impacting your ability to stick to a ketogenic lifestyle.

Stress Management: Chronic stress can affect blood sugar levels and hinder weight loss. Implement stress-reduction techniques such as mindfulness, meditation, yoga, or deep breathing exercises.

Hydration: Adequate water intake is crucial for overall well-being. Proper hydration supports metabolic functions and can help alleviate keto-related side effects like constipation.

4. Balancing Macros for Exercise:

Protein Intake: Ensure an adequate protein intake to support muscle repair and recovery after exercise. Protein also plays a role in preserving lean muscle mass.

Adjusting Carbs: Some individuals may benefit from strategic carb intake around workouts, known as targeted or cyclical ketogenic approaches. Experiment with carb intake to find what works best for your energy needs.

5. Mindful Eating and Exercise Timing:

Pre-Workout Nutrition: Consider a small keto-friendly snack before workouts if needed for energy. Options include a handful of nuts, a piece of cheese, or a low-carb protein shake.

Post-Workout Nutrition: Opt for a combination of protein and healthy fats post-workout to support recovery. This could be a protein-rich meal or a keto-friendly protein shake.

6. Consulting Healthcare Professionals:

Individualization: Every person's health and fitness needs are unique. Consult with healthcare professionals, including a physician and a fitness or nutrition expert, to tailor an exercise and diet plan that suits your specific requirements.

Monitoring Health Markers: Regularly monitor health markers such as blood pressure, cholesterol levels, and overall well-being to ensure the ketogenic lifestyle is benefiting your health.

7. Enjoyable Physical Activities:

Find What You Love: Choose physical activities that you enjoy to make exercise a sustainable part of your routine. Whether it's hiking, dancing, or playing a sport, make it enjoyable.

8. Holistic Wellness Check-In:

Mind-Body Connection: Embrace practices that foster the mind-body connection, such as yoga or tai chi.

Set Realistic Goals: Establish holistic wellness goals that go beyond physical appearance, including mental and emotional well-being.

9. Adapting Exercise to Your Keto Journey:

During Adaptation: Understand that during the initial stages of keto adaptation, energy levels may fluctuate. Modify the intensity and duration of exercise as needed during this period.

Long-Term Adaptation: As your body becomes more accustomed to ketosis, energy levels and exercise performance are likely to stabilize and improve.

10. Listening to Your Body:

Rest and Recovery: Recognize the importance of rest and recovery days. Overtraining can hinder progress and may lead to burnout.

Adjusting Intensity: Modify the intensity of your workouts based on your energy levels, especially during the adaptation phase.

11. Community and Support:

Connect with Others: Join keto or fitness communities for support, motivation, and shared experiences. Building a supportive network can enhance your overall well-being.

12. Holistic Self-Care Practices:

Self-Care Rituals: Implement self-care practices that align with holistic well-being, such as taking Epsom salt baths, getting massages, or spending time in nature.

13. Celebrating Non-Scale Victories:

Non-Scale Achievements: Acknowledge and celebrate non-scale victories related to your well-being, such as improved energy levels, enhanced mood, or better sleep quality.

14. Evaluating Sustainability:

Sustainable Habits: Strive to create habits that are sustainable in the long term. This includes finding joy in both your ketogenic lifestyle and exercise routine.

15. Staying Adaptable:

Adjusting as Needed: Recognize that both the ketogenic lifestyle and exercise routines may need adjustments over time. Be adaptable and willing to make changes based on your evolving needs.

By integrating exercise and embracing holistic well-being practices, you can enhance the benefits of the ketogenic lifestyle, promoting not only physical health but also mental and emotional wellness. Always consult with healthcare professionals to ensure your chosen approach aligns with your individual health goals and needs.

30-Day Meal Plan

DAYS	BREAKFAST	LUNCH	DINNER	SNACK/DESSERT
1	Chocolate Chip Waffle P 15	Fish Fillets with Lemon-Dill Sauce P 36	Basil Turkey Meatballs P 47	Salami Chips with Pesto P 70
2	Mexican Breakfast Beef Chili P 15	Chicken with Asparagus & Root Vegetables P 48	Foil-Packet Salmon P 36	Red Wine Mushrooms P 70
3	Spinach and Mushroom Mini Quiche P 15	Salmon Romesco P 41	Crispy Thighs & Mash P 47	Keto Taco Shells P 70
4	Cajun Breakfast Sausage P 16	Stewed Chicken and Sausage P 47	Pistachio-Crusted Salmon P 36	Cool Ranch Dorito Crackers P 71
5	Chunky Cobb-Style Egg Salad P 16	Mouthwatering Cod over Creamy Leek Noodles P 37	Chicken and Bacon Rolls P 48	Chocolate Soft-Serve Ice Cream P 71
6	Pizza Pâté P 20	Poblano Chicken P 49	Golden Shrimp P 36	Buttered Cabbage P 71
7	Pulled Pork Hash P 16	Shrimp Stuffed Zucchini P 38	Ethiopian Chicken with Cauliflower P 48	Keto Crackers-Two Ways P 72
8	Brad's "Ketoatmeal" P 16	Turkey Stew with Salsa Verde P 50	Tuna Steak P 37	Bacon-Pepper Fat Bombs P 72
9	Smoked Salmon and Cream Cheese Roll-Ups P 20	Red Cabbage Tilapia Taco Bowl P 39	Chicken, Eggplant and Gruyere Gratin P 49	Taste of the Mediterranean Fat Bombs P 70
10	Mixed Berry Smoothie P 21	Caprese Chicken Skillet P 49	Sardine Fritter Wraps P 39	Almond Sesame Crackers P 72
11	Nutty "Oatmeal" P 20	Hot Pork with Dill Pickles P 58	Lemon-Thyme Poached Halibut P 44	Warm Herbed Olives P 72
12	Cheese Stuffed Avocados P 17	Mackerel and Broccoli Casserole P 37	Sausage and Peppers P 58	Crab Salad–Stuffed Avocado P 73
13	Coconut & Walnut Chia Pudding P 18	Pork Fried Cauliflower Rice P 61	Simple Flounder in Brown Butter Lemon Sauce P 45	Cheesy Spinach Puffs P 73
14	Cheddar Eggs P 19	Cajun Salmon P 41	Sweet Beef Curry P 58	Avocado Salsa P 74
15	Smoked Ham and Egg Muffins P 20	Hawaiian Pulled Pork Roast with Cabbage P 59	Snapper with Shallot and Tomato P 45	Devilish Eggs P 75
16	Tahini Banana Detox Smoothie P 19	Souvlaki Spiced Salmon Bowls P 44	Jalapeño Popper Pork Chops P 60	Strawberry Panna Cotta P 91

DAYS	BREAKFAST	LUNCH	DINNER	SNACK/DESSERT
17	Smoky Sausage Patties P 17	Herby Beef & Veggie Stew P 58	Tuna Avocado Bites P 41	Lush Chocolate Cake P 91
18	Bacon Spaghetti Squash Fritters P 17	Sour Cream Salmon with Parmesan P 37	Beef Tenderloin with Red Wine Sauce P 60	Chocolate Chip Almond Cookies P 95
19	Keto Breakfast Pudding P 21	#N/A	Tuna Cakes P 45	Electrolyte Gummies P 91
20	Breakfast Sammies P 19	Grilled Calamari P 44	Classic Pork and Cauliflower Keema P 61	Olive Oil Cake P 93
21	Cinnamon Crunch Cereal P 18	Turkey Enchilada Bowl P 55	Peppercorn-Crusted Beef Tenderloin P 66	Jelly Pie Jars P 92
22	Eggs & Crabmeat with Creme Fraiche Salsa P 21	Chicken Breasts with Spinach & Artichoke P 53	Parmesan Pork Chops and Roasted Asparagus P 67	Sweetened Condensed Coconut Milk P 93
23	Cheddar Chicken Casserole P 22	Italian Beef Burgers P 66	Chipotle Dry-Rub Wings P 55	Cholesterol Caring Nut Clusters P 94
24	Pumpkin Spice Latte Overnight "Oats" P 22	Lazy Lasagna Chicken P 55	Fajita Meatball Lettuce Wraps P 68	Chocolate Macadamia Bark P 92
25	Traditional Porridge P 17	Pork Chops with Pecan Crust P 67	Blackened Cajun Chicken Tenders P 54	Coffee Fat Bombs P 95
26	Cinnamon-Nut Cottage Cheese P 19	Chicken & Squash Traybake P 55	Pork Larb Lettuce Wraps P 65	Hazelnut Butter Cookies P 93
27	PB&J Overnight Hemp P 22	Apple and Pumpkin Ham P 64	Chili Turkey Patties with Cucumber Salsa P 54	Whipped Cream P 92
28	Pepper Sausage Fry P 22	Blackened Chicken P 48	Pork and Mushroom Bake P 65	Baked Cheesecake P 95
29	Jalapeño Popper Egg Cups P 15	Easy Zucchini Beef Lasagna P 65	Jalapeño Cheddar Chicken Casserole P 51	Hazelnut Butter Cookies P 93
30	Jerky Cookies P 23	Beef Burger P 67	Chettinad Chicken P 53	Cheesecake P 93

Chapter ❷

Breakfasts

Chocolate Chip Waffle

Prep time: 5 minutes | Cook time: 5 minutes | Serves 1

- ⅓ cup blanched almond flour
- ½ tablespoon coconut flour
- ¼ teaspoon baking powder
- 2 large eggs
- ¼ teaspoon vanilla extract
- 4 drops liquid stevia
- 1 tablespoon stevia-sweetened chocolate chips
- For Topping (optional)
- Swerve confectioners'-style sweetener
- Sugar-free syrup
- Salted butter

1. Preheat a waffle maker to medium-high heat. 2. Place all the ingredients except the chocolate chips in a large bowl and blend until smooth. Fold in the chocolate chips. 3. Spray the hot waffle maker with nonstick cooking spray. 4. Pour the batter into the hot waffle iron and cook for 3 to 5 minutes, until light golden brown. 5. Serve dusted with Swerve confectioners'-style sweetener and topped with sugar-free syrup and butter, if desired.

Per Serving:

1 waffle: calories: 398 | fat: 31g | protein: 23g | carbs: 14g | net carbs: 6g | fiber: 8g

Mexican Breakfast Beef Chili

Prep time: 5 minutes | Cook time: 45 minutes | Serves 4

- 2 tablespoons coconut oil
- 1 pound (454 g) ground grass-fed beef
- 1 (14-ounce / 397-g) can sugar-free or low-sugar diced tomatoes
- ½ cup shredded full-fat Cheddar cheese (optional)
- 1 teaspoon hot sauce
- ½ teaspoon chili powder
- ½ teaspoon crushed red pepper
- ½ teaspoon ground cumin
- ½ teaspoon kosher salt
- ½ teaspoon freshly ground black pepper

1. Set the Instant Pot to Sauté and melt the oil. 2. Pour in ½ cup of filtered water, then add the beef, tomatoes, cheese, hot sauce, chili powder, red pepper, cumin, salt, and black pepper to the Instant Pot, stirring thoroughly. 3. Close the lid, set the pressure release to Sealing, and hit Cancel to stop the current program. Select Manual, set the Instant Pot to 45 minutes on High Pressure and let cook. 4. Once cooked, let the pressure naturally disperse from the Instant Pot for about 10 minutes, then carefully switch the pressure release to Venting. 5. Open the Instant Pot, serve, and enjoy!

Per Serving:

calories: 351 | fat: 19g | protein: 39g | carbs: 6g | net carbs: 4g | fiber: 2g

Jalapeño Popper Egg Cups

Prep time: 10 minutes | Cook time: 10 minutes | Serves 2

- 4 large eggs
- ¼ cup chopped pickled jalapeños
- 2 ounces (57 g) full-fat
- cream cheese
- ½ cup shredded sharp Cheddar cheese

1. In a medium bowl, beat the eggs, then pour into four silicone muffin cups. 2. In a large microwave-safe bowl, place jalapeños, cream cheese, and Cheddar. Microwave for 30 seconds and stir. Take a spoonful, approximately ¼ of the mixture, and place it in the center of one of the egg cups. Repeat with remaining mixture. 3. Place egg cups into the air fryer basket. 4. Adjust the temperature to 320°F (160°C) and bake for 10 minutes. 5. Serve warm.

Per Serving:

calories: 381 | fat: 32g | protein: 21g | carbs: 3g | net carbs: 2g | fiber: 1g

Spinach and Mushroom Mini Quiche

Prep time: 10 minutes | Cook time: 15 minutes | Serves 4

- 1 teaspoon olive oil, plus more for spraying
- 1 cup coarsely chopped mushrooms
- 1 cup fresh baby spinach, shredded
- 4 eggs, beaten
- ½ cup shredded Cheddar cheese
- ½ cup shredded Mozzarella cheese
- ¼ teaspoon salt
- ¼ teaspoon black pepper

1. Spray 4 silicone baking cups with olive oil and set aside. 2. In a medium sauté pan over medium heat, warm 1 teaspoon of olive oil. Add the mushrooms and sauté until soft, 3 to 4 minutes. 3. Add the spinach and cook until wilted, 1 to 2 minutes. Set aside. 4. In a medium bowl, whisk together the eggs, Cheddar cheese, Mozzarella cheese, salt, and pepper. 5. Gently fold the mushrooms and spinach into the egg mixture. 6. Pour ¼ of the mixture into each silicone baking cup. 7. Place the baking cups into the air fryer basket and air fry at 350°F (177°C) for 5 minutes. Stir the mixture in each ramekin slightly and air fry until the egg has set, an additional 3 to 5 minutes.

Per Serving:

calories: 210 | fat: 15g | protein: 16g | carbs: 3g | net carbs: 2g | fiber: 1g

Cajun Breakfast Sausage

Prep time: 10 minutes | Cook time: 15 to 20 minutes | Serves 8

- 1½ pounds (680 g) 85% lean ground turkey
- 3 cloves garlic, finely chopped
- ¼ onion, grated
- 1 teaspoon Tabasco
- sauce
- 1 teaspoon Creole seasoning
- 1 teaspoon dried thyme
- ½ teaspoon paprika
- ½ teaspoon cayenne

1. Preheat the air fryer to 370ºF (188ºC). 2. In a large bowl, combine the turkey, garlic, onion, Tabasco, Creole seasoning, thyme, paprika, and cayenne. Mix with clean hands until thoroughly combined. Shape into 16 patties, about ½ inch thick. (Wet your hands slightly if you find the sausage too sticky to handle.) 3. Working in batches if necessary, arrange the patties in a single layer in the air fryer basket. Pausing halfway through the cooking time to flip the patties, air fry for 15 to 20 minutes until a thermometer inserted into the thickest portion registers 165ºF (74ºC).

Per Serving:

calories: 164 | fat: 9g | protein: 19g | carbs: 2g | net carbs: 2g | fiber: 0g

Chunky Cobb-Style Egg Salad

Prep time: 5 minutes | Cook time: 10 minutes | Serves 6

- 8 cups water
- 1 dozen large eggs, room temperature
- ¼ cup mayonnaise, homemade or store-bought
- 2 tablespoons chopped fresh chives
- 2 tablespoons chopped fresh dill
- 2 tablespoons minced shallots or red onions
- 12 slices cooked bacon, chopped
- Sea salt and ground black pepper, to taste
- Microgreens, for serving
- Sliced cucumbers, for serving (optional)

1. Fill a large pot with the water and bring to a boil. Fill a large bowl with ice water. 2. Place the eggs in the boiling water and cook for 10 minutes. Transfer the eggs to the ice water and chill for 10 minutes. This will keep them from turning green around the yolks. 3. Peel the eggs, place them in a large bowl, and mash them with a potato masher or large fork. Mix in the mayonnaise, chives, dill, and shallots. Stir in the bacon so it is evenly distributed. 4. Season with salt and pepper to taste and serve over microgreens and with sliced cucumbers on the side, if desired.

Per Serving:

calories: 498 | fat: 46g | protein: 20g | carbs: 2g | net carbs: 2g | fiber: 0g

Pulled Pork Hash

Prep time: 10 minutes | Cook time: 15 minutes | Serves 4

- 4 eggs
- 10 ounces (283 g) pulled pork, shredded
- 1 teaspoon coconut oil
- 1 teaspoon red pepper
- 1 teaspoon chopped fresh cilantro
- 1 tomato, chopped
- ¼ cup water

1. Melt the coconut oil in the instant pot on Sauté mode. 2. Then add pulled pork, red pepper, cilantro, water, and chopped tomato. 3. Cook the ingredients for 5 minutes. 4. Then stir it well with the help of the spatula and crack the eggs over it. 5. Close the lid. 6. Cook the meal on Manual mode (High Pressure) for 7 minutes. Then make a quick pressure release.

Per Serving:

calories: 275 | fat: 18g | protein: 22g | carbs: 6g | net carbs: 5g | fiber: 1g

Brad's "Ketoatmeal"

Prep time: 5 minutes | Cook time: 10 minutes | Serves 2

- ½ cup coconut milk
- 3 large egg yolks
- ¼ cup coconut flakes
- ½ teaspoon ground cinnamon
- 1 teaspoon vanilla extract
- ½ cup puréed nuts (walnuts, almonds,
- pecans, macadamias, or a combo)
- 2 tablespoons almond butter
- ⅛ teaspoon salt (omit if almond butter contains salt)
- 1 tablespoon cacao nibs (optional)

Toppings:
- ¼ cup coconut milk
- 2 teaspoons cacao nibs
- (optional)

1. Mix the coconut milk, egg yolks, coconut flakes, cinnamon, vanilla, nut purée, almond butter, salt, and cacao nibs (if using) in a medium saucepan. Heat over medium-low heat, stirring continuously, for 3 to 4 minutes. 2. Remove from the heat and scoop into two small bowls. Top each with 2 tablespoons coconut milk and 1 teaspoon cacao nibs (if using). Eat immediately.

Per Serving:

calories: 682 | fat: 62g | protein: 15g | carbs: 16g | net carbs: 10g | fiber: 6g

Smoky Sausage Patties

Prep time: 30 minutes | Cook time: 9 minutes | Serves 8

- 1 pound (454 g) ground pork
- 1 tablespoon coconut aminos
- 2 teaspoons liquid smoke
- 1 teaspoon dried sage
- 1 teaspoon sea salt
- ½ teaspoon fennel seeds
- ½ teaspoon dried thyme
- ½ teaspoon freshly ground black pepper
- ¼ teaspoon cayenne pepper

1. In a large bowl, combine the pork, coconut aminos, liquid smoke, sage, salt, fennel seeds, thyme, black pepper, and cayenne pepper. Work the meat with your hands until the seasonings are fully incorporated. 2. Shape the mixture into 8 equal-size patties. Using your thumb, make a dent in the center of each patty. Place the patties on a plate and cover with plastic wrap. Refrigerate the patties for at least 30 minutes. 3. Working in batches if necessary, place the patties in a single layer in the air fryer, being careful not to overcrowd them. 4. Set the air fryer to 400°F (204°C) and air fry for 5 minutes. Flip and cook for about 4 minutes more.

Per Serving:

calories: 177 | fat: 13g | protein: 13g | carbs: 2g | net carbs: 1g | fiber: 1g

Bacon Spaghetti Squash Fritters

Prep time: 20 minutes | Cook time: 15 minutes | Serves 4

- ½ cooked spaghetti squash
- 2 tablespoons cream cheese
- ½ cup shredded whole-milk Mozzarella cheese
- 1 egg
- ½ teaspoon salt
- ¼ teaspoon pepper
- 1 stalk green onion, sliced
- 4 slices cooked bacon, crumbled
- 2 tablespoons coconut oil

1. Remove seeds from cooked squash and use fork to scrape strands out of shell. Place strands into cheesecloth or kitchen towel and squeeze to remove as much excess moisture as possible. 2. Place cream cheese and Mozzarella in small bowl and microwave for 45 seconds to melt together. Mix with spoon and place in large bowl. Add all ingredients except coconut oil to bowl. Mixture will be wet like batter. 3. Press the Sauté button and then press the Adjust button to set heat to Less. Add coconut oil to Instant Pot. When fully preheated, add 2 to 3 tablespoons of batter to pot to make a fritter. Let fry until firm and completely cooked through.

Per Serving:

calories: 202 | fat: 16g | protein: 9g | carbs: 2g | net carbs: 1g | fiber: 1g

Traditional Porridge

Prep time: 5 minutes | Cook time: 4 minutes | Serves 4

- 2 tablespoons coconut oil
- 1 cup full-fat coconut milk
- 2 tablespoons blanched almond flour
- 2 tablespoons sugar-free chocolate chips
- 1 cup heavy whipping cream
- ½ cup chopped cashews
- ½ cup chopped pecans
- ½ teaspoon ground cinnamon
- ½ teaspoon erythritol, or more to taste
- ¼ cup unsweetened coconut flakes

1. Set the Instant Pot to Sauté and melt the coconut oil. 2. Pour in the coconut milk, 1 cup of filtered water, then combine and mix the flour, chocolate chips, whipping cream, cashews, pecans, cinnamon, erythritol, and coconut flakes, inside the Instant Pot. 3. Close the lid, set the pressure release to Sealing, and hit Cancel to stop the current program. Select Manual, set the Instant Pot to 4 minutes on High Pressure, and let cook. 4. Once cooked, perform a quick release by carefully switching the pressure valve to Venting. 5. Open the Instant Pot, serve, and enjoy!

Per Serving:

calories: 533 | fat: 51g | protein: 7g | carbs: 16g | net carbs: 11g | fiber: 5g

Cheese Stuffed Avocados

Prep time: 10 minutes | Cook time: 17 minutes | Serves 4

- 3 avocados, halved and pitted, skin on
- ½ cup feta cheese, crumbled
- ½ cup cheddar cheese, grated
- 2 eggs, beaten
- Salt and black pepper, to taste
- 1 tablespoon fresh basil, chopped

1. Set oven to 360°F and lay the avocado halves in an ovenproof dish. 2. In a mixing dish, mix both types of cheeses, black pepper, eggs, and salt. 3. Split the mixture equally into the avocado halves. 4. Bake thoroughly for 15 to 17 minutes. 5. Decorate with fresh basil before serving.

Per Serving:

calories: 365 | fat: 32g | protein: 12g | carbs: 13g | net carbs: 5g | fiber: 10g

Coconut & Walnut Chia Pudding

Prep time: 10 minutes | Cook time: 10 minutes | Serves 1

- ½ teaspoon vanilla extract
- ½ cup water
- 1 tablespoon chia seeds
- 2 tablespoons hemp seeds
- 1 tablespoon flax seed meal
- 2 tablespoons almond meal
- 2 tablespoons shredded coconut
- ¼ teaspoon granulated stevia
- 1 tablespoon walnuts, chopped

1. Put chia seeds, hemp seeds, flaxseed meal, almond meal, granulated stevia, and shredded coconut in a nonstick saucepan and pour over the water. Simmer over medium heat, occasionally stirring, until creamed and thickened, for about 3-4 minutes. Stir in vanilla. When the pudding is ready, spoon into a serving bowl, sprinkle with walnuts and serve warm.

Per Serving:

calories: 365 | fat: 31g | protein: 11g | carbs: 16g | net carbs: 8g | fiber: 10g

Cinnamon Crunch Cereal

Prep time: 5 minutes | Cook time: 12 minutes | Serves 6

- 3½ cups (14 ounces / 397 g) blanched almond flour
- ½ cup erythritol
- 2 teaspoons ground cinnamon

Cinnamon Coating:

- ½ cup erythritol
- 1 tablespoon ground cinnamon
- ½ teaspoon sea salt
- 2 large eggs, beaten
- 1 teaspoon vanilla extract
- 2 tablespoons coconut oil, melted

1. Preheat the oven to 350ºF (180ºC). 2. In a large bowl, stir together the almond flour, erythritol, cinnamon, and sea salt. 3. In a small bowl, whisk together the eggs and vanilla. Add to the flour mixture and mix well until a dough forms. 4. Place the dough between two large greased pieces of parchment paper, at least 20 × 14 inches in size. Use a rolling pin to roll the dough out into a very thin rectangle, about 1/16 inch thick. It will tend to form an oval shape, so just rip off pieces and reattach to form a more angular shape. You can split the dough into two or more smaller batches if you can't get it to roll thin enough between your 20 × 14-inch pieces of parchment, or don't have a pan that large. 5. Place the bottom piece of parchment paper onto an extra-large baking sheet, at least 20 × 14 inches in size (or two 10 × 14-inch pans, if you've split your dough into smaller batches). 6. Cut the dough into ½-inch-wide strips. Rotate the pan 90 degrees and cut the dough strips into ½-inch-wide strips again, so you are left with ½-inch squares. You don't need to separate the squares; just cutting the dough is sufficient. 7. Transfer the pan(s) to the oven and bake for 8 to 12 minutes, until golden brown and crispy. 8. Meanwhile, make the cinnamon coating: In a large zip-seal bag, combine the erythritol and cinnamon and shake to mix. 9. When the cereal is finished baking, remove from the oven and cool at room temperature to crisp up. 10. Brush the cereal on both sides with melted coconut oil. Then break apart the squares and add to the bag with the cinnamon-erythritol mixture. Shake to coat. Store in an airtight container in the pantry.

Per Serving:

calories: 446 | fat: 39g | protein: 16g | carbs: 26g | net carbs: 7g | fiber: 19g

Prosciutto Baked Eggs with Spinach

Prep time: 5 minutes | Cook time: 20 minutes | Serves 6

- 1 (12 ounces / 340 g) bag frozen spinach, thawed and drained
- 6 ounces (170 g) prosciutto, very thinly sliced (about 12 large, ultra-thin slices)
- 1 tablespoon avocado oil
- 6 cloves garlic, minced
- ¼ cup finely chopped sun-dried tomatoes
- ⅛ teaspoon sea salt
- Pinch of black pepper
- 12 large eggs

1. Preheat the oven to 350ºF (180ºC). 2. Place the thawed spinach into a kitchen towel and squeeze well over the sink, getting rid of as much liquid as possible. Set aside. 3. Line 12 cups of a muffin tin with a thin layer of prosciutto, overlapping the prosciutto pieces slightly if necessary. Wrap around the sides first, then patch any holes and the bottom. Set aside. 4. In a large skillet, heat the oil over medium-high heat. Add the minced garlic and sauté for about 30 seconds, until fragrant. Add the spinach and sun-dried tomatoes. Season with the sea salt and black pepper. Sauté for 5 minutes. 5. Divide the spinach mixture evenly among the prosciutto-lined muffin cups. Crack an egg into each muffin cup. 6. Transfer the pan to the oven and bake until the eggs are done to your liking, approximately as follows: a. Runny yolks: 13 to 15 minutes b. Semi-firm yolks: 16 to 18 minutes c. Firm yolks: 18 to 20 minutes 7. Allow the egg muffins to cool in the pan for a few minutes before removing.

Per Serving:

calories: 314 | fat: 22g | protein: 20g | carbs: 7g | net carbs: 5g | fiber: 2g

Cinnamon-Nut Cottage Cheese

Prep time: 5 minutes | Cook time: 0 minutes | Serves 1

- ½ cup cottage cheese
- 1 stevia packet or a few squirts liquid stevia or substitute
- 2 teaspoons to 1 tablespoon cinnamon
- ¼ cup chopped pecans

1. In a bowl, combine the cottage cheese and stevia, mixing well. 2. Add the cinnamon and mix just to incorporate. Add more cinnamon or stevia to taste. 3. Sprinkle the pecans on top and enjoy!

Per Serving:

calories: 324 | fat: 27g | protein: 15g | carbs: 10g | net carbs: 6g | fiber: 4g

Breakfast Sammies

Prep time: 15 minutes | Cook time: 20 minutes | Serves 5

Biscuits:
- 6 large egg whites
- 2 cups blanched almond flour, plus more if needed
- 1½ teaspoons baking powder
- ½ teaspoon fine sea salt
- ¼ cup (½ stick) very cold unsalted butter (or lard for dairy-free), cut into ¼-inch pieces

Eggs:
- 5 large eggs
- ½ teaspoon fine sea salt
- ¼ teaspoon ground black pepper
- 5 (1 ounce / 28 g) slices Cheddar cheese (omit for dairy-free)
- 10 thin slices ham

1. Spray the air fryer basket with avocado oil. Preheat the air fryer to 350ºF (177ºC). Grease two pie pans or two baking pans that will fit inside your air fryer. 2. Make the biscuits: In a medium-sized bowl, whip the egg whites with a hand mixer until very stiff. Set aside. 3. In a separate medium-sized bowl, stir together the almond flour, baking powder, and salt until well combined. Cut in the butter. Gently fold the flour mixture into the egg whites with a rubber spatula. If the dough is too wet to form into mounds, add a few tablespoons of almond flour until the dough holds together well. 4. Using a large spoon, divide the dough into 5 equal portions and drop them about 1 inch apart on one of the greased pie pans. (If you're using a smaller air fryer, work in batches if necessary.) Place the pan in the air fryer and bake for 11 to 14 minutes, until the biscuits are golden brown. Remove from the air fryer and set aside to cool. 5. Make the eggs: Set the air fryer to 375ºF (191ºC). Crack the eggs into the remaining greased pie pan and sprinkle with the salt and pepper. Place the eggs in the air fryer to bake for 5 minutes, or until they are cooked to your liking. 6. Open the air fryer and top each egg yolk with a slice of cheese (if using). Bake for another minute, or until the cheese is melted. 7. Once the biscuits are cool, slice them in half lengthwise. Place 1 cooked egg topped with cheese and 2 slices of ham in each biscuit. 8. Store leftover biscuits, eggs, and ham in separate airtight containers in the fridge for up to 3 days. Reheat the biscuits and eggs on a baking sheet in a preheated 350ºF (177ºC) air fryer for 5 minutes, or until warmed through.

Per Serving:

calories: 454 | fat: 35g | protein: 27g | carbs: 8g | net carbs: 4g | fiber: 4g

Tahini Banana Detox Smoothie

Prep time: 10 minutes | Cook time: 0 minutes | Serves 2

- 1½ cups unsweetened almond milk
- ½ cup heavy (whipping) cream
- 1 banana
- 2 scoops (25–28 grams)
- vanilla protein powder
- 2 tablespoons tahini
- ½ teaspoon ground cinnamon
- 5 ice cubes

1. Blend the smoothie. Put the almond milk, cream, banana, protein powder, tahini, cinnamon, and ice in a blender and blend until smooth and creamy. 2. Serve. Pour into two tall glasses and serve.

Per Serving:

calories: 425 | fat: 29g | protein: 25g | carbs: 16g | net carbs: 10g | fiber: 6g

Cheddar Eggs

Prep time: 5 minutes | Cook time: 15 minutes | Serves 2

- 4 large eggs
- 2 tablespoons unsalted butter, melted
- ½ cup shredded sharp Cheddar cheese

1. Crack eggs into a round baking dish and whisk. Place dish into the air fryer basket. 2. Adjust the temperature to 400ºF (204ºC) and set the timer for 10 minutes. 3. After 5 minutes, stir the eggs and add the butter and cheese. Let cook 3 more minutes and stir again. 4. Allow eggs to finish cooking an additional 2 minutes or remove if they are to your desired liking. 5. Use a fork to fluff. Serve warm.

Per Serving:

calories: 328 | fat: 27g | protein: 20g | carbs: 1g | net carbs: 1g | fiber: 0g

Smoked Ham and Egg Muffins

Prep time: 5 minutes | Cook time: 25 minutes | Serves 9

- 2 cups chopped smoked ham
- ⅓ cup grated Parmesan cheese
- ¼ cup almond flour
- 9 eggs
- ⅓ cup mayonnaise, sugar-free
- ¼ teaspoon garlic powder
- ¼ cup chopped onion
- Sea salt to taste

1. Preheat your oven to 370°F. 2. Lightly grease nine muffin pans with cooking spray and set aside. Place the onion, ham, garlic powder, and salt, in a food processor, and pulse until ground. Stir in the mayonnaise, almond flour, and Parmesan cheese. Press this mixture into the muffin cups. 3. Make sure it goes all the way up the muffin sides so that there will be room for the egg. Bake for 5 minutes. Crack an egg into each muffin cup. Return to the oven and bake for 20 more minutes or until the tops are firm to the touch and eggs are cooked. Leave to cool slightly before serving.

Per Serving:

calories: 165 | fat: 11g | protein: 14g | carbs: 2g | net carbs: 1g | fiber: 1g

Nutty "Oatmeal"

Prep time: 5 minutes | Cook time: 4 minutes | Serves 4

- 2 tablespoons coconut oil
- 1 cup full-fat coconut milk
- 1 cup heavy whipping cream
- ½ cup macadamia nuts
- ½ cup chopped pecans
- ⅓ cup Swerve, or more
- to taste
- ¼ cup unsweetened coconut flakes
- 2 tablespoons chopped hazelnuts
- 2 tablespoons chia seeds
- ½ teaspoon ground cinnamon

1. Before you get started, soak the chia seeds for about 5 to 10 minutes (can be up to 20, if desired) in 1 cup of filtered water. After soaking, set the Instant Pot to Sauté and add the coconut oil. Once melted, pour in the milk, whipping cream, and 1 cup of filtered water. Then add the macadamia nuts, pecans, Swerve, coconut flakes, hazelnuts, chia seeds, and cinnamon. Mix thoroughly inside the Instant Pot. 2. Close the lid, set the pressure release to Sealing, and hit Cancel to stop the current program. Select Manual, set the Instant Pot to 4 minutes on High Pressure, and let cook. 3. Once cooked, carefully switch the pressure release to Venting. 4. Open the Instant Pot, serve, and enjoy!

Per Serving:

calories: 506 | fat: 53g | protein: 6g | carbs: 11g | net carbs: 5g | fiber: 6g

Pizza Pâté

Prep time: 10 minutes | Cook time: 0 minutes | Makes 2½ cups

- 1 cup (190 g) chopped pepperoni
- ¾ cup (120 g) raw almonds, soaked for 12 hours, then drained and rinsed ½ cup (120 ml) melted coconut oil
- ⅓ cup (80 ml) tomato sauce
- ¼ cup (17 g) nutritional
- yeast
- 2 teaspoons apple cider vinegar
- 2 teaspoons onion powder
- 1 teaspoon garlic powder
- ¼ teaspoon finely ground gray sea salt
- 1 tablespoon finely chopped fresh basil

1. Place all the ingredients except the basil in a high-powered blender or food processor. Blend or pulse until smooth, about 1 minute. 2. Add the basil and pulse until just mixed in.

Per Serving:

calories: 144 | fat: 13g | protein: 5g | carbs: 3g | net carbs: 1g | fiber: 1g

Smoked Salmon and Cream Cheese Roll-Ups

Prep time: 25 minutes | Cook time: 0 minutes | Serves 2

- 4 ounces cream cheese, at room temperature
- 1 teaspoon grated lemon zest
- 1 teaspoon Dijon mustard
- 2 tablespoons chopped scallions, white and
- green parts
- Pink Himalayan salt
- Freshly ground black pepper
- 1 (4-ounce) package cold-smoked salmon (about 12 slices)

1. Put the cream cheese, lemon zest, mustard, and scallions in a food processor (or blender), and season with pink Himalayan salt and pepper. Process until fully mixed and smooth. 2. Spread the cream-cheese mixture on each slice of smoked salmon, and roll it up. Place the rolls on a plate seam-side down. 3. Serve immediately or refrigerate, covered in plastic wrap or in a lidded container, for up to 3 days.

Per Serving:

calories: 268 | fat: 22g | protein: 14g | carbs: 4g | net carbs: 3g | fiber: 1g

Mixed Berry Smoothie

Prep time: 5 minutes | Cook time: 0 minutes | Serves 2

- ½ cup fresh or frozen strawberries
- ½ cup fresh or frozen blueberries
- ½ cup fresh or frozen raspberries
- 1 cup ice cubes
- ½ cup heavy (whipping) cream
- ½ cup Two Good vanilla yogurt
- 2 tablespoons MCT oil
- ¼ to ½ cup water, as needed

1. Fill a high-speed blender with the berries, ice cubes, cream, yogurt, and MCT oil. 2. Blend until smooth. If your blender struggles with the thickness, slowly add the water until it begins to blend. 3. Divide the mixture between 2 glasses and enjoy!

Per Serving:

calories: 408 | fat: 38g | protein: 4g | carbs: 16g | net carbs: 12g | fiber: 4g

Sausage and Gruyère Breakfast Casserole

Prep time: 15 minutes | Cook time: 50 minutes | Makes 8

- ¾ pound unseasoned ground pork
- 1 bunch scallions, chopped
- ½ teaspoon red pepper flakes
- Pinch of ground cloves
- 1 teaspoon pink Himalayan salt
- ¼ teaspoon ground black pepper
- 1 tablespoon chopped fresh sage
- 1 teaspoon chopped fresh marjoram
- 8 large eggs
- ¼ cup heavy whipping cream
- 1¼ cups shredded Gruyère cheese (about 5 ounces), divided

1. Preheat the oven to 350°F and grease a 1¾-quart baking dish with coconut oil spray. 2. In a large skillet over medium-high heat, partially cook the pork, stirring to break it up, about 5 minutes. Add the scallions, red pepper flakes, cloves, salt, and pepper and stir to combine. Continue to cook until the pork is fully cooked and browned, an additional 5 minutes. 3. Add the sage and marjoram and stir to combine—now you have your own seasoned breakfast sausage! Pour the cooked sausage into the greased baking dish. 4. In a bowl, whisk together the eggs, cream, and 1 cup of the shredded cheese. Pour over the sausage in the casserole dish. 5. Sprinkle the remaining Gruyère over the top of the casserole and bake for 40 minutes, or until the eggs are fully set in the center and the top is golden brown.

Per Serving:

calories: 282 | fat: 22g | protein: 19g | carbs: 1g | net carbs: 1g | fiber: 0g

Keto Breakfast Pudding

Prep time: 5 minutes | Cook time: 0 minutes | Serves 3

- 1½ cups (350 ml) full-fat coconut milk
- 1 cup (110 g) frozen raspberries
- ¼ cup (60 ml) MCT oil or melted coconut oil, or ¼ cup (40 g) unflavored MCT oil powder
- ¼ cup (40 g) collagen

Toppings (optional):
- Unsweetened shredded coconut
- peptides or protein powder
- 2 tablespoons chia seeds
- 1 tablespoon apple cider vinegar
- 1 teaspoon vanilla extract
- 1 tablespoon erythritol, or 4 drops liquid stevia

- Hulled hemp seeds
- Fresh berries of choice

1. Place all the pudding ingredients in a blender or food processor and blend until smooth. Serve in bowls with your favorite toppings, if desired.

Per Serving:

calories: 403 | fat: 34g | protein: 15g | carbs: 9g | net carbs: 6g | fiber: 3g

Eggs & Crabmeat with Creme Fraiche Salsa

Prep time: 10 minutes | Cook time: 10 minutes | Serves 3

- 1 tablespoon olive oil
- 6 eggs, whisked
- 1 (6 ounces) can

For the Salsa:
- ¾ cup crème fraiche
- ½ cup scallions, chopped
- ½ teaspoon garlic powder
- crabmeat, flaked
- Salt and black pepper to taste

- Salt and black pepper to taste
- ½ teaspoon fresh dill, chopped

1. Set a sauté pan over medium heat and warm olive oil. Crack in eggs and scramble them. Stir in crabmeat and season with salt and black pepper; cook until cooked thoroughly. 2. In a mixing dish, combine all salsa ingredients. Equally, split the egg/crabmeat mixture among serving plates; serve alongside the scallions and salsa to the side.

Per Serving:

calories: 364 | fat: 26g | protein: 25g | carbs: 5g | net carbs: 5g | fiber: 0g

Cheddar Chicken Casserole

Prep time: 10 minutes | Cook time: 20 minutes | Serves 6

- 1 cup ground chicken
- 1 teaspoon olive oil
- 1 teaspoon chili flakes
- 1 teaspoon salt
- 1 cup shredded Cheddar cheese
- ½ cup coconut cream

1. Press the Sauté button on the Instant Pot and heat the oil. Add the ground chicken, chili flakes and salt to the pot and sauté for 10 minutes. Stir in the remaining ingredients. 2. Set the lid in place. Select the Manual mode and set the cooking time for 10 minutes on High Pressure. When the timer goes off, do a quick pressure release. Carefully open the lid. 3. Let the dish cool for 10 minutes before serving.

Per Serving:

calories: 172 | fat: 13.4g | protein: 12.0g | carbs: 1.3g | net carbs: 0.8g | fiber: 0.5g

Pumpkin Spice Latte Overnight "Oats"

Prep time: 5 minutes | Cook time: 0 minutes | Serves 2

- ½ cup (75 g) hulled hemp seeds
- ⅓ cup (80 ml) milk (nondairy or regular), plus more for serving
- ⅓ cup (80 ml) brewed coffee (decaf or regular)
- 2 tablespoons canned pumpkin puree
- 1 tablespoon chia seeds
- 2 teaspoons erythritol, or

Toppings (Optional):
- Chopped raw or roasted pecans
- Ground cinnamon
- Additional hulled hemp

- 3 drops liquid stevia
- ½ teaspoon vanilla extract
- ½ teaspoon ground cinnamon
- ¼ teaspoon ground nutmeg
- ⅛ teaspoon ground cloves
- Pinch of finely ground sea salt

seeds
- Toasted unsweetened shredded coconut

1. Place all the ingredients in a 12-ounce (350-ml) or larger container with a lid and stir until combined. Cover and set in the fridge to soak overnight, or for at least 8 hours. 2. The following day, add more milk until the desired consistency is reached. Divide between 2 small bowls, top as desired, and enjoy.

Per Serving:

calories: 337 | fat: 26g | protein: 15g | carbs: 9g | net carbs: 2g | fiber: 7g

PB&J Overnight Hemp

Prep time: 5 minutes | Cook time: 0 minutes | serves 6

- 3 cups unsweetened almond milk, plus more for serving
- 1 tablespoon sugar-free peanut butter
- 4 drops liquid stevia or sugar-free sweetener of choice
- 1½ cups hemp hearts
- 2 tablespoons chia seeds
- ¼ cup cacao nibs
- ⅛ cup unsweetened coconut flakes
- ¼ cup freeze-dried raspberries

1. In a large mixing bowl, whisk together the almond milk, peanut butter, and stevia. 2. Once well combined, add the hemp hearts, chia seeds, cacao nibs, coconut, and raspberries, and stir together. 3. Pour the mixture into a lidded storage container and place in the refrigerator for at least 8 hours. 4. Divide the mixture among 6 small serving bowls and top with a splash of almond milk.

Per Serving:

calories: 324 | fat: 24g | protein: 16g | carbs: 10g | net carbs: 2g | fiber: 8g

Pepper Sausage Fry

Prep time: 5 minutes | Cook time: 20 minutes | Serves 4

- ¼ cup (60 ml) avocado oil, or ¼ cup (55 g) coconut oil
- 12 ounces (340 g) smoked sausages, thinly sliced
- 1 small green bell pepper, thinly sliced
- 1 small red bell pepper, thinly sliced
- 1½ teaspoons garlic
- powder
- 1 teaspoon dried oregano leaves
- 1 teaspoon paprika
- ¼ teaspoon finely ground sea salt
- ¼ teaspoon ground black pepper
- ¼ cup (17 g) chopped fresh parsley

1. Heat the oil in a large frying pan over medium-low heat until it shimmers. 2. When the oil is shimmering, add the rest of the ingredients, except the parsley. Cover and cook for 15 minutes, until the bell peppers are fork-tender. 3. Remove the lid and continue to cook for 5 to 6 minutes, until the liquid evaporates. 4. Remove from the heat, stir in the parsley, and serve.

Per Serving:

calories: 411 | fat: 38g | protein: 11g | carbs: 6g | net carbs: 5g | fiber: 2g

Jerky Cookies

Prep time: 10 minutes | Cook time: 6 hours | Serves 18

- 1 pound (455 g) ground beef (10% fat)
- 2 tablespoons coconut aminos
- 1 teaspoon smoked sea salt
- 1 teaspoon ground black pepper
- ½ teaspoon garlic powder
- ½ teaspoon red pepper flakes

1. Place 2 oven racks as close to the middle of the oven as possible. Preheat the oven to 170°F (77°C) and line 2 baking sheets with parchment paper or a silicone baking mat. 2. Place all the ingredients in a medium-sized bowl and combine with your hands until well mixed. 3. Scooping a heaping tablespoon of the meat mixture into your palm, roll it into a ball, and then flatten it into a 2-inch (5-cm) round. Transfer to a prepared baking sheet and repeat with the remaining mixture. 4. Bake the cookies for 6 hours, flipping them over halfway through cooking. From time to time, rotate the pans from one oven rack to the other to ensure even baking. The cookies are done when they are chewy like jerky. 5. Transfer the cookies to a cooling rack and allow to cool for 30 minutes.

Per Serving:

calories: 47 | fat: 2g | protein: 8g | carbs: 1g | net carbs: 1g | fiber: 0g

Bacon and Mushrooms with Soft-Boiled Eggs

Prep time: 8 minutes | Cook time: 15 minutes | Serves 4

- ½ pound (227 g) bacon, diced
- 12 ounces (340 g) baby portobello mushrooms, stemmed and quartered
- ¼ cup diced onions
- 4 large eggs (omit for egg-free)
- 3 tablespoons plus 2 teaspoons coconut vinegar or red wine vinegar
- 3 tablespoons MCT oil or extra-virgin olive oil
- 1 teaspoon Dijon mustard
- ½ teaspoon fine sea salt
- ¼ teaspoon freshly ground black pepper
- 1 teaspoon Swerve confectioners'-style sweetener or equivalent amount of liquid or powdered sweetener (optional)
- Chopped fresh chives, for garnish

1. Place the diced bacon in a skillet and sauté over medium heat until crispy, about 5 minutes. Using a slotted spoon, remove the bacon but leave the drippings in the pan. Add the mushrooms and onions and sauté in the drippings for 10 minutes, or until the mushrooms are golden brown and cooked through. 2. Meanwhile, make the soft-boiled eggs: Place the eggs in a pot of simmering, not boiling, water, cover, and simmer for 6 minutes. Immediately rinse under cold water. Peel and set aside. 3. Add the vinegar, oil, mustard, salt, pepper, and sweetener, if using, to the sauté pan with the mushrooms and stir well. Add the crispy bacon and stir to combine. 4. Place the mushroom mixture on a serving platter. Slice the eggs in half and place them yolk side up on top of the mushroom mixture. Garnish with fresh chives. 5. Store extras in an airtight container in the fridge for up to 4 days. Best served fresh.

Per Serving:

calories: 528 | fat: 44g | protein: 28g | carbs: 5g | net carbs: 4g | fiber: 1g

Golden Gate Granola

Prep time: 10 minutes | Cook time: 1 hour | Makes 4 cups

- ¼ cup (½ stick) unsalted butter
- ¼ cup powdered erythritol
- ¼ teaspoon plus 10 drops of liquid stevia
- 1 teaspoon ground cinnamon
- ½ teaspoon vanilla
- extract
- 1 cup raw almonds
- 1 cup raw hazelnuts
- 1 cup unsweetened coconut flakes
- ½ cup raw pumpkin seeds
- ¼ cup hemp hearts

1. Preheat the oven to 275°F and line a rimmed baking sheet with parchment paper or a silicone baking mat. 2. In a small saucepan over medium heat, combine the butter, erythritol, stevia, cinnamon, and vanilla extract. Stirring occasionally, heat until the butter and erythritol are melted and dissolved. Remove from the heat and set aside. 3. In a large bowl, combine the nuts, coconut flakes, pumpkin seeds, and hemp hearts. Pour the melted butter mixture over the nut mixture and toss using a rubber spatula, making sure that everything is well coated. 4. Pour the granola onto the lined baking sheet and spread it out into an even layer. Bake for 1 hour, stirring every 15 minutes or so, until dark golden brown. 5. Let the granola cool in the pan for at least 1 hour to allow it to harden and form clumps. Store in a sealed jar or zip-top plastic bag for up to 3 weeks. It does not need to be refrigerated.

Per Serving:

calories: 200 | fat: 18g | protein: 5g | carbs: 5g | net carbs: 2g | fiber: 3g

Mocha Protein Keto Coffee

Prep time: 5 minutes | Cook time: 1 minutes | Serves 1

- 12 ounces hot brewed coffee
- 2 tablespoons heavy whipping cream
- 1 tablespoon unsalted butter
- 1 tablespoon cocoa
- powder
- 1 scoop chocolate-flavored protein powder
- 1 scoop unflavored collagen peptides
- 10 drops of liquid stevia

1. Place all the ingredients in a blender and blend until smooth and frothy. Pour into a 16-ounce mug and serve immediately, or pour it into a Thermos and take it on the go!

Per Serving:

calories: 361 | fat: 24g | protein: 37g | carbs: 4g | net carbs: 2g | fiber: 2g

Egg Roll in a Bowl

Prep time: 10 minutes | Cook time: 10 minutes | Serves 2

- 2 large eggs
- 2 tablespoons sesame oil, divided
- 2 tablespoons soy sauce, divided
- 2 tablespoons extra-virgin olive oil
- 6 ounces (170 g) ground pork
- 1 tablespoon chopped fresh ginger (or 1 teaspoon ground ginger)
- 2 cloves garlic, minced
- 2 cups finely chopped cabbage (or bagged
- coleslaw mix; no dressing)
- 2 ribs celery, diced
- ½ small red bell pepper, diced
- 2 tablespoons lime juice, divided
- 2 scallions, minced (green and white parts)
- 2 tablespoons mayonnaise
- 1 teaspoon sriracha or other hot sauce
- ½ teaspoon garlic powder

1. In a small bowl, beat together the eggs, 1 tablespoon of sesame oil, and 1 tablespoon of soy sauce and set aside. 2. Heat the olive oil in a large skillet over medium heat. Sauté the ground pork, breaking it apart, until browned and no longer pink, 4 to 5 minutes. Add the ginger and garlic and sauté for an additional 30 seconds. 3. Add the cabbage, celery, and bell pepper and sauté, stirring constantly, until the vegetables are wilted and fragrant, another 2 to 3 minutes. 4. Push the vegetables and pork to one side of the skillet and add the egg mixture to the other side. Reduce heat to low and scramble the egg until cooked through, 1 to 2 minutes. Remove the skillet from the heat and mix the egg into the pork and cabbage. 5. In a small bowl, whisk together the remaining 1 tablespoon of sesame oil, the remaining 1 tablespoon of soy sauce, 1 tablespoon of lime juice, and the scallions. Pour over the cooked pork mixture and stir to combine well, reserving the bowl. 6. In the same small bowl, combine the remaining 1 tablespoon of lime juice, the mayonnaise, sriracha, and garlic powder. 7. Divide the pork mixture evenly between two bowls and drizzle each with half of the spicy mayo. Serve warm.

Per Serving:

calories: 695 | fat: 61g | protein: 25g | carbs: 16g | net carbs: 10g | fiber: 4g

Keto Chai

Prep time: 3 minutes | Cook time: 10 to 15 minutes | Serves 7

- 8 whole cloves
- 7 cardamom pods
- 2 cinnamon sticks
- 1½ teaspoons black peppercorns
- 1 (2-inch) piece fresh ginger, sliced into thin rounds
- 5 cups cold water
- 5 bags black tea
- 2 cups unsweetened (unflavored or vanilla-flavored) cashew milk,
- homemade or store-bought, or almond milk (or hemp milk for nut-free)
- 2 to 4 tablespoons Swerve confectioners'-style sweetener or equivalent amount of liquid or powdered sweetener
- 1 tablespoon coconut oil per cup of tea

1. Place the spices and ginger in a medium saucepan. Toast on low heat while lightly crushing the spices with the back of a spoon. 2. Add the water and bring to a boil. Once boiling, cover the pan, lower the heat, and simmer for 5 to 10 minutes (the longer time will create a stronger chai flavor). Remove from the heat. 3. Place the teabags in the saucepan and steep for 4 minutes. Remove the teabags and add the cashew milk and 2 tablespoons of the sweetener. Stir, taste, and add more sweetener if desired. 4. Bring the chai to a bare simmer over medium heat, then strain it into a teapot. Just before serving, place a tablespoon of coconut oil in each teacup, pour the hot tea over it, and whisk to blend the coconut oil into the tea. Store extra tea in an airtight container in the fridge for up to 1 week.

Per Serving:

calories: 35 | fat: 3g | protein: 1g | carbs: 1g | net carbs: 1g | fiber: 0g

Slow-Cooked Granola with Nuts

Prep time: 5 minutes | Cook time: 2 hours 30 minutes | Serves 10

- 1 cup raw almonds
- 1 cup pumpkin seeds
- 1 cup raw walnuts
- 1 cup raw cashews
- 1 tablespoon coconut oil
- ¼ cup unsweetened coconut chips
- 1 teaspoon sea salt
- 1 teaspoon cinnamon

1. In a large bowl, stir together the almonds, pumpkin seeds, walnuts, cashews and coconut oil. Make sure all the nuts are coated with the coconut oil. Place the nut mixture in the Instant Pot and cover the pot with a paper towel. 2. Lock the lid. Select the Slow Cook mode and set the cooking time for 1 hour on More. When the timer goes off, stir the nuts. Set the timer for another hour. 3. Again, when the timer goes off, stir the nut mixture and add the coconut chips. Set the timer for another 30 minutes. The cashews should become a nice golden color. 4. When the timer goes off, transfer the nut mixture to a baking pan to cool and sprinkle with the sea salt and cinnamon. Serve.

Per Serving:

calories: 311 | fat: 28g | protein: 10g | carbs:11| net carbs:7| fiber: 4g

Pumpkin Spice Smoothie

Prep time: 5 minutes | Cook time: 0 minutes | Serves 2

- 1 cup full-fat coconut, nut, or dairy milk
- ¾ cup canned pumpkin
- ½ cup frozen riced cauliflower
- 1 cup water
- 1 teaspoon ground cinnamon, plus extra for garnish if desired
- 1 teaspoon pumpkin pie spice
- 1 teaspoon pure vanilla extract
- Small handful of ice (optional)
- 2 scoops collagen peptides
- ⅛ teaspoon green stevia, or 2 or 3 drops stevia extract (optional)
- 1 tablespoon coconut chips, for garnish (optional)

1. Place all the ingredients except the coconut chips in a blender and blend until smooth. If you prefer a thinner smoothie, add more water or milk to your liking. 2. Garnish with ground cinnamon and coconut chips before serving, if desired.

Per Serving:

calories: 302 | fat: 24g | protein: 13g | carbs: 12g | net carbs: 9g | fiber: 3g

Chapter 3

Stews and Soups

Beef and Okra Stew

Prep time: 15 minutes | Cook time: 25 minutes | Serves 3

- 8 ounces (227 g) beef sirloin, chopped
- ¼ teaspoon cumin seeds
- 1 teaspoon dried basil
- 1 tablespoon avocado oil
- ¼ cup coconut cream
- 1 cup water
- 6 ounces (170 g) okra, chopped

1. Sprinkle the beef sirloin with cumin seeds and dried basil and put in the Instant Pot. 2. Add avocado oil and roast the meat on Sauté mode for 5 minutes. Flip occasionally. 3. Add coconut cream, water, and okra. 4. Close the lid and select Manual mode. Set cooking time for 25 minutes on High Pressure. 5. When timer beeps, use a natural pressure release for 10 minutes, the release any remaining pressure. Open the lid. 6. Serve warm.

Per Serving:

calories: 216 | fat: 10g | protein: 25g | carbs: 6g | net carbs: 3g | fiber: 3g

Bacon, Leek, and Cauliflower Soup

Prep time: 15 minutes | Cook time: 15 minutes | Serves 6

- 6 slices bacon
- 1 leek, remove the dark green end and roots, sliced in half lengthwise, rinsed, cut into ½-inch-thick slices crosswise
- ½ medium yellow onion, sliced
- 4 cloves garlic, minced
- 3 cups chicken broth
- 1 large head cauliflower,
- roughly chopped into florets
- 1 cup water
- 1 teaspoon kosher salt
- 1 teaspoon ground black pepper
- ⅔ cup shredded sharp Cheddar cheese, divided
- ½ cup heavy whipping cream

1. Set the Instant Pot to Sauté mode. When heated, place the bacon on the bottom of the pot and cook for 5 minutes or until crispy. 2. Transfer the bacon slices to a plate. Let stand until cool enough to handle, crumble it with forks. 3. Add the leek and onion to the bacon fat remaining in the pot. Sauté for 5 minutes or until fragrant and the onion begins to caramelize. Add the garlic and sauté for 30 seconds more or until fragrant. 4. Stir in the chicken broth, cauliflower florets, water, salt, pepper, and three-quarters of the crumbled bacon. 5. Secure the lid. Press the Manual button and set cooking time for 3 minutes on High Pressure. 6. When timer beeps, perform a quick pressure release. Open the lid. 7. Stir in ½ cup of the Cheddar and the cream. Use

an immersion blender to purée the soup until smooth. 8. Ladle into bowls and garnish with the remaining Cheddar and crumbled bacon. Serve immediately.

Per Serving:

calories: 251 | fat: 19g | protein: 11g | carbs: 12g | net carbs: 9g | fiber: 3g

Lamb and Broccoli Soup

Prep time: 10 minutes | Cook time: 25 minutes | Serves 4

- 7 ounces (198 g) lamb fillet, chopped
- 1 tablespoon avocado oil
- ½ cup broccoli, roughly chopped
- ¼ daikon, chopped
- 2 bell peppers, chopped
- ¼ teaspoon ground cumin
- 5 cups beef broth

1. Sauté the lamb fillet with avocado oil in the Instant Pot for 5 minutes. 2. Add the broccoli, daikon, bell peppers, ground cumin, and beef broth. 3. Close the lid. Select Manual mode and set cooking time for 20 minutes on High Pressure. 4. When timer beeps, use a natural pressure release for 10 minutes, then release any remaining pressure. Open the lid. 5. Serve warm.

Per Serving:

calories: 169 | fat: 6g | protein: 21g | carbs: 7g | net carbs: 6g | fiber: 1g

Power Green Soup

Prep time: 10 minutes | Cook time: 15 minutes | Serves 6

- 1 broccoli head, chopped
- 1 cup spinach
- 1 onion, chopped
- 2 garlic cloves, minced
- ½ cup watercress
- 5 cups veggie stock
- 1 cup coconut milk
- 1 tablespoon ghee
- 1 bay leaf
- Salt and black pepper, to taste

1. Melt the ghee in a large pot over medium heat. Add onion and garlic, and cook for 3 minutes. Add broccoli and cook for an additional 5 minutes. Pour the stock over and add the bay leaf. Close the lid, bring to a boil, and reduce the heat. Simmer for about 3 minutes. 2. At the end, add spinach and watercress, and cook for 3 more minutes. Stir in the coconut cream, salt and black pepper. Discard the bay leaf, and blend the soup with a hand blender.

Per Serving:

calories: 392 | fat: 38g | protein: 5g | carbs: 7g | net carbs: 6g | fiber: 1g

Chilled Cilantro and Avocado Soup

Prep time: 10 minutes | Cook time: 7 minutes | Serves 6

- 2 to 3 tablespoons olive oil
- 1 large white onion, diced
- 3 garlic cloves, crushed
- 1 serrano chile, seeded and diced
- Salt and freshly ground black pepper, to taste
- 4 or 5 ripe avocados,
- peeled, halved, and pitted
- 4 cups chicken broth, or vegetable broth
- 2 cups water
- Juice of 1 lemon
- ¼ cup chopped fresh cilantro, plus more for garnish
- ½ cup sour cream

1. In a large pan over medium heat, heat the olive oil. 2. Add the onion and garlic. Sauté for 5 to 7 minutes until the onion is softened and translucent. 3. Add the serrano, season with salt and pepper, and remove from the heat. 4. In a blender, combine the avocados, chicken broth, water, lemon juice, cilantro, and onion-garlic-chile mixture. Purée until smooth (you may have to do this in batches), strain through a fine-mesh sieve, and season with more salt and pepper. Refrigerate, covered, for about 3 hours or until chilled through. 5. To serve, top with sour cream and a sprinkle of chopped cilantro. Refrigerate leftovers in an airtight container for up to 1 week.

Per Serving:

calories: 513 | fat: 45g | protein: 7g | carbs: 20g | net carbs: 8g | fiber: 12g

Garlic Beef Soup

Prep time: 12 minutes | Cook time: 42 minutes | Serves 8

- 10 strips bacon, chopped
- 1 medium white onion, chopped
- Cloves squeezed from 3 heads roasted garlic, or 6 cloves garlic, minced
- 1 to 2 jalapeño peppers, seeded and chopped (optional)
- 2 pounds (907 g)

For Garnish:

- 1 avocado, peeled, pitted, and diced
- 2 radishes, very thinly
- boneless beef chuck roast, cut into 4 equal-sized pieces
- 5 cups beef broth
- 1 cup chopped fresh cilantro, plus more for garnish
- 2 teaspoons fine sea salt
- 1 teaspoon ground black pepper

- sliced
- 2 tablespoons chopped fresh chives

1. Place the bacon in the Instant Pot and press Sauté. Cook, stirring occasionally, for 4 minutes, or until the bacon is crisp. Remove the bacon with a slotted spoon, leaving the drippings in the pot. Set the bacon on a paper towel-lined plate to drain. 2. Add the onion, garlic, and jalapeños, if using, to the Instant Pot and sauté for 3 minutes, or until the onion is soft. Press Cancel to stop the Sauté. 3. Add the beef, broth, cilantro, salt, and pepper. Stir to combine. 4. Seal the lid, press Manual, and set the timer for 35 minutes. Once finished, let the pressure release naturally. 5. Remove the lid and shred the beef with two forks. Taste the liquid and add more salt, if needed. 6. Ladle the soup into bowls. Garnish with the reserved bacon, avocado, radishes, chives, and more cilantro.

Per Serving:

calories: 456 | fat: 36g | protein: 25g | carbs: 6g | net carbs: 4g | fiber: 2g

Bacon Soup

Prep time: 10 minutes | Cook time: 1 hour 20 minutes | Serves 6

- ⅓ cup (69 g) lard
- 1 pound (455 g) pork stewing pieces
- ¾ cup (110 g) sliced shallots
- 10 strips bacon (about 10 ounces/285 g), cut into about ½-inch (1.25-cm) pieces
- 1¾ cups (415 ml) chicken bone broth
- 3 medium turnips (about 12½ ounces/355 g), cubed
- ¼ cup (60 ml) white
- wine, such as Pinot Grigio, Sauvignon Blanc, or
- unoaked Chardonnay
- 1 tablespoon prepared yellow mustard
- 4 sprigs fresh thyme
- ½ cup (120 ml) full-fat coconut milk
- 2 tablespoons apple cider vinegar
- 2 tablespoons unflavored gelatin
- 1 tablespoon dried tarragon leaves

1. Melt the lard in a large saucepan over medium heat. Once the lard has melted, add the pork pieces and cook for 8 minutes, or until lightly browned on the outside. 2. Add the sliced shallots and bacon pieces. Sauté for an additional 5 minutes or until the shallots become fragrant. 3. Add the bone broth, turnips, wine, mustard, and thyme sprigs. Cover and bring to a boil, then reduce the heat to medium-low and cook until the meat and turnips are fork-tender, about 1 hour. 4. Remove the thyme sprigs and add the coconut milk, vinegar, gelatin, and tarragon. Increase the heat to medium and boil, covered, for another 10 minutes. 5. Divide the soup among 6 small bowls and serve.

Per Serving:

calories: 571 | fat: 41g | protein: 40g | carbs: 10g | net carbs: 9g | fiber: 1g

Avocado-Lime Soup

Prep time: 5 minutes | Cook time: 20 minutes | serves 8

- 2 tablespoons cold-pressed olive oil
- ½ yellow onion, chopped
- 1 teaspoon ground cumin
- 1 teaspoon ground coriander
- 1 teaspoon chili powder
- ¼ cup hemp hearts
- 1 medium tomato, chopped
- 1 cup chopped cabbage (set some aside for garnish)
- ½ cup chopped fresh cilantro
- ½ cup chopped celery
- ½ jalapeño pepper, chopped
- 8 cups vegetable broth
- Juice of 2 limes
- 1 avocado, peeled, pitted, and cut into cubes
- 3 flax crackers

1. Heat the olive oil in a large stockpot over medium heat and add the onion, cumin, coriander, and chili powder. Sauté, stirring occasionally, until the onion becomes tender, about 5 minutes. 2. Add the hemp hearts, tomato, cabbage, cilantro, celery, and jalapeño to the pot. Stir to coat the spices and allow to cook for 4 minutes. 3. Pour the broth into the pot and simmer on low for 20 minutes. 4. Remove the pot from the heat and stir in the lime juice. 5. Divide the avocado equally among 4 serving bowls. 6. Pour the soup over the avocado in the bowls and garnish with additional cabbage and cilantro. 7. Break the flax crackers over the top of the soup to create a "tortilla soup" vibe.

Per Serving:

calories: 130 | fat: 9g | protein: 3g | carbs: 9g | net carbs: 5g | fiber: 4g

Chicken Cauliflower Rice Soup

Prep time: 5 minutes | Cook time: 20 minutes | Serves 4

- 4 tablespoons butter
- ¼ cup diced onion
- 2 stalks celery, chopped
- ½ cup fresh spinach
- ½ teaspoon salt
- ¼ teaspoon pepper
- ¼ teaspoon dried thyme
- ¼ teaspoon dried parsley
- 1 bay leaf
- 2 cups chicken broth
- 2 cups diced cooked chicken
- ¾ cup uncooked cauliflower rice
- ½ teaspoon xanthan gum (optional)

1. Press the Sauté button and add butter to Instant Pot. Add onions and sauté until translucent. Place celery and spinach into Instant Pot and sauté for 2 to 3 minutes until spinach is wilted. Press the Cancel button. 2. Sprinkle seasoning into Instant Pot and add bay leaf, broth, and cooked chicken. Click lid closed. Press the Soup button and adjust time for

10 minutes. 3. When timer beeps, quick-release the pressure and stir in cauliflower rice. Leave Instant Pot on Keep Warm setting to finish cooking cauliflower rice additional 10 minutes. Serve warm. 4. For a thicker soup, stir in xanthan gum.

Per Serving:

calories: 228 | fat: 14g | protein: 22g | carbs: 3g | net carbs: 2g | fiber: 1g

Cauliflower Soup

Prep time: 10 minutes | Cook time: 6 minutes | Serves 4

- 2 cups chopped cauliflower
- 2 tablespoons fresh cilantro
- 1 cup coconut cream
- 2 cups beef broth
- 3 ounces (85 g) Provolone cheese, chopped

1. Put cauliflower, cilantro, coconut cream, beef broth, and cheese in the Instant Pot. Stir to mix well. 2. Select Manual mode and set cooking time for 6 minutes on High Pressure. 3. When timer beeps, allow a natural pressure release for 4 minutes, then release any remaining pressure. Open the lid. 4. Blend the soup and ladle in bowls to serve.

Per Serving:

calories: 244 | fat: 21g | protein: 10g | carbs: 7g | net carbs: 4g | fiber: 3g

Green Minestrone Soup

Prep time: 10 minutes | Cook time: 20 minutes | Serves 4

- 2 tablespoons ghee
- 2 tablespoons onion-garlic puree
- 2 heads broccoli, cut in florets
- 2 stalks celery, chopped
- 5 cups vegetable broth
- 1 cup baby spinach
- Salt and black pepper to taste
- 2 tablespoons Gruyere cheese, grated

1. Melt the ghee in a saucepan over medium heat and sauté the onion-garlic puree for 3 minutes until softened. Mix in the broccoli and celery, and cook for 4 minutes until slightly tender. Pour in the broth, bring to a boil, then reduce the heat to medium-low and simmer covered for about 5 minutes. 2. Drop in the spinach to wilt, adjust the seasonings, and cook for 4 minutes. Ladle soup into serving bowls. Serve with a sprinkle of grated Gruyere cheese.

Per Serving:

calories: 123 | fat: 9g | protein: 5g | carbs: 8g | net carbs: 6g | fiber: 2g

Chicken Zucchini Soup

Prep time: 8 minutes | Cook time: 14 minutes | Serves 6

- ¼ cup coconut oil or unsalted butter
- 1 cup chopped celery
- ¼ cup chopped onions
- 2 cloves garlic, minced
- 1 pound (454 g) boneless, skinless chicken breasts, cut into 1-inch cubes
- 6 cups chicken broth
- 1 tablespoon dried parsley
- 1 teaspoon fine sea salt
- ½ teaspoon dried marjoram
- ½ teaspoon ground black pepper
- 1 bay leaf
- 2 cups zucchini noodles

1. Place the coconut oil in the Instant Pot and press Sauté. Once melted, add the celery, onions, and garlic and cook, stirring occasionally, for 4 minutes, or until the onions are soft. Press Cancel to stop the Sauté. 2. Add the cubed chicken, broth, parsley, salt, marjoram, pepper, and bay leaf. Seal the lid, press Manual, and set the timer for 10 minutes. Once finished, let the pressure release naturally. 3. Remove the lid and stir well. Place the noodles in bowls, using ⅓ cup per bowl. Ladle the soup over the noodles and serve immediately; if it sits too long, the noodles will get too soft.

Per Serving:

calories: 253 | fat: 15g | protein: 21g | carbs: 11g | net carbs: 10g | fiber: 1g

Tomato-Basil Parmesan Soup

Prep time: 5 minutes | Cook time: 12 minutes | Serves 12

- 2 tablespoons unsalted butter or coconut oil
- ½ cup finely diced onions
- Cloves squeezed from 1 head roasted garlic , or 2 cloves garlic, minced
- 1 tablespoon dried basil leaves
- 1 teaspoon dried oregano leaves
- 1 (8 ounces / 227 g) package cream cheese,
- softened
- 4 cups chicken broth
- 2 (14½ ounces / 411 g) cans diced tomatoes
- 1 cup shredded Parmesan cheese, plus more for garnish
- 1 teaspoon fine sea salt
- ¼ teaspoon ground black pepper
- Fresh basil leaves, for garnish

1. Place the butter in the Instant Pot and press Sauté. Once melted, add the onions, garlic, basil, and oregano and cook, stirring often, for 4 minutes, or until the onions are soft. Press Cancel to stop the Sauté. 2. Add the cream cheese and whisk to loosen. (If you don't use a whisk to loosen the cream cheese, you will end up with clumps in your soup.) Slowly whisk in the broth. Add the tomatoes, Parmesan, salt, and pepper and stir to combine. 3. Seal the lid, press Manual, and set the timer for 8 minutes. Once finished, turn the valve to venting for a quick release. 4. Remove the lid and purée the soup with a stick blender, or transfer the soup to a regular blender or food processor and process until smooth. If using a regular blender, you may need to blend the soup in two batches; if you overfill the blender jar, the soup will not purée properly. 5. Season with salt and pepper to taste, if desired. Ladle the soup into bowls and garnish with more Parmesan and basil leaves.

Per Serving:

calories: 146 | fat: 10g | protein: 8g | carbs: 4g | net carbs: 3g | fiber: 1g

Chicken Poblano Pepper Soup

Prep time: 10 minutes | Cook time: 20 minutes | Serves 8

- 1 cup diced onion
- 3 poblano peppers, chopped
- 5 garlic cloves
- 2 cups diced cauliflower
- 1½ pounds (680 g) chicken breast, cut into large chunks
- ¼ cup chopped fresh cilantro
- 1 teaspoon ground coriander
- 1 teaspoon ground cumin
- 1 to 2 teaspoons salt
- 2 cups water
- 2 ounces (57 g) cream cheese, cut into small chunks
- 1 cup sour cream

1. To the inner cooking pot of the Instant Pot, add the onion, poblanos, garlic, cauliflower, chicken, cilantro, coriander, cumin, salt, and water. 2. Lock the lid into place. Select Manual and adjust the pressure to High. Cook for 15 minutes. When the cooking is complete, let the pressure release naturally for 10 minutes, then quick-release any remaining pressure. Unlock the lid. 3. Remove the chicken with tongs and place in a bowl. 4. Tilting the pot, use an immersion blender to roughly purée the vegetable mixture. It should still be slightly chunky. 5. Turn the Instant Pot to Sauté and adjust to high heat. When the broth is hot and bubbling, add the cream cheese and stir until it melts. Use a whisk to blend in the cream cheese if needed. 6. Shred the chicken and stir it back into the pot. Once it is heated through, serve, topped with sour cream, and enjoy.

Per Serving:

calories: 202 | fat: 10g | protein: 20g | carbs: 8g | net carbs: 5g | fiber: 3g

Chicken Creamy Soup

Prep time: 5 minutes | Cook time: 10 minutes | Serves 4

- 2cups cooked and shredded chicken
- 3 tablespoons butter, melted
- 4 cups chicken broth
- 4 tablespoons chopped
- cilantro
- ⅓ cup buffalo sauce
- ½ cup cream cheese
- Salt and black pepper, to taste

1. Blend the butter, buffalo sauce, and cream cheese, in a food processor, until smooth. Transfer to a pot, add chicken broth and heat until hot but do not bring to a boil. Stir in chicken, salt, black pepper and cook until heated through. When ready, remove to soup bowls and serve garnished with cilantro.

Per Serving:

calories: 480 | fat: 41g | protein: 16g | carbs: 13g | net carbs: 12g | fiber: 1g

Thai Shrimp and Mushroom Soup

Prep time: 15 minutes | Cook time: 10 minutes | Serves 6

- 2 tablespoons unsalted butter, divided
- ½ pound (227 g) medium uncooked shrimp, shelled and deveined
- ½ medium yellow onion, diced
- 2 cloves garlic, minced
- 1 cup sliced fresh white mushrooms
- 1 tablespoon freshly grated ginger root
- 4 cups chicken broth
- 2 tablespoons fish sauce
- 2½ teaspoons red curry
- paste
- 2 tablespoons lime juice
- 1 stalk lemongrass, outer stalk removed, crushed, and finely chopped
- 2 tablespoons coconut aminos
- 1 teaspoon sea salt
- ½ teaspoon ground black pepper
- 13½ ounces (383 g) can unsweetened, full-fat coconut milk
- 3 tablespoons chopped fresh cilantro

1. Select the Instant Pot on Sauté mode. Add 1 tablespoon butter. 2. Once the butter is melted, add the shrimp and sauté for 3 minutes or until opaque. Transfer the shrimp to a medium bowl. Set aside. 3. Add the remaining butter to the pot. Once the butter is melted, add the onions and garlic and sauté for 2 minutes or until the garlic is fragrant and the onions are softened. 4. Add the mushrooms, ginger root, chicken broth, fish sauce, red curry paste, lime juice, lemongrass, coconut aminos, sea salt, and black pepper to the pot. Stir to combine. 5. Lock the lid. Select Manual mode and set cooking time for 5 minutes on High Pressure. 6. When cooking is complete, allow the pressure to release naturally for 5 minutes, then release the remaining pressure. 7. Open the lid. Stir in the cooked shrimp and coconut milk. 8. Select Sauté mode. Bring the soup to a boil and then press Keep Warm / Cancel. Let the soup rest in the pot for 2 minutes. 9. Ladle the soup into bowls and sprinkle the cilantro over top. Serve hot.

Per Serving:

calories: 237 | fat: 20g | protein: 9g | carbs: 9g | net carbs: 6g | fiber: 2g

Spicy Sausage and Chicken Stew

Prep time: 10 minutes | Cook time: 25 minutes | Serves 10

- 1 tablespoon coconut oil
- 2 pounds (907 g) bulk Italian sausage
- 2 boneless, skinless chicken thighs, cut into ½-inch pieces
- ½ cup chopped onions
- 1 (28 ounces / 794 g) can whole peeled tomatoes, drained
- 1 cup sugar-free tomato sauce
- 1 (4½ ounces / 128 g) can green chilies
- 3 tablespoons minced garlic
- 2 tablespoons smoked
- paprika
- 1 tablespoon ground cumin
- 1 tablespoon dried oregano leaves
- 2 teaspoons fine sea salt
- 1 teaspoon cayenne pepper
- 1 cup chicken broth
- 1 ounce (28 g) unsweetened baking chocolate, chopped
- ¼ cup lime juice
- Chopped fresh cilantro leaves, for garnish
- Red pepper flakes, for garnish

1. Place the coconut oil in the Instant Pot and press Sauté. Once melted, add the sausage, chicken, and onions and cook, stirring to break up the sausage, until the sausage is starting to cook through and the onions are soft, about 5 minutes. 2. Meanwhile, make the tomato purée: Place the tomatoes, tomato sauce, and chilies in a food processor and process until smooth. 3. Add the garlic, paprika, cumin, oregano, salt, and cayenne pepper to the Instant Pot and stir to combine. Then add the tomato purée, broth, and chocolate and stir well. Press Cancel to stop the Sauté. 4. Seal the lid, press Manual, and set the timer for 20 minutes. Once finished, let the pressure release naturally. 5. Just before serving, stir in the lime juice. Ladle the stew into bowls and garnish with cilantro and red pepper flakes.

Per Serving:

calories: 341 | fat: 23g | protein: 21g | carbs: 10g | net carbs: 8g | fiber: 2g

Keto Pho with Shirataki Noodles

Prep time: 20 minutes | Cook time: 10 minutes | Makes 4 bowls

- 8 ounces (227 g) sirloin, very thinly sliced
- 3 tablespoons coconut oil (or butter or ghee)
- 2 garlic cloves, minced
- 2 tablespoons liquid or coconut aminos
- 2 tablespoons fish sauce
- 1 teaspoon freshly grated or ground ginger
- 8 cups bone broth
- 4 (7-ounce / 198-g) packages shirataki noodles, drained and rinsed
- 1 cup bean sprouts
- 1 scallion, chopped
- 1 tablespoon toasted sesame seeds (optional)

1. Put the sirloin in the freezer while you prepare the broth and other ingredients (about 15 to 20 minutes). This makes it easier to slice. 2. In a large pot over medium heat, melt the coconut oil. Add the garlic and cook for 3 minutes. Then add the aminos, fish sauce, ginger, and bone broth. Bring to a boil. 3. Remove the beef from the freezer and slice it very thin. 4. Divide the noodles, beef, and bean sprouts evenly among four serving bowls. Carefully ladle 2 cups of broth into each bowl. Cover the bowls with plates and let sit for 3 to 5 minutes to cook the meat. 5. Serve garnished with the chopped scallion and sesame seeds (if using).

Per Serving:

1 bowl: calories: 385 | fat: 29g | protein: 23g | carbs: 8g | net carbs: 4g | fiber: 4g

Bacon Curry Soup

Prep time: 10 minutes | Cook time: 20 minutes | Serves 4

- 3 ounces (85 g) bacon, chopped
- 1 tablespoon chopped scallions
- 1 teaspoon curry powder
- 1 cup coconut milk
- 3 cups beef broth
- 1 cup Cheddar cheese, shredded

1. Heat the the Instant Pot on Sauté mode for 3 minutes and add bacon. Cook for 5 minutes. Flip constantly. 2. Add the scallions and curry powder. Sauté for 5 minutes more. 3. Pour in the coconut milk and beef broth. Add the Cheddar cheese and stir to mix well. 4. Select Manual mode and set cooking time for 10 minutes on High Pressure. 5. When timer beeps, use a quick pressure release. Open the lid. 6. Blend the soup with an immersion blender until smooth. Serve warm.

Per Serving:

calories: 398 | fat: 34g | protein: 20g | carbs: 5g | net carbs:

4g | fiber: 2g

Broc Obama Cheese Soup

Prep time: 25 minutes | Cook time: 25 minutes | Serves 8

- 8 cups chicken broth
- 2 large heads broccoli, chopped into bite-sized florets
- 1 clove garlic, peeled and minced
- ¼ cup heavy whipping cream
- ¼ cup shredded Cheddar cheese
- ⅛ teaspoon salt
- ⅛ teaspoon black pepper

1. In a medium pot over medium heat, add broth and bring to boil (about 5 minutes). Add broccoli and garlic. Reduce heat to low, cover pot, and simmer until vegetables are fully softened, about 15 minutes. 2. Remove from heat and blend using a hand immersion blender to desired consistency while still in pot. Leave some chunks of varying sizes for variety. 3. Return pot to medium heat and add cream and cheese. Stir 3 to 5 minutes until fully blended. Add salt and pepper. 4. Remove from heat, let cool 10 minutes, and serve.

Per Serving:

calories: 82 | fat: 4g | protein: 5g | carbs: 8g | net carbs: 5g | fiber: 3g

Salsa Verde Chicken Soup

Prep time: 5 minutes | Cook time: 10 minutes | Serves 4

- ½ cup salsa verde
- 2 cups cooked and shredded chicken
- 2 cups chicken broth
- 1 cup shredded cheddar cheese
- 4 ounces cream cheese
- ½ teaspoon chili powder
- ½ teaspoon ground cumin
- ½ teaspoon fresh cilantro, chopped
- Salt and black pepper, to taste

1. Combine the cream cheese, salsa verde, and broth, in a food processor; pulse until smooth. Transfer the mixture to a pot and place over medium heat. Cook until hot, but do not bring to a boil. Add chicken, chili powder, and cumin and cook for about 3-5 minutes, or until it is heated through. 2. Stir in cheddar cheese and season with salt and pepper to taste. If it is very thick, add a few tablespoons of water and boil for 1-3 more minutes. Serve hot in bowls sprinkled with fresh cilantro.

Per Serving:

calories: 346 | fat: 23g | protein: 25g | carbs: 4g | net carbs: 3g | fiber: 1g

Jalapeño Popper Chicken Soup

Prep time: 5 minutes | Cook time: 25 minutes | Serves 4

- 2 tablespoons butter
- ½ medium diced onion
- ¼ cup sliced pickled jalapeños
- ¼ cup cooked crumbled bacon
- 2 cups chicken broth
- 2 cups cooked diced chicken
- 4 ounces (113 g) cream cheese
- 1 teaspoon salt
- ½ teaspoon pepper
- ¼ teaspoon garlic powder
- ⅓ cup heavy cream
- 1 cup shredded sharp Cheddar cheese

1. Press the Sauté button. Add butter, onion, and sliced jalapeños to Instant Pot. Sauté for 5 minutes, until onions are translucent. Add bacon and press the Cancel button. 2. Add broth, cooked chicken, cream cheese, salt, pepper, and garlic to Instant Pot. Click lid closed. Press the Soup button and adjust time for 20 minutes. 3. When timer beeps, quick-release the steam. Stir in heavy cream and Cheddar. Continue stirring until cheese is fully melted. Serve warm.

Per Serving:

calories: 524 | fat: 36g | protein: 35g | carbs: 9g | net carbs: 8g | fiber: 1g

Chicken and Kale Soup

Prep time: 5 minutes | Cook time: 5 minutes | Serves 4

- 2 cups chopped cooked chicken breast
- 12 ounces (340 g) frozen kale
- 1 onion, chopped
- 2 cups water
- 1 tablespoon powdered chicken broth base
- ½ teaspoon ground
- cinnamon
- Pinch ground cloves
- 2 teaspoons minced garlic
- 1 teaspoon freshly ground black pepper
- 1 teaspoon salt
- 2 cups full-fat coconut milk

1. Put the chicken, kale, onion, water, chicken broth base, cinnamon, cloves, garlic, pepper, and salt in the inner cooking pot of the Instant Pot. 2. Lock the lid into place. Select Manual and adjust the pressure to High. Cook for 5 minutes. When the cooking is complete, let the pressure release naturally for 10 minutes, then quick-release any remaining pressure. Unlock the lid. 3. Stir in the coconut milk. Taste and adjust any seasonings as needed before serving.

Per Serving:

calories: 387 | fat: 27g | protein: 26g | carbs: 10g | net carbs: 8g | fiber: 2g

Summer Vegetable Soup

Prep time: 10 minutes | Cook time: 6 minutes | Serves 6

- 3 cups finely sliced leeks
- 6 cups chopped rainbow chard, stems and leaves separated
- 1 cup chopped celery
- 2 tablespoons minced garlic, divided
- 1 teaspoon dried oregano
- 1 teaspoon salt
- 2 teaspoons freshly ground black pepper
- 3 cups chicken broth, plus more as needed
- 2 cups sliced yellow summer squash, ½-inch slices
- ¼ cup chopped fresh parsley
- ¾ cup heavy (whipping) cream
- 4 to 6 tablespoons grated Parmesan cheese

1. Put the leeks, chard, celery, 1 tablespoon of garlic, oregano, salt, pepper, and broth into the inner cooking pot of the Instant Pot. 2. Lock the lid into place. Select Manual and adjust the pressure to High. Cook for 3 minutes. When the cooking is complete, quick-release the pressure. Unlock the lid. 3. Add more broth if needed. 4. Turn the pot to Sauté and adjust the heat to high. Add the yellow squash, parsley, and remaining 1 tablespoon of garlic. 5. Allow the soup to cook for 2 to 3 minutes, or until the squash is softened and cooked through. 6. Stir in the cream and ladle the soup into bowls. Sprinkle with the Parmesan cheese and serve.

Per Serving:

calories: 210 | fat: 14g | protein: 10g | carbs: 12g | net carbs: 8g | fiber: 4g

Pork and Daikon Stew

Prep time: 15 minutes | Cook time: 3 minutes | Serves 6

- 1 pound (454 g) pork tenderloin, chopped
- 1 ounce (28 g) green onions, chopped
- ½ cup daikon, chopped
- 1 lemon slice
- 1 tablespoon heavy cream
- 1 tablespoon butter
- 1 teaspoon ground black pepper
- 3 cups water

1. Put all ingredients in the Instant Pot and stir to mix with a spatula. 2. Seal the lid. Set Manual mode and set cooking time for 20 minutes on High Pressure. 3. When cooking is complete, use a natural pressure release for 15 minutes, then release any remaining pressure. Open the lid. 4. Serve warm.

Per Serving:

calories: 137 | fat: 6g | protein: 20g | carbs: 1g | net carbs: 1g | fiber: 0g

Slow Cooker Beer Soup with Cheddar & Sausage

Prep time: 15 minutes | Cook time: 8 hours | Serves 8

- 1 cup heavy cream
- 10 ounces sausages, sliced
- 1 cup celery, chopped
- 1 cup carrots, chopped
- 4 garlic cloves, minced
- 8 ounces cream cheese
- 1 teaspoon red pepper flakes
- 6 ounces beer
- 16 ounces beef stock
- 1 onion, diced
- 1 cup cheddar cheese, grated
- Salt and black pepper, to taste
- Fresh cilantro, chopped, to garnish

1. Turn on the slow cooker. Add beef stock, beer, sausages, carrots, onion, garlic, celery, salt, red pepper flakes, and black pepper, and stir to combine. Pour in enough water to cover all the ingredients by roughly 2 inches. Close the lid and cook for 6 hours on Low. 2. Open the lid and stir in the heavy cream, cheddar, and cream cheese, and cook for 2 more hours. Ladle the soup into bowls and garnish with cilantro before serving. Yummy!

Per Serving:

calories: 387| fat: 28g | protein: 24g | carbs: 12g | net carbs: 9g | fiber: 2g

Broccoli Cheddar Soup

Prep time: 5 minutes | Cook time: 10 minutes | Serves 4

- 2 tablespoons butter
- ⅛ cup onion, diced
- ½ teaspoon garlic powder
- ½ teaspoon salt
- ¼ teaspoon pepper
- 2 cups chicken broth
- 1 cup chopped broccoli
- 1 tablespoon cream cheese, softened
- ¼ cup heavy cream
- 1 cup shredded Cheddar cheese

1. Press the Sauté button and add butter to Instant Pot. Add onion and sauté until translucent. Press the Cancel button and add garlic powder, salt, pepper, broth, and broccoli to pot. 2. Click lid closed. Press the Soup button and set time for 5 minutes. When timer beeps, stir in heavy cream, cream cheese, and Cheddar.

Per Serving:

calories: 250 | fat: 20g | protein: 9g | carbs: 4g | net carbs: 3g | fiber: 1g

Broccoli-Cheese Soup

Prep time: 5 minutes | Cook time: 20 minutes | Serves 4

- 2 tablespoons butter
- 1 cup broccoli florets, finely chopped
- 1 cup heavy (whipping) cream
- 1 cup chicken or vegetable broth
- Pink Himalayan salt
- Freshly ground black pepper
- 1 cup shredded cheese, some reserved for topping (I use sharp Cheddar)

1. In a medium saucepan over medium heat, melt the butter. 2. Add the broccoli and sauté in the butter for about 5 minutes, until tender. 3. Add the cream and the chicken broth, stirring constantly. Season with pink Himalayan salt and pepper. Cook, stirring occasionally, for 10 to 15 minutes, until the soup has thickened. 4. Turn down the heat to low, and begin adding the shredded cheese. Reserve a small handful of cheese for topping the bowls of soup. (Do not add all the cheese at once, or it may clump up.) Add small amounts, slowly, while stirring constantly. 5. Pour the soup into four bowls, top each with half of the reserved cheese, and serve.

Per Serving:

calories: 383 | fat: 37g | protein: 10g | carbs: 4g | net carbs: 4g | fiber: 0g

Green Garden Soup

Prep time: 20 minutes | Cook time: 29 minutes | Serves 5

- 1 tablespoon olive oil
- 1 garlic clove, diced
- ½ cup cauliflower florets
- 1 cup kale, chopped
- 2 tablespoons chives, chopped
- 1 teaspoon sea salt
- 6 cups beef broth

1. Heat the olive oil in the Instant Pot on Sauté mode for 2 minutes and add the garlic. Sauté for 2 minutes or until fragrant. 2. Add cauliflower, kale, chives, sea salt, and beef broth. 3. Close the lid. Select Manual mode and set cooking time for 5 minutes on High Pressure. 4. When timer beeps, use a quick pressure release and open the lid. 5. Ladle the soup into the bowls. Serve warm.

Per Serving:

calories: 80 | fat: 5g | protein: 7g | carbs: 2g | net carbs: 2g | fiber: 1g

Chapter 4

Fish and Seafood

Fish Fillets with Lemon-Dill Sauce

Prep time: 5 minutes | Cook time: 7 minutes | Serves 4

- 1 pound (454 g) snapper, grouper, or salmon fillets
- Sea salt and freshly ground black pepper, to taste
- 1 tablespoon avocado oil
- ¼ cup sour cream
- ¼ cup sugar-free
- mayonnaise
- 2 tablespoons fresh dill, chopped, plus more for garnish
- 1 tablespoon freshly squeezed lemon juice
- ½ teaspoon grated lemon zest

1. Pat the fish dry with paper towels and season well with salt and pepper. Brush with the avocado oil. 2. Set the air fryer to 400ºF (204ºC). Place the fillets in the air fryer basket and air fry for 1 minute. 3. Lower the air fryer temperature to 325ºF (163ºC) and continue cooking for 5 minutes. Flip the fish and cook for 1 minute more or until an instant-read thermometer reads 145ºF (63ºC). (If using salmon, cook it to 125ºF / 52ºC for medium-rare.) 4. While the fish is cooking, make the sauce by combining the sour cream, mayonnaise, dill, lemon juice, and lemon zest in a medium bowl. Season with salt and pepper and stir until combined. Refrigerate until ready to serve. 5. Serve the fish with the sauce, garnished with the remaining dill.

Per Serving:

calories: 223 | fat: 12g | protein: 25g | carbs: 4g | net carbs: 3g | fiber: 1g

Foil-Packet Salmon

Prep time: 2 minutes | Cook time: 7 minutes | Serves 2

- 2 (3-ounce / 85-g) salmon fillets
- ¼ teaspoon garlic powder
- 1 teaspoon salt
- ¼ teaspoon pepper
- ¼ teaspoon dried dill
- ½ lemon
- 1 cup water

1. Place each filet of salmon on a square of foil, skin-side down. 2. Season with garlic powder, salt, and pepper and squeeze the lemon juice over the fish. 3. Cut the lemon into four slices and place two on each filet. Close the foil packets by folding over edges. 4. Add the water to the Instant Pot and insert a trivet. Place the foil packets on the trivet. 5. Secure the lid. Select the Steam mode and set the cooking time for 7 minutes at Low Pressure. 6. Once cooking is complete, do a quick pressure release. Carefully open the lid. 7. Check the internal temperature with a meat thermometer to ensure the thickest part of the filets reached at least 145ºF (63ºC).

Salmon should easily flake when fully cooked. Serve immediately.

Per Serving:

calories: 128 | fat: 5g | protein: 19g | carbs: 0g | net carbs: 0g | fiber: 0g

Pistachio-Crusted Salmon

Prep time: 5 minutes | Cook time: 20 minutes | Serves 4

- 4 salmon fillets
- ½ teaspoon pepper
- 1 teaspoon salt
- ¼ cup mayonnaise
- ½ cup chopped pistachios
- Sauce
- 1 chopped shallot
- 2 teaspoons lemon zest
- 1 tablespoon olive oil
- A pinch of black pepper
- 1 cup heavy cream

1. Preheat the oven to 370ºF. 2. Brush the salmon with mayonnaise and season with salt and pepper. Coat with pistachios, place in a lined baking dish and bake for 15 minutes. 3. Heat olive oil in a saucepan and sauté the shallot for 3 minutes. Stir in the rest of the sauce ingredients. Bring the mixture to a boil and cook until thickened. Serve the fish with the sauce.

Per Serving:

calories: 473 | fat: 33g | protein: 36g | carbs: 8g | net carbs: 6g | fiber: 2g

Golden Shrimp

Prep time: 20 minutes | Cook time: 7 minutes | Serves 4

- 2 egg whites
- ½ cup coconut flour
- 1 cup Parmigiano-Reggiano, grated
- ½ teaspoon celery seeds
- ½ teaspoon porcini powder
- ½ teaspoon onion powder
- 1 teaspoon garlic powder
- ½ teaspoon dried rosemary
- ½ teaspoon sea salt
- ½ teaspoon ground black pepper
- 1½ pounds (680 g) shrimp, deveined

1. Whisk the egg with coconut flour and Parmigiano-Reggiano. Add in seasonings and mix to combine well. 2. Dip your shrimp in the batter. Roll until they are covered on all sides. 3. Cook in the preheated air fryer at 390ºF (199ºC) for 5 to 7 minutes or until golden brown. Work in batches. Serve with lemon wedges if desired.

Per Serving:

calories: 265 | fat: 11g | protein: 33g | carbs: 7g | net carbs: 6g | fiber: 1g

Tuna Steak

Prep time: 10 minutes | Cook time: 12 minutes | Serves 4

- 1 pound (454 g) tuna steaks, boneless and cubed
- 1 tablespoon mustard
- 1 tablespoon avocado oil
- 1 tablespoon apple cider vinegar

1. Mix avocado oil with mustard and apple cider vinegar. 2. Then brush tuna steaks with mustard mixture and put in the air fryer basket. 3. Cook the fish at 360ºF (182ºC) for 6 minutes per side.

Per Serving:
calories: 180 | fat: 9g | protein: 25g | carbs: 1g | net carbs: 1g | fiber: 0g

Mouthwatering Cod over Creamy Leek Noodles

Prep time: 10 minutes | Cook time: 24 minutes | Serves 4

- 1 small leek, sliced into long thin noodles (about 2 cups)
- ½ cup heavy cream
- 2 cloves garlic, minced
- 1 teaspoon fine sea salt, Coating:
- ¼ cup grated Parmesan cheese
- 2 tablespoons mayonnaise
- 2 tablespoons unsalted butter, softened
- divided
- 4 (4-ounce / 113-g) cod fillets (about 1 inch thick)
- ½ teaspoon ground black pepper
- 1 tablespoon chopped fresh thyme, or ½ teaspoon dried thyme leaves, plus more for garnish

1. Preheat the air fryer to 350ºF (177ºC). 2. Place the leek noodles in a casserole dish or a pan that will fit in your air fryer. 3. In a small bowl, stir together the cream, garlic, and ½ teaspoon of the salt. Pour the mixture over the leeks and cook in the air fryer for 10 minutes, or until the leeks are very tender. 4. Pat the fish dry and season with the remaining ½ teaspoon of salt and the pepper. When the leeks are ready, open the air fryer and place the fish fillets on top of the leeks. Air fry for 8 to 10 minutes, until the fish flakes easily with a fork (the thicker the fillets, the longer this will take). 5. While the fish cooks, make the coating: In a small bowl, combine the Parmesan, mayo, butter, and thyme. 6. When the fish is ready, remove it from the air fryer and increase the heat to 425ºF (218ºC) (or as high as your air fryer can go). Spread the fillets with a ½-inch-thick to ¾-inch-thick

layer of the coating. 7. Place the fish back in the air fryer and air fry for 3 to 4 minutes, until the coating browns. 8. Garnish with fresh or dried thyme, if desired. Store leftovers in an airtight container in the refrigerator for up to 3 days. Reheat in a casserole dish in a preheated 350ºF (177ºC) air fryer for 6 minutes, or until heated through.

Per Serving:
calories: 380 | fat: 28g | protein: 24g | carbs: 6g | net carbs: 5g | fiber: 1g

Mackerel and Broccoli Casserole

Prep time: 15 minutes | Cook time: 15 minutes | Serves 5

- 1 cup shredded broccoli
- 10 ounces (283 g) mackerel, chopped
- ½ cup shredded Cheddar
- cheese
- 1 cup coconut milk
- 1 teaspoon ground cumin
- 1 teaspoon salt

1. Sprinkle the chopped mackerel with ground cumin and salt and transfer in the instant pot. 2. Top the fish with shredded broccoli and Cheddar cheese, 3. Then add coconut milk. Close and seal the lid. 4. Cook the casserole on Manual mode (High Pressure) for 15 minutes. 5. Allow the natural pressure release for 10 minutes and open the lid.

Per Serving:
calories: 312 | fat: 25g | protein: 18g | carbs: 4g | net carbs: 2g | fiber: 2g

Sour Cream Salmon with Parmesan

Prep time: 10 minutes | Cook time: 17 minutes | Serves 4

- 1 cup sour cream
- ½ tbsp minced dill
- ½ lemon, zested and juiced
- Pink salt and black
- pepper to season
- 4 salmon steaks
- ½ cup grated Parmesan cheese

1. Preheat oven to 400ºF and line a baking sheet with parchment paper; set aside. In a bowl, mix the sour cream, dill, lemon zest, juice, salt and black pepper, and set aside. 2. Season the fish with salt and black pepper, drizzle lemon juice on both sides of the fish and arrange them in the baking sheet. Spread the sour cream mixture on each fish and sprinkle with Parmesan. 3. Bake the fish for 15 minutes and after broil the top for 2 minutes with a close watch for a nice a brown color. Plate the fish and serve with buttery green beans.

Per Serving:
calories: 529 | fat: 38g | protein: 41g | carbs: 6g | net carbs: 6g | fiber: 0g

Almond Catfish

Prep time: 10 minutes | Cook time: 12 minutes | Serves 4

- ➤ 2 pounds (907 g) catfish fillet
- ➤ ½ cup almond flour
- ➤ 2 eggs, beaten
- ➤ 1 teaspoon salt
- ➤ 1 teaspoon avocado oil

1. Sprinkle the catfish fillet with salt and dip in the eggs. 2. Then coat the fish in the almond flour and put in the air fryer basket. Sprinkle the fish with avocado oil. 3. Cook the fish for 6 minutes per side at 380ºF (193ºC).

Per Serving:

calories: 360 | fat: 21g | protein: 36g | carbs: 7g | net carbs: 5g | fiber: 2g

Clam Chowder

Prep time: 5 minutes | Cook time: 15 minutes | Serves 4

- ➤ 4 slices bacon, chopped into ½-inch squares
- ➤ 2 tablespoons unsalted butter
- ➤ ½ small yellow onion, chopped
- ➤ 4 ribs celery, cut into ¼-inch-thick half-moons
- ➤ 1 cup chopped cauliflower florets, cut to about ½ inch thick
- ➤ 4 ounces (113 g) chopped mushrooms
- ➤ 4 cloves garlic, minced
- ➤ 1 teaspoon dried tarragon
- ➤ 1 teaspoon salt
- ➤ ¼ teaspoon freshly ground black pepper
- ➤ 8 ounces (227 g) bottled clam juice
- ➤ 1 cup vegetable stock or broth
- ➤ ½ cup heavy cream
- ➤ 8 ounces (227 g) cream cheese, room temperature
- ➤ 3 (6½-ounce / 184-g) cans chopped clams, with juice
- ➤ ¼ cup freshly chopped Italian parsley

1. Place the bacon in a medium saucepan over medium heat. Fry until just browned and most of the fat has been rendered, 3 to 4 minutes. Remove the bacon with a slotted spoon, reserving the rendered fat. 2. Add the butter to the pan with the fat and melt over medium heat. Add the onion, celery, cauliflower, and mushrooms and sauté until vegetables are just tender, 4 to 5 minutes. Add the garlic, tarragon, salt, and pepper and sauté for another 30 seconds or until fragrant. 3. Add the clam juice, stock, cream, and cream cheese and whisk until the cheese is melted and creamy, 2 to 3 minutes. Add the clams and their juice, bring to a simmer, and cook for 1 to 2 minutes so the flavors meld. Stir in the parsley and serve warm.

Per Serving:

calories: 671 | fat: 54g | protein: 34g | carbs: 15g | net carbs:

13g | fiber: 2g

Shrimp Stuffed Zucchini

Prep time: 15 minutes | Cook time: 25 minutes | Serves 4

- ➤ 4 medium zucchinis
- ➤ 1 pound small shrimp, peeled, deveined
- ➤ 1 tablespoon minced onion
- ➤ 2 teaspoons butter
- ➤ ¼ cup chopped tomatoes
- ➤ Salt and black pepper to taste
- ➤ 1 cup pork rinds, crushed
- ➤ 1 tablespoon chopped basil leaves
- ➤ 2 tablespoons melted butter

1. Preheat the oven to 350ºF and trim off the top and bottom ends of the zucchinis. Lay them flat on a chopping board, and cut a ¼ -inch off the top to create a boat for the stuffing. Scoop out the seeds with a spoon and set the zucchinis aside. 2. Melt the firm butter in a small skillet and sauté the onion and tomato for 6 minutes. Transfer the mixture to a bowl and add the shrimp, half of the pork rinds, basil leaves, salt, and black pepper. 3. Combine the ingredients and stuff the zucchini boats with the mixture. Sprinkle the top of the boats with the remaining pork rinds and drizzle the melted butter over them. 4. Place on a baking sheet and bake for 15 to 20 minutes. The shrimp should no longer be pink by this time. Remove the zucchinis after and serve with a tomato and mozzarella salad.

Per Serving:

calories: 300 | fat: 16g | protein: 26g | carbs: 10g | net carbs: 6g | fiber: 4g

Louisiana Shrimp Gumbo

Prep time: 10 minutes | Cook time: 4 minutes | Serves 6

- ➤ 1 pound (454 g) shrimp
- ➤ ¼ cup chopped celery stalk
- ➤ 1 chili pepper, chopped
- ➤ ¼ cup chopped okra
- ➤ 1 tablespoon coconut oil
- ➤ 2 cups chicken broth
- ➤ 1 teaspoon sugar-free tomato paste

1. Put all ingredients in the instant pot and stir until you get a light red color. 2. Then close and seal the lid. 3. Cook the meal on Manual mode (High Pressure) for 4 minutes. 4. When the time is finished, allow the natural pressure release for 10 minutes.

Per Serving:

calories: 126 | fat: 4g | protein: 19g | carbs: 2g | net carbs: 2g | fiber: 0g

Red Cabbage Tilapia Taco Bowl

Prep time: 15 minutes | Cook time: 10 minutes | Serves 4

- 2 cups cauli rice
- 2 teaspoons ghee
- 4 tilapia fillets, cut into cubes
- ¼ teaspoon taco seasoning
- Salt and chili pepper to taste
- ¼ head red cabbage, shredded
- 1 ripe avocado, pitted and chopped

1. Sprinkle cauli rice in a bowl with a little water and microwave for 3 minutes. Fluff after with a fork and set aside. Melt ghee in a skillet over medium heat, rub the tilapia with the taco seasoning, salt, and chili pepper, and fry until brown on all sides, for about 8 minutes in total. 2. Transfer to a plate and set aside. In 4 serving bowls, share the cauli rice, cabbage, fish, and avocado. Serve with chipotle lime sour cream dressing.

Per Serving:

calories: 315 | fat: 23g | protein: 21g | carbs: 6g | net carbs: 3g | fiber: 3g

Sardine Fritter Wraps

Prep time: 5 minutes | Cook time: 8 minutes | Serves 4

- ⅓ cup (80 ml) refined avocado oil, for frying

Fritters:

- 2 (4.375 ounces/125 g) cans sardines, drained
- ½ cup (55 g) blanched almond flour
- 2 large eggs
- 2 tablespoons finely chopped fresh parsley
- 2 tablespoons finely diced red bell pepper
- 2 cloves garlic, minced
- ½ teaspoon finely ground gray sea salt
- ¼ teaspoon ground black pepper

For Serving:

- 8 romaine lettuce leaves
- 1 small English cucumber, sliced thin
- 8 tablespoons (105 g)
- mayonnaise
- Thinly sliced green onions

1. Pour the avocado oil into a large frying pan. Heat on medium for a couple of minutes. 2. Meanwhile, prepare the fritters: Place the fritter ingredients in a medium-sized bowl and stir to combine, being careful not to mash the heck out of the sardines. Spoon about 1 tablespoon of the mixture into the palm of your hand and roll it into a ball, then flatten it like a burger patty. Repeat with the remaining fritter mixture, making a total of 16 small patties. 3. Fry the fritters in the hot oil for 2 minutes per side, then transfer to a cooling rack. You may have to fry the fritters in batches if your pan isn't large enough to fit them all without overcrowding. 4. Meanwhile, divide the lettuce leaves among 4 dinner plates. Top with the sliced cucumber. When the fritters are done, place 2 fritters on each leaf. Top with a dollop of mayonnaise, sprinkle with sliced green onions, and serve!

Per Serving:

calories: 612 | fat: 56g | protein: 23g | carbs: 6g | net carbs: 4g | fiber: 2g

Bacon-Wrapped Shrimp

Prep time: 10 minutes | Cook time: 15 minutes | Serves 4

- 1 pound (454 g) shrimp, peeled, deveined, tails
- still attached
- 20 slices bacon

1. Preheat the oven to 400ºF (205ºC). Line a baking sheet with parchment paper. 2. Wrap each shrimp with a slice of bacon, secure with a toothpick, and place on the prepared baking sheet. 3. Bake about 15 minutes or until the bacon looks crispy.

Per Serving:

5 shrimp: calories: 335 | fat: 19g | protein: 38g | carbs: 2g | net carbs: 2g | fiber: 0g

Muffin Top Tuna Pops

Prep time: 10 minutes | Cook time: 25 minutes | Serves 6

- 1 (5-ounce) can tuna in water, drained
- 2 large eggs
- ¾ cup shredded Cheddar cheese
- ¾ cup shredded pepper jack cheese
- ¼ cup full-fat sour cream
- ¼ cup full-fat mayonnaise
- ¼ cup chopped yellow onion
- 1 tablespoon dried parsley
- ¼ teaspoon salt
- 18 pieces sliced jalapeño from jar
- 2 tablespoons unsalted butter

1. Preheat oven to 350°F. Grease six cups of a muffin tin. 2. Combine all ingredients except the jalapeño slices and butter in a medium mixing bowl. 3. Evenly fill six muffin cups with the mixture, topping each with three jalapeño slices. 4. Bake 25 minutes. Serve warm with butter.

Per Serving:

calories: 275 | fat: 22g | protein: 14g | carbs: 1g | net carbs: 1g | fiber: 0g

Shrimp Fry

Prep time: 5 minutes | Cook time: 20 minutes | Serves 4

- ¼ cup (55 g) coconut oil
- 1 pound (455 g) medium shrimp, peeled, deveined, and tails removed
- 12 ounces (340 g) smoked sausage (chicken, pork, beef—anything goes), cubed
- 5 asparagus spears, woody ends snapped off, thinly sliced
- 4 ounces (115 g) cremini mushrooms, sliced
- 1 medium zucchini, cubed
- 1 tablespoon paprika
- 2 teaspoons garlic powder
- 1 teaspoon onion powder
- 1 teaspoon dried thyme leaves
- ½ teaspoon finely ground sea salt
- ¼ teaspoon ground black pepper
- Pinch of cayenne pepper (optional)
- Handful of fresh parsley leaves, chopped, for serving

1. Melt the oil in a large frying pan over medium heat. 2. Add the remaining ingredients, except the parsley. Toss to coat in the oil, then cover and cook for 15 to 20 minutes, until the asparagus is tender and the shrimp has turned pink. 3. Divide the mixture among 4 serving plates, sprinkle with parsley, and serve.

Per Serving:

calories: 574 | fat: 40g | protein: 45g | carbs: 8g | net carbs: 6g | fiber: 2g

Sole Meunière

Prep time: 5 minutes | Cook time: 10 minutes | Serves 2

- ½ cup almond flour
- 4 (6-ounce / 170-g) sole fillets
- Salt, to taste
- Freshly ground black pepper, to taste
- 6 tablespoons butter, divided
- Juice of ½ lemon
- 2 tablespoons minced fresh parsley leaves
- 4 lemon wedges (from the other half of the lemon), for serving

1. Put the almond flour into a shallow dish. 2. Pat the fish dry with a paper towel and coat each side with almond flour. Season with salt and pepper. 3. In a large skillet over medium heat, melt 3 tablespoons of butter. 4. Add the fish to the skillet and cook for 2 to 3 minutes per side or until the fish is completely opaque. Transfer the fish to a serving platter. 5. Return the skillet to the heat and add the remaining 3 tablespoons of butter and the lemon juice. When melted, pour it over the fish, garnish with the parsley, and serve

with the lemon wedges. Refrigerate leftovers in an airtight container for up to 4 days.

Per Serving:

calories: 624 | fat: 40g | protein: 65g | carbs: 2g | net carbs: 2g | fiber: 0g

Oregano Tilapia Fingers

Prep time: 15 minutes | Cook time: 9 minutes | Serves 4

- 1 pound (454 g) tilapia fillet
- ½ cup coconut flour
- 2 eggs, beaten
- ½ teaspoon ground paprika
- 1 teaspoon dried oregano
- 1 teaspoon avocado oil

1. Cut the tilapia fillets into fingers and sprinkle with ground paprika and dried oregano. 2. Then dip the tilapia fingers in eggs and coat in the coconut flour. 3. Sprinkle fish fingers with avocado oil and cook in the air fryer at 370ºF (188ºC) for 9 minutes.

Per Serving:

calories: 230 | fat: 8g | protein: 32g | carbs: 10g | net carbs: 7g | fiber: 3g

Shrimp Alfredo

Prep time: 10 minutes | Cook time: 10 minutes | Serves 2

- 2 tablespoons butter
- 2 tablespoons olive oil, divided
- 1 garlic clove, minced
- 1 cup heavy (whipping) cream
- ¾ cup grated Parmesan
- cheese
- Salt, to taste
- Freshly ground black pepper, to taste
- 1 pound (454 g) shrimp, shells and tails removed, deveined

1. In a small saucepan over medium-low heat, melt together the butter and 1 tablespoon of olive oil. 2. Stir in the garlic and cream. Bring to a low simmer and cook for 5 to 7 minutes until thickened. 3. Slowly add the Parmesan, stirring well to mix as it melts. Continue to stir until smooth. Season with salt and pepper. Set aside. 4. In a skillet over medium heat, heat the remaining 1 tablespoon of olive oil. 5. Add the shrimp and sauté for about 3 minutes per side or until they turn pink. Remove from the heat and toss with the Alfredo sauce. Serve immediately. Refrigerate leftovers in an airtight container for up to 5 days.

Per Serving:

calories: 1034 | fat: 84g | protein: 63g | carbs: 7g | net carbs: 7g | fiber: 0g

Scallops in Lemon-Butter Sauce

Prep time: 10 minutes | Cook time: 6 minutes | Serves 2

- 8 large dry sea scallops (about ¾ pound / 340 g)
- Salt and freshly ground black pepper, to taste
- 2 tablespoons olive oil
- 2 tablespoons unsalted butter, melted
- 2 tablespoons chopped
- flat-leaf parsley
- 1 tablespoon fresh lemon juice
- 2 teaspoons capers, drained and chopped
- 1 teaspoon grated lemon zest
- 1 clove garlic, minced

1. Preheat the air fryer to 400ºF (204ºC). 2. Use a paper towel to pat the scallops dry. Sprinkle lightly with salt and pepper. Brush with the olive oil. Arrange the scallops in a single layer in the air fryer basket. Pausing halfway through the cooking time to turn the scallops, air fry for about 6 minutes until firm and opaque. 3. Meanwhile, in a small bowl, combine the oil, butter, parsley, lemon juice, capers, lemon zest, and garlic. Drizzle over the scallops just before serving.

Per Serving:

calories: 304 | fat: 22g | protein: 21g | carbs: 5g | net carbs: 4g | fiber: 1g

Salmon Romesco

Prep time: 10 minutes | Cook time: 30 minutes | Serves 4

- ½ cup almonds
- 4 garlic cloves, peeled
- 1 tomato
- 4 (6-ounce / 170-g) salmon fillets
- 2 red bell peppers
- ¼ cup olive oil
- 2 tablespoons white wine
- vinegar
- 1 tablespoon smoked paprika
- 1 teaspoon ground cayenne pepper
- Salt, to taste
- Freshly ground black pepper, to taste

1. Preheat the oven to 375ºF (190ºC). 2. On a large baking sheet, spread out the almonds and add the garlic and tomato. Roast for 10 minutes or until the almonds are fragrant and just starting to brown. Remove the almonds and continue roasting the garlic and tomato for 15 to 20 minutes more until the garlic is browned and the tomato has softened. 3. While the almonds, garlic, and tomato roast, on a separate baking sheet, bake the salmon for 30 to 35 minutes or until the flesh is opaque and flakes easily with a fork. 4. Meanwhile, roast the red peppers for 3 to 5 minutes over an open flame or on a hot (medium high) grill until the skins are blackened. Cover with plastic wrap and let sweat until cool enough to handle.

Peel off the blackened skin and remove the seeds. 5. In a food processor, combine the almonds, garlic, tomato, bell peppers, olive oil, vinegar, paprika, cayenne, and some salt and pepper. Purée until smooth. Serve over the salmon and enjoy immediately.

Per Serving:

calories: 513 | fat: 37g | protein: 37g | carbs: 8g | net carbs: 4g | fiber: 4g

Cajun Salmon

Prep time: 5 minutes | Cook time: 7 minutes | Serves 2

- 2 (4 ounces / 113 g) salmon fillets, skin removed
- 2 tablespoons unsalted butter, melted
- ⅛ teaspoon ground
- cayenne pepper
- ½ teaspoon garlic powder
- 1 teaspoon paprika
- ¼ teaspoon ground black pepper

1. Brush each fillet with butter. 2. Combine remaining ingredients in a small bowl and then rub onto fish. Place fillets into the air fryer basket. 3. Adjust the temperature to 390ºF (199ºC) and air fry for 7 minutes. 4. When fully cooked, internal temperature will be 145ºF (63ºC). Serve immediately.

Per Serving:

calories: 213 | fat: 12g | protein: 24g | carbs: 1g | net carbs: 0g | fiber: 1g

Tuna Avocado Bites

Prep time: 10 minutes | Cook time: 7 minutes | Makes 12 bites

- 1 (10-ounce / 283-g) can tuna, drained
- ¼ cup full-fat mayonnaise
- 1 stalk celery, chopped
- 1 medium avocado,
- peeled, pitted, and mashed
- ½ cup blanched finely ground almond flour, divided
- 2 teaspoons coconut oil

1. In a large bowl, mix tuna, mayonnaise, celery, and mashed avocado. Form the mixture into balls. 2. Roll balls in almond flour and spritz with coconut oil. Place balls into the air fryer basket. 3. Adjust the temperature to 400ºF (204ºC) and set the timer for 7 minutes. 4. Gently turn tuna bites after 5 minutes. Serve warm.

Per Serving:

2 bites: calories: 170 | fat: 13g | protein: 12g | carbs: 4g | net carbs: 1g | fiber: 3g

Shrimp in Curry Sauce

Prep time: 10 minutes | Cook time: 5 minutes | Serves 2

- ½ ounce grated Parmesan cheese
- 1 egg, beaten
- ¼ teaspoon curry powder
- 2 teaspoons almond flour
- 12 shrimp, shelled
- 3 tablespoons coconut oil
- Sauce
- 2 tablespoons curry leaves
- 2 tablespoons butter
- ½ onion, diced
- ½ cup heavy cream
- ½ ounce cheddar cheese, shredded

1. Combine all dry ingredients for the batter. Melt the coconut oil in a skillet over medium heat. Dip the shrimp in the egg first, and then coat with the dry mixture. Fry until golden and crispy. 2. In another skillet, melt butter. Add onion and cook for 3 minutes. Add curry leaves and cook for 30 seconds. Stir in heavy cream and cheddar and cook until thickened. Add shrimp and coat well. Serve.

Per Serving:

calories: 772 | fat: 73g | protein: 20g | carbs: 11g | net carbs: 8g | fiber: 3g

Spicy Tuna Hand Rolls

Prep time: 10 minutes | Cook time: 0 minutes | Serves 6

Tuna:
- 12 ounces sushi-grade ahi tuna, finely chopped
- 2 tablespoons Sriracha sauce
- 1 tablespoon

mayonnaise, homemade or store-bought
- 1 teaspoon toasted sesame oil

Hand Rolls:
- 3 sheets nori
- 1 medium-sized avocado, thinly sliced
- ½ cucumber, julienned
- Black and white sesame seeds, for garnish (optional)
- Soy sauce, for serving

1. Put the tuna, Sriracha, mayonnaise, and sesame oil in a small bowl and mix with a spoon. 2. Cut the nori sheets in half lengthwise to create 6 rectangular wrappers. 3. Place a wrapper on the palm of one of your hands. Put 2 ounces of tuna and 3 or 4 slices each of avocado and cucumber on the left end of the wrapper, on a diagonal to make rolling easier. Starting from the bottom-left corner, tightly roll into a cone shape, moistening the edge of the nori to create a seal. Garnish the top of the roll with sesame seeds, if desired. Repeat with the remaining ingredients. 4. Serve the rolls with soy sauce. These are best eaten immediately, as they don't store well.

Per Serving:

calories: 133 | fat: 6g | protein: 15g | carbs: 4g | net carbs: 2g | fiber: 2g

Blackened Salmon

Prep time: 10 minutes | Cook time: 8 minutes | Serves 2

- 10 ounces (283 g) salmon fillet
- ½ teaspoon ground coriander
- 1 teaspoon ground cumin
- 1 teaspoon dried basil
- 1 tablespoon avocado oil

1. In the shallow bowl, mix ground coriander, ground cumin, and dried basil. 2. Then coat the salmon fillet in the spices and sprinkle with avocado oil. 3. Put the fish in the air fryer basket and cook at 395ºF (202ºC) for 4 minutes per side.

Per Serving:

calories: 270 | fat: 17g | protein: 25g | carbs: 2g | net carbs: 0g | fiber: 2g

Garam Masala Fish

Prep time: 10 minutes | Cook time: 10 minutes | Serves 4

- 2 tablespoons sesame oil
- ½ teaspoon cumin seeds
- ½ cup chopped leeks
- 1 teaspoon ginger-garlic paste
- 1 pound (454 g) cod fillets, boneless and sliced
- 2 ripe tomatoes, chopped
- 1½ tablespoons fresh lemon juice
- ½ teaspoon garam masala
- ½ teaspoon turmeric
- powder
- 1 tablespoon chopped fresh dill leaves
- 1 tablespoon chopped fresh curry leaves
- 1 tablespoon chopped fresh parsley leaves
- Coarse sea salt, to taste
- ½ teaspoon smoked cayenne pepper
- ¼ teaspoon ground black pepper, or more to taste

1. Set the Instant Pot to Sauté. Add and heat the sesame oil until hot. Sauté the cumin seeds for 30 seconds. 2. Add the leeks and cook for another 2 minutes until translucent. Add the ginger-garlic paste and cook for an additional 40 seconds. 3. Stir in the remaining ingredients. 4. Lock the lid. Select the Manual mode and set the cooking time for 6 minutes at Low Pressure. 5. When the timer beeps, perform a quick pressure release. Carefully remove the lid. 6. Serve immediately.

Per Serving:

calories: 166 | fat: 8g | protein: 18g | carbs: 6g | net carbs: 4g | fiber: 2g

Italian Tuna Roast

Prep time: 15 minutes | Cook time: 21 to 24 minutes | Serves 8

- Cooking spray
- 1 tablespoon Italian seasoning
- ⅛ teaspoon ground black pepper
- 1 tablespoon extra-light
- olive oil
- 1 teaspoon lemon juice
- 1 tuna loin (approximately 2 pounds / 907 g, 3 to 4 inches thick)

1. Spray baking dish with cooking spray and place in air fryer basket. Preheat the air fryer to 390ºF (199ºC). 2. Mix together the Italian seasoning, pepper, oil, and lemon juice. 3. Using a dull table knife or butter knife, pierce top of tuna about every half inch: Insert knife into top of tuna roast and pierce almost all the way to the bottom. 4. Spoon oil mixture into each of the holes and use the knife to push seasonings into the tuna as deeply as possible. 5. Spread any remaining oil mixture on all outer surfaces of tuna. 6. Place tuna roast in baking dish and roast at 390ºF (199ºC) for 20 minutes. Check temperature with a meat thermometer. Cook for an additional 1 to 4 minutes or until temperature reaches 145ºF (63ºC). 7. Remove basket from the air fryer and let tuna sit in the basket for 10 minutes.

Per Serving:
calories: 206 | fat: 6g | protein: 35g | carbs: 1g | net carbs: 1g | fiber: 0g

Shrimp and Avocado Lettuce Cups

Prep time: 10 minutes | Cook time: 5 minutes | Serves 2

- 1 tablespoon ghee
- ½ pound shrimp (I use defrosted Trader Joe's Frozen Medium Cooked Shrimp, which are peeled and deveined, with tail off)
- ½ cup halved grape tomatoes
- ½ avocado, sliced
- Pink Himalayan salt
- Freshly ground black pepper
- 4 butter lettuce leaves, rinsed and patted dry
- 1 tablespoon Spicy Red Pepper Miso Mayo

1. In a medium skillet over medium-high heat, heat the ghee. Add the shrimp and cook. (I use cooked shrimp, so they take only about 1 minute to heat through, and I flip them halfway through cooking. Uncooked shrimp take about 2 minutes to cook.) Season with pink Himalayan salt and pepper. Shrimp are cooked when they turn pink and opaque. 2. Season the tomatoes and avocado with pink Himalayan salt and pepper. 3. Divide the lettuce cups between two plates. Fill each

cup with shrimp, tomatoes, and avocado. Drizzle the mayo sauce on top and serve.

Per Serving:
calories: 326 | fat: 11g | protein: 33g | carbs: 7g | net carbs: 4g | fiber: 3g

Parmesan Mackerel with Coriander

Prep time: 10 minutes | Cook time: 7 minutes | Serves 2

- 12 ounces (340 g) mackerel fillet
- 2 ounces (57 g) Parmesan, grated
- 1 teaspoon ground coriander
- 1 tablespoon olive oil

1. Sprinkle the mackerel fillet with olive oil and put it in the air fryer basket. 2. Top the fish with ground coriander and Parmesan. 3. Cook the fish at 390ºF (199ºC) for 7 minutes.

Per Serving:
calories: 504 | fat: 36g | protein: 42g | carbs: 3g | net carbs: 2g | fiber: 0g

Crunchy Fish Sticks

Prep time: 30 minutes | Cook time: 9 minutes | Serves 4

- 1 pound (454 g) cod fillets
- 1½ cups finely ground blanched almond flour
- 2 teaspoons Old Bay seasoning
- ½ teaspoon paprika
- Sea salt and freshly
- ground black pepper, to taste
- ¼ cup sugar-free mayonnaise
- 1 large egg, beaten
- Avocado oil spray
- Tartar sauce, for serving

1. Cut the fish into ¾-inch-wide strips. 2. In a shallow bowl, stir together the almond flour, Old Bay seasoning, paprika, and salt and pepper to taste. In another shallow bowl, whisk together the mayonnaise and egg. 3. Dip the cod strips in the egg mixture, then the almond flour, gently pressing with your fingers to help adhere to the coating. 4. Place the coated fish on a parchment paper-lined baking sheet and freeze for 30 minutes. 5. Spray the air fryer basket with oil. Set the air fryer to 400ºF (204ºC). Place the fish in the basket in a single layer, and spray each piece with oil. 6. Cook for 5 minutes. Flip and spray with more oil. Cook for 4 minutes more, until the internal temperature reaches 140ºF (60ºC). Serve with the tartar sauce.

Per Serving:
calories: 500 | fat: 38g | protein: 33g | carbs: 12g | net carbs: 6g | fiber: 6g

Grilled Calamari

Prep time: 10 minutes | Cook time: 5 minutes | Serves 4

- 2 pounds calamari tubes and tentacles, cleaned
- ½ cup good-quality olive oil
- Zest and juice of 2 lemons
- 2 tablespoons chopped
- fresh oregano
- 1 tablespoon minced garlic
- ¼ teaspoon sea salt
- ⅛ teaspoon freshly ground black pepper

1. Prepare the calamari. Score the top layer of the calamari tubes about 2 inches apart. 2. Marinate the calamari. In a large bowl, stir together the olive oil, lemon zest, lemon juice, oregano, garlic, salt, and pepper. Add the calamari and toss to coat it well, then place it in the refrigerator to marinate for at least 30 minutes and up to 1 hour. 3. Grill the calamari. Preheat a grill to high heat. Grill the calamari, turning once, for about 3 minutes total, until it's tender and lightly charred. 4. Serve. Divide the calamari between four plates and serve it hot.

Per Serving:

calories: 455 | fat: 30g | protein: 35g | carbs: 8g | net carbs: 7g | fiber: 1g

Souvlaki Spiced Salmon Bowls

Prep time: 10 minutes | Cook time: 20 minutes | Serves 4

- For The Salmon
- ¼ cup good-quality olive oil
- Juice of 1 lemon
- 2 tablespoons chopped fresh oregano
- 1 tablespoon minced garlic
- 1 tablespoon balsamic vinegar
- 1 tablespoon smoked sweet paprika
- ½ teaspoon sea salt
- ¼ teaspoon freshly ground black pepper
- 4 (4-ounce) salmon fillets
- For The Bowls
- 2 tablespoons good-quality olive oil
- 1 red bell pepper, cut into strips
- 1 yellow bell pepper, cut into strips
- 1 zucchini, cut into ½-inch strips lengthwise
- 1 cucumber, diced
- 1 large tomato, chopped
- ½ cup sliced Kalamata olives
- 6 ounces feta cheese, crumbled
- ½ cup sour cream

Make The Salmon: 1. Marinate the fish. In a medium bowl, stir together the olive oil, lemon juice, oregano, garlic,

vinegar, paprika, salt, and pepper. Add the salmon and turn to coat it well with the marinade. Cover the bowl and let the salmon sit marinating for 15 to 20 minutes. 2. Grill the fish. Preheat the grill to medium-high heat and grill the fish until just cooked through, 4 to 5 minutes per side. Set the fish aside on a plate. Make The Bowls: 1. Grill the vegetables. In a medium bowl, toss together the oil, red and yellow bell peppers, and zucchini. Grill the vegetables, turning once, until they're lightly charred and soft, about 3 minutes per side. 2. Assemble and serve. Divide the grilled vegetables between four bowls. Top each bowl with cucumber, tomato, olives, feta cheese, and the sour cream. Place one salmon fillet on top of each bowl and serve immediately.

Per Serving:

calories: 553 | fat: 44g | protein: 30g | carbs: 10g | net carbs: 7g | fiber: 3g

Lemon-Thyme Poached Halibut

Prep time: 5 minutes | Cook time: 15 minutes | Serves 4

- 1 lemon, thinly sliced
- ½ cup extra-virgin olive oil or MCT oil, plus more for drizzling
- 4 (6-ounce / 170-g) halibut steaks
- 1 teaspoon fine sea salt
- ½ teaspoon freshly ground black pepper
- 1 sprig fresh thyme or other herb of choice
- Coarse sea salt, for garnish (preferably Hawaiian alaea sea salt for color)
- 1 tablespoon capers, for garnish (optional)

1. Line the bottom of a large enameled cast-iron skillet with the lemon slices. Pour the oil over the top of the lemon slices. Place the halibut steaks in the skillet and add enough water to cover the fish. Season the poaching liquid with the salt and pepper, then add the sprig of thyme. 2. Heat on medium-low until the poaching liquid is steaming but not boiling (about 165ºF / 74ºC). Once the liquid is steaming, poach the halibut steaks until they are cooked through and opaque, 10 to 12 minutes (depending on thickness). Remove the steaks from the poaching liquid. 3. Serve with a drizzle of olive oil and garnished with coarse sea salt and capers, if desired. 4. Store extras in an airtight container in the fridge for up to 3 days. To reheat, place the halibut in a heat-safe dish with a few tablespoons of water, cover, and place in a preheated 350ºF (180ºC) oven until warmed.

Per Serving:

calories: 305 | fat: 29g | protein: 9g | carbs: 2g | net carbs: 1g | fiber: 1g

Snapper with Shallot and Tomato

Prep time: 20 minutes | Cook time: 15 minutes | Serves 2

- 2 snapper fillets
- 1 shallot, peeled and sliced
- 2 garlic cloves, halved
- 1 bell pepper, sliced
- 1 small-sized serrano pepper, sliced
- 1 tomato, sliced
- 1 tablespoon olive oil
- ¼ teaspoon freshly ground black pepper
- ½ teaspoon paprika
- Sea salt, to taste
- 2 bay leaves

1. Place two parchment sheets on a working surface. Place the fish in the center of one side of the parchment paper. 2. Top with the shallot, garlic, peppers, and tomato. Drizzle olive oil over the fish and vegetables. Season with black pepper, paprika, and salt. Add the bay leaves. 3. Fold over the other half of the parchment. Now, fold the paper around the edges tightly and create a half moon shape, sealing the fish inside. 4. Cook in the preheated air fryer at 390ºF (199ºC) for 15 minutes. Serve warm.

Per Serving:

calories: 259 | fat: 12g | protein: 31g | carbs: 10g | net carbs: 6g | fiber: 4g

Tuna Cakes

Prep time: 10 minutes | Cook time: 10 minutes | Serves 4

- 4 (3-ounce / 85-g) pouches tuna, drained
- 1 large egg, whisked
- 2 tablespoons peeled and chopped white onion
- ½ teaspoon Old Bay seasoning

1. In a large bowl, mix all ingredients together and form into four patties. 2. Place patties into ungreased air fryer basket. Adjust the temperature to 400ºF (204ºC) and air fry for 10 minutes. Patties will be browned and crispy when done. Let cool 5 minutes before serving.

Per Serving:

calories: 110 | fat: 2g | protein: 20g | carbs: 2g | net carbs: 2g | fiber: 0g

Simple Flounder in Brown Butter Lemon Sauce

Prep time: 10 minutes | Cook time: 10 minutes | Serves 4

- For The Sauce
- ½ cup unsalted grass-fed butter, cut into pieces
- Juice of 1 lemon
- Sea salt, for seasoning
- Freshly ground black pepper, for seasoning
- For The Fish
- 4 (4-ounce) boneless flounder fillets
- Sea salt, for seasoning
- Freshly ground black pepper, for seasoning
- ¼ cup almond flour
- 2 tablespoons good-quality olive oil
- 1 tablespoon chopped fresh parsley

Make The Sauce: 1. Brown the butter. In a medium saucepan over medium heat, cook the butter, stirring it once in a while, until it is golden brown, about 4 minutes. 2. Finish the sauce. Remove the saucepan from the heat and stir in the lemon juice. Season the sauce with salt and pepper and set it aside. Make The Fish 1. Season the fish. Pat the fish fillets dry and season them lightly with salt and pepper. Spoon the almond flour onto a plate, then roll the fish fillets through the flour until they're lightly coated. 2. Cook the fish. In a large skillet over medium-high heat, warm the olive oil. Add the fish fillets and fry them until they're crispy and golden on both sides, 2 to 3 minutes per side. 3. Serve. Transfer the fish to a serving plate and drizzle with the sauce. Top with the parsley and serve it hot.

Per Serving:

calories: 389 | fat: 33g | protein: 22g | carbs: 1g | net carbs: 1g | fiber: 0g

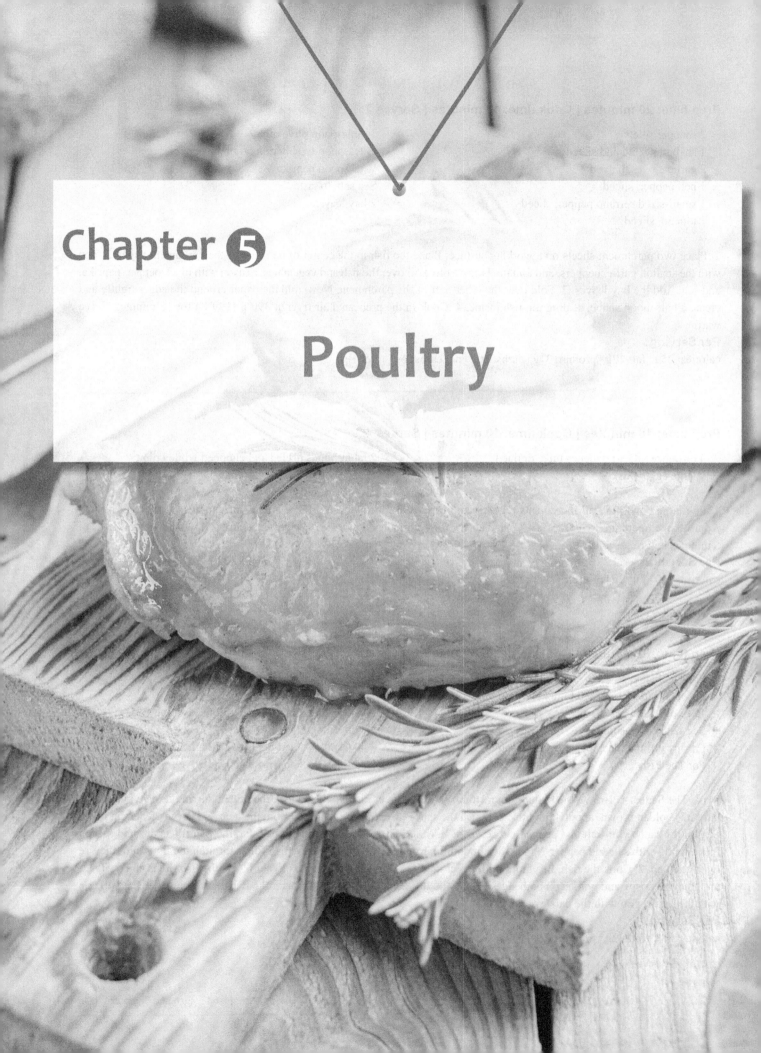

Chapter 5

Poultry

Basil Turkey Meatballs

Prep time: 5 minutes | Cook time: 10 minutes | Serves 4

- 1 pound ground turkey
- 2 tablespoons chopped sun-dried tomatoes
- 2 tablespoons chopped basil
- ½ teaspoon garlic powder
- 1 egg
- ½ teaspoon salt
- ¼ cup almond flour
- 2 tablespoons olive oil
- ½ cup shredded mozzarella cheese
- ¼ teaspoon pepper

1. Place everything, except the oil in a bowl. Mix with your hands until combined. Form into 16 balls. Heat the olive oil in a skillet over medium heat. Cook the meatballs for 4-5 minutes per each side. Serve.

Per Serving:

calories: 343 | fat: 22g | protein: 28g | carbs: 7g | net carbs: 5g | fiber: 2g

Crispy Thighs & Mash

Prep time: 15 minutes | Cook time: 30 minutes | Serves 6

Crispy Chicken:

- 6 small or 3 large boneless, skinless chicken thighs (about 1 pound/455 g)
- ¼ cup (60 ml) melted coconut oil or avocado oil

Butternut Mash:

- 1 medium butternut squash (about 1¼ pounds/570 g)
- 2 tablespoons coconut oil or ghee
- ½ teaspoon finely ground sea salt
- 1 teaspoon garlic powder
- ½ teaspoon onion powder
- ¼ teaspoon finely ground sea salt
- ¼ teaspoon ground black pepper
- ⅛ teaspoon ground black pepper
- ⅓ cup (80 ml) milk (nondairy or regular)
- 1½ tablespoons chicken bone broth

1. Cook the chicken: Preheat the oven to 400°F (205°C). If using large chicken thighs, cut them in half to make 6 pieces. Place the chicken on a rimmed baking sheet. Pour the oil over the thighs and dust them with the spices. Turn the thighs until they're fully coated in the oil and spices. Bake for 25 to 30 minutes, until the internal temperature of the chicken reaches 165°F (74°C). Cut the chicken into ½-inch (1.25-cm) slices. 2. Meanwhile, make the mash: Peel and seed the squash, then cut the flesh into cubes. Measure 3 cups (455 g) of the cubes for the mash; store any remaining squash in the fridge for another use. 3. Heat the oil in a large frying pan over medium heat. Add the squash, salt, and pepper. Cover and cook for 10 to 15 minutes, until the squash is lightly browned. Add the milk and broth, cover, and continue to cook for 15 minutes, or until the squash is soft enough to mash easily. When the squash is done, mash it with the back of a fork right there in the pan. 4. To serve, divide the mash among 6 dinner plates. Top each portion with an equal amount of the sliced chicken thighs and enjoy!

Per Serving:

calories: 331 | fat: 26g | protein: 16g | carbs: 10g | net carbs: 8g | fiber: 2g

Stewed Chicken and Sausage

Prep time: 10 minutes | Cook time: 1 hour 10 minutes | Serves 8

- 2 pounds (907 g) Mexican-style fresh (raw) chorizo
- 1 tablespoon coconut oil
- 2 boneless, skinless chicken thighs, cut into ½-inch pieces
- 1 cup chopped onions
- 1½ (18-ounce / 510-g) jars whole peeled tomatoes with juices
- 3 chipotle chiles in adobo sauce
- 3 tablespoons minced garlic
- 2 tablespoons smoked paprika
- 1 tablespoon ground cumin
- 1 tablespoon dried oregano leaves
- 2 teaspoons fine sea salt
- 1 teaspoon cayenne pepper
- 2 cups chicken bone broth, homemade or store-bought
- ¼ cup lime juice
- ¼ cup chopped fresh cilantro

1. Slice 1 pound (454 g) of the chorizo into rounds; crumble the remaining pound. 2. Heat the oil in large soup pot over medium-high heat. Add the sliced and crumbled chorizo, chicken, and onions and cook until the onions are soft and the chicken is cooked through, about 5 minutes, stirring to break up the crumbled chorizo. 3. Meanwhile, place the tomatoes and their juices and the chiles in a food processor. Purée until smooth; set aside. 4. Add the garlic, paprika, cumin, oregano, salt, and cayenne pepper to the soup pot and sauté for another minute while stirring. 5. Add the puréed tomato mixture and broth to the soup pot. Bring to a gentle boil, then reduce the heat to low and simmer for 1 hour to allow the flavors to open up. Just before serving, stir in the lime juice and cilantro. 6. Store extras in an airtight container in the fridge for up to 2 days. Reheat in a saucepan over medium heat until warmed.

Per Serving:

calories: 415 | fat: 33g | protein: 20g | carbs: 10g | net carbs: 8g | fiber: 2g

Chicken and Bacon Rolls

Prep time: 10 minutes | Cook time: 35 minutes | Serves 4

- 1 tablespoon fresh chives, chopped
- 8 ounces blue cheese
- 2 pounds chicken breasts, skinless,
- boneless, halved
- 12 bacon slices
- 2 tomatoes, chopped
- Salt and ground black pepper, to taste

1. Set a pan over medium heat, place in the bacon, cook until halfway done, remove to a plate. 2. In a bowl, stir together blue cheese, chives, tomatoes, pepper and salt. 3. Use a meat tenderizer to flatten the chicken breasts, season and lay blue cheese mixture on top. 4 Roll them up, and wrap each in a bacon slice. 5 Place the wrapped chicken breasts in a greased baking dish, and roast in the oven at 370ºF for 30 minutes. 6 Serve on top of wilted kale.

Per Serving:

calories: 632 | fat: 38g | protein: 67g | carbs: 6g | net carbs: 5g | fiber: 1g

Ethiopian Chicken with Cauliflower

Prep time: 15 minutes | Cook time: 28 minutes | Serves 6

- 2 handful fresh Italian parsley, roughly chopped
- ½ cup fresh chopped chives
- 2 sprigs thyme
- 6 chicken drumsticks
- 1½ small-sized head cauliflower, broken into large-sized florets
- 2 teaspoons mustard powder
- ⅓ teaspoon porcini powder
- 1½ teaspoons berbere spice
- ⅓ teaspoon sweet paprika
- ½ teaspoon shallot powder
- 1 teaspoon granulated garlic
- 1 teaspoon freshly cracked pink peppercorns
- ½ teaspoon sea salt

1. Simply combine all items for the berbere spice rub mix. After that, coat the chicken drumsticks with this rub mix on all sides. Transfer them to the baking dish. 2. Now, lower the cauliflower onto the chicken drumsticks. Add thyme, chives and Italian parsley and spritz everything with a pan spray. Transfer the baking dish to the preheated air fryer. 3. Next step, set the timer for 28 minutes; roast at 355ºF (179ºC), turning occasionally. Bon appétit!

Per Serving:

calories: 235 | fat: 12g | protein: 25g | carbs: 5g | net carbs: 3g | fiber: 2g

Blackened Chicken

Prep time: 10 minutes | Cook time: 20 minutes | Serves 4

- 1 large egg, beaten
- ¾ cup Blackened seasoning
- 2 whole boneless,
- skinless chicken breasts (about 1 pound / 454 g each), halved
- 1 to 2 tablespoons oil

1. Place the beaten egg in one shallow bowl and the Blackened seasoning in another shallow bowl. 2. One at a time, dip the chicken pieces in the beaten egg and the Blackened seasoning, coating thoroughly. 3. Preheat the air fryer to 360ºF (182ºC). Line the air fryer basket with parchment paper. 4. Place the chicken pieces on the parchment and spritz with oil. 5. Cook for 10 minutes. Flip the chicken, spritz it with oil, and cook for 10 minutes more until the internal temperature reaches 165ºF (74ºC) and the chicken is no longer pink inside. Let sit for 5 minutes before serving.

Per Serving:

calories: 270 | fat: 6g | protein: 48g | carbs: 2g | net carbs: 2g | fiber: 0g

Chicken with Asparagus & Root Vegetables

Prep time: 25 minutes | Cook time: 37 minutes | Serves 4

- 2 cups whipping cream
- 3 chicken breasts, boneless, skinless, chopped
- 3 tablespoons butter
- ½ cup onion, chopped
- ¾ cup carrot, chopped
- 5 cups chicken stock
- Salt and black pepper, to
- taste
- 1 bay leaf
- 1 turnip, chopped
- 1 parsnip, chopped
- 17 ounces asparagus, trimmed
- 3 teaspoons fresh thyme, chopped

1. Set a pan over medium heat and add whipping cream, allow simmering, and cook until it's reduced by half, about 7 minutes. 2. Set another pan over medium heat and warm butter, sauté the onion for 3 minutes. Pour in the chicken stock, carrots, turnip, and parsnip, chicken, and bay leaf, bring to a boil, and simmer for 20 minutes. 3. Add in the asparagus and cook for 7 minutes. Discard the bay leaf, stir in the reduced whipping cream, adjust the seasoning and ladle the stew into serving bowls. Scatter with fresh thyme.

Per Serving:

calories: 502 | fat: 33g | protein: 39g | carbs: 11g | net carbs: 6g | fiber: 5g

Poblano Chicken

Prep time: 10 minutes | Cook time: 29 minutes | Serves 4

- 2 Poblano peppers, sliced
- 16 ounces (454 g) chicken fillet
- ½ teaspoon salt
- ½ cup coconut cream
- 1 tablespoon butter
- ½ teaspoon chili powder

1. Heat up the butter on Sauté mode for 3 minutes. 2. Add Poblano and cook them for 3 minutes. 3. Meanwhile, cut the chicken fillet into the strips and sprinkle with salt and chili powder. 4. Add the chicken strips to the instant pot. 5. Then add coconut cream and close the lid. Cook the meal on Sauté mode for 20 minutes.

Per Serving:

calories: 320 | fat: 18g | protein: 34g | carbs: 4g | net carbs: 3g | fiber: 1g

Caprese Chicken Skillet

Prep time: 10 minutes | Cook time: 15 minutes | Serves 4

- 1 tablespoon extra-virgin olive oil
- 1 pound boneless, skinless chicken thighs
- 1½ teaspoons pink Himalayan salt, divided
- ½ teaspoon ground black pepper
- 1 teaspoon minced garlic
- 12 cherry tomatoes,
- halved (about 3 ounces)
- ¼ teaspoon red pepper flakes
- 1 medium-sized zucchini, spiral-sliced into noodles
- 3 or 4 large fresh basil leaves, minced
- 3 ounces mini mozzarella balls, halved

1. Heat the olive oil in a large skillet over medium-high heat. 2. Chop the chicken into 1-inch pieces and season with 1 teaspoon of the salt and the black pepper. 3. Put the chicken in the hot skillet and cook through, 5 to 7 minutes. (When fully cooked, the chicken will no longer be pink in the middle.) Remove from the skillet and set aside. 4. Turn the heat down to low and use a spatula to scrape up the drippings from the bottom of the skillet. Add the garlic and cook for 20 seconds. Add the tomatoes, remaining ½ teaspoon of salt, and red pepper flakes. Stir to combine and cover with a lid. Cook for 5 to 7 minutes, until the tomatoes have burst and softened. 5. Turn the heat back up to high, add the zucchini noodles and basil, and cook for 1 minute, until the noodles are slightly tender but not mushy. Remove from the heat, add the chicken and mozzarella, and toss to combine. Serve immediately.

Per Serving:

calories: 226 | fat: 12g | protein: 26g | carbs: 4g | net carbs:

3g | fiber: 1g

Chicken, Eggplant and Gruyere Gratin

Prep time: 10 minutes | Cook time: 50 minutes | Serves 4

- 3 tablespoons butter
- 1 eggplant, chopped
- 2 tablespoons gruyere cheese, grated
- Salt and black pepper, to taste
- 2 garlic cloves, minced
- 6 chicken thighs

1. Set a pan over medium heat and warm 1 tablespoon butter, place in the chicken thighs, season with pepper and salt, cook each side for 3 minutes and lay them in a baking dish. In the same pan melt the rest of the butter and cook the garlic for 1 minute. 2. Stir in the eggplant, pepper, and salt, and cook for 10 minutes. Ladle this mixture over the chicken, spread with the cheese, set in the oven at 350ºF, and bake for 30 minutes. Turn on the oven's broiler, and broil everything for 2 minutes. Split among serving plates and enjoy.

Per Serving:

calories: 500 | fat: 35g | protein: 34g | carbs: 9g | net carbs: 8g | fiber: 2g

Chicken Stew with Sun-Dried Tomatoes

Prep time: 15 minutes | Cook time: 45 minutes | Serves 4

- 2 carrots, chopped
- 2 tablespoons olive oil
- 2 celery stalks, chopped
- 2 cups chicken stock
- 1 shallot, chopped
- 28 ounces chicken thighs, skinless, boneless
- 3 garlic cloves, peeled and minced
- ½ teaspoon dried
- rosemary
- 2 ounces sun-dried tomatoes, chopped
- 1 cup spinach
- ¼ teaspoon dried thyme
- ½ cup heavy cream
- Salt and ground black pepper, to taste
- A pinch of xanthan gum

1. In a pot, heat the olive oil over medium heat and add garlic, carrots, celery, and shallot; season with salt and pepper and sauté for 5-6 minutes until tender. Stir in the chicken and cook for 5 minutes. 2. Pour in the stock, tomatoes, rosemary, and thyme, and cook for 30 minutes covered. Stir in xanthan gum, cream, and spinach; cook for 5 minutes. Adjust the seasonings and separate into bowls.

Per Serving:

calories: 511 | fat: 35g | protein: 36g | carbs: 12g | net carbs: 9g | fiber: 3g

Turkey Stew with Salsa Verde

Prep time: 10 minutes | Cook time: 20 minutes | Serves 6

- 4 cups leftover turkey meat, chopped
- 2 cups green beans
- 6 cups chicken stock
- Salt and ground black pepper, to taste
- 1 fresh chipotle pepper, chopped
- ½ cup salsa verde
- 1 teaspoon ground coriander
- 2 teaspoons cumin
- ¼ cup sour cream
- 1 tablespoon fresh cilantro, chopped

1. Set a pan over medium heat. Add in the stock and heat. Stir in green beans, and cook for 10 minutes. Place in the turkey, ground coriander, salt, salsa verde, chipotle pepper, cumin, and black pepper, and cook for 10 minutes. Stir in the sour cream, kill the heat, and separate into bowls. Top with chopped cilantro to serve.

Per Serving:

calories: 253 | fat: 13g | protein: 32g | carbs: 2g | net carbs: 2g | fiber: 0g

One Pot Chicken with Mushrooms

Prep time: 10 minutes | Cook time: 20 minutes | Serves 6

- 2 cups sliced mushrooms
- ½ teaspoon onion powder
- ½ teaspoon garlic powder
- ¼ cup butter
- 1 teaspoon Dijon
- mustard
- 1 tablespoon tarragon, chopped
- 2 pounds chicken thighs
- Salt and black pepper, to taste

1. Season the thighs with salt, pepper, garlic, and onion powder. Melt the butter in a skillet, and cook the chicken until browned; set aside. Add mushrooms to the same fat and cook for about 5 minutes. 2. Stir in Dijon mustard and ½ cup of water. Return the chicken to the skillet. Season to taste with salt and pepper, reduce the heat and cover, and let simmer for 15 minutes. Stir in tarragon. Serve warm.

Per Serving:

calories: 404 | fat: 32g | protein: 27g | carbs: 2g | net carbs: 1g | fiber: 1g

Chicken Tacos with Fried Cheese Shells

Prep time: 5 minutes | Cook time: 25 minutes | Serves 6

Chicken:
- 4 (6-ounce / 170-g) boneless, skinless chicken breasts
- 1 cup chicken broth
- 1 teaspoon salt
- ¼ teaspoon pepper
- 1 tablespoon chili powder
- 2 teaspoons garlic powder
- 2 teaspoons cumin

Cheese Shells:
- 1½ cups shredded whole-   milk Mozzarella cheese

1. Combine all ingredients for the chicken in the Instant Pot. 2. Secure the lid. Select the Manual mode and set the cooking time for 20 minutes at High Pressure. 3. Once cooking is complete, do a quick pressure release. Carefully open the lid. 4. Shred the chicken and serve in bowls or cheese shells. 5. Make the cheese shells: Heat a nonstick skillet over medium heat. 6. Sprinkle ¼ cup of Mozzarella cheese in the skillet and fry until golden. Flip and turn off the heat. Allow the cheese to get brown. Fill with chicken and fold. The cheese will harden as it cools. Repeat with the remaining cheese and filling. 7. Serve warm.

Per Serving:

calories: 233 | fat: 8g | protein: 32g | carbs: 2g | net carbs: 2g | fiber: 2g

Quick Chicken Fajitas

Prep time: 10 minutes | Cook time: 15 minutes | Serves 2

- 10 ounces (283 g) boneless, skinless chicken breast, sliced into ¼-inch strips
- 2 tablespoons coconut oil, melted
- 1 tablespoon chili powder
- ½ teaspoon cumin
- ½ teaspoon paprika
- ½ teaspoon garlic powder
- ¼ medium onion, peeled and sliced
- ½ medium green bell pepper, seeded and sliced
- ½ medium red bell pepper, seeded and sliced

1. Place chicken and coconut oil into a large bowl and sprinkle with chili powder, cumin, paprika, and garlic powder. Toss chicken until well coated with seasoning. Place chicken into the air fryer basket. 2. Adjust the temperature to 350ºF (177ºC) and air fry for 15 minutes. 3. Add onion and peppers into the basket when the cooking time has 7 minutes remaining. 4. Toss the chicken two or three times during cooking. Vegetables should be tender and chicken fully cooked to at least 165ºF (74ºC) internal temperature when finished. Serve warm.

Per Serving:

calories: 309 | fat: 18g | protein: 29g | carbs: 8g | net carbs: 5g | fiber: 3g

Lemon & Rosemary Chicken in a Skillet

Prep time: 5 minutes | Cook time: 14 minutes | Serves 4

- 8 chicken thighs
- 1 teaspoon salt
- 2 tablespoons lemon juice
- 1 teaspoon lemon zest
- 2 tablespoons olive oil
- 1 tablespoon chopped rosemary
- ¼ teaspoon black pepper
- 1 garlic clove, minced

1. Combine all ingredients in a bowl. Place in the fridge for one hour. Heat a skillet over medium heat. Add the chicken along with the juices and cook until crispy, about 7 minutes per side.

Per Serving:

calories: 457 | fat: 33g | protein: 37g | carbs: 3g | net carbs: 2g | fiber: 1g

Jalapeño Cheddar Chicken Casserole

Prep time: 10 minutes | Cook time: 35 minutes | Serves 2

- 1 tablespoon extra-virgin olive oil
- 1 pound (454 g) boneless, skinless chicken thighs, cut into ½-inch cubes
- 4 ounces (113 g) full-fat cream cheese
- 2 jalapeño peppers, sliced, seeds and membranes removed
- ¼ cup heavy (whipping) cream
- ¼ cup chicken broth
- ½ teaspoon pink Himalayan sea salt
- ¼ teaspoon garlic powder
- ¼ teaspoon onion powder
- ½ cup shredded Cheddar cheese, divided
- 1 cup cooked cauliflower rice

1. Preheat the oven to 375ºF (190ºC). 2. In a medium sauté pan or skillet, heat the olive oil over medium-high heat and add the chicken. Cook for 10 to 12 minutes, until the chicken is no longer pink. 3. In a medium saucepan, combine the cream cheese, jalapeños, cream, broth, salt, garlic powder, and onion powder over medium heat. Stir until the cream cheese melts into the sauce. Add ¼ cup of Cheddar cheese, and continue to stir until it melts into the sauce. 4. In an 8-inch square baking dish, combine the chicken and cauliflower rice. 5. Pour in the cheese sauce, then sprinkle the remaining ¼ cup of Cheddar cheese over the top. 6. Bake for 20 minutes, until the sauce is bubbling. Let cool for 10 minutes, then serve.

Per Serving:

calories: 994 | fat: 85g | protein: 50g | carbs: 9g | net carbs: 7g | fiber: 2g

Chicken Legs with Leeks

Prep time: 30 minutes | Cook time: 18 minutes | Serves 6

- 2 leeks, sliced
- 2 large-sized tomatoes, chopped
- 3 cloves garlic, minced
- ½ teaspoon dried oregano
- 6 chicken legs, boneless and skinless
- ½ teaspoon smoked cayenne pepper
- 2 tablespoons olive oil
- A freshly ground nutmeg

1. In a mixing dish, thoroughly combine all ingredients, minus the leeks. Place in the refrigerator and let it marinate overnight. 2. Lay the leeks onto the bottom of the air fryer basket. Top with the chicken legs. 3. Roast chicken legs at 375ºF (191ºC) for 18 minutes, turning halfway through. Serve with hoisin sauce.

Per Serving:

calories: 275 | fat: 15g | protein: 25g | carbs: 10g | net carbs: 8g | fiber: 2g

Turkey with Mushroom Gravy

Prep time: 10 minutes | Cook time: 45 minutes | Serves 4

- 1 (2-pound / 907-g) piece of turkey breast
- ½ teaspoon pink Himalayan sea salt, plus more for seasoning
- ¼ teaspoon freshly ground black pepper, plus more for seasoning
- 4 tablespoons (½ stick) butter
- 2 cups sliced fresh mushrooms
- ½ medium onion, chopped
- 1 cup chicken broth
- ¼ cup sour cream

1. Preheat the oven to 450ºF (235ºC). 2. Slice the turkey breast into 4 cutlets that are roughly 2 inches thick. 3. Place the cutlets in an 8-inch square baking dish and season lightly with a little salt and pepper. Bake for 30 minutes. 4. In a medium saucepan, melt the butter over medium heat. Add the mushrooms and onion and cook for 3 to 5 minutes, until the onion is almost translucent. 5. Add the broth, sour cream, ½ teaspoon of salt, and ¼ teaspoon of pepper to the pan. Stir to form a sauce, then simmer over low heat for about 5 minutes, until it reaches your desired thickness. Keep warm. 6. When the turkey is almost finished baking, pour the gravy over it and bake for an additional 5 to 10 minutes, until the gravy is bubbling. Serve.

Per Serving:

calories: 499 | fat: 30g | protein: 51g | carbs: 3g | net carbs: 2g | fiber: 1g

Spice-Rubbed Turkey Breast

Prep time: 5 minutes | Cook time: 45 to 55 minutes | Serves 10

- 1 tablespoon sea salt
- 1 teaspoon paprika
- 1 teaspoon onion powder
- 1 teaspoon garlic powder
- ½ teaspoon freshly
- ground black pepper
- 4 pounds (1.8 kg) bone-in, skin-on turkey breast
- 2 tablespoons unsalted butter, melted

1. In a small bowl, combine the salt, paprika, onion powder, garlic powder, and pepper. 2. Sprinkle the seasonings all over the turkey. Brush the turkey with some of the melted butter. 3. Set the air fryer to 350ºF (177ºC). Place the turkey in the air fryer basket, skin-side down, and roast for 25 minutes. 4. Flip the turkey and brush it with the remaining butter. Continue cooking for another 20 to 30 minutes, until an instant-read thermometer reads 160ºF (71ºC). 5. Remove the turkey breast from the air fryer. Tent a piece of aluminum foil over the turkey, and allow it to rest for about 5 minutes before serving.

Per Serving:

calories: 302 | fat: 14g | protein: 40g | carbs: 1g | net carbs: 1g | fiber: 0g

Verde Chicken Enchiladas

Prep time: 20 minutes | Cook time: 20 minutes | Serves 8

- 2 (4.2-ounce) boneless, skinless chicken breasts, cooked
- ½ cup cooked, diced mushrooms
- ½ cup cooked, diced zucchini
- 8 small low-carb flour tortillas
- 1 cup green enchilada
- sauce
- 1 cup shredded Cheddar cheese
- 1 medium green onion, finely chopped
- ¼ cup freshly minced cilantro, divided
- ¼ cup sliced black olives
- ⅓ cup full-fat sour cream

1. Preheat oven to 350°F. Grease a 9" × 9" baking dish. 2. In a medium bowl, finely shred cooked chicken breasts. Add mushrooms and zucchini and stir to combine. 3. On a large baking sheet or clean cutting board, lay out tortillas one at a time and evenly distribute chicken and vegetable mixture in center of each tortilla. Roll each tortilla over chicken and vegetables to make tight rolls. 4. Put rolls in baking dish. Cover with green enchilada sauce and evenly top with cheese, green onion, half of the cilantro, and olives. 5. Bake 15–20 minutes until cheese melts. 6. Let cool 10 minutes. Top with sour cream and remaining cilantro and serve.

Per Serving:

calories: 289 | fat: 15g | protein: 18g | carbs: 21g | net carbs: 17g | fiber: 4g

Authentic Chicken Shawarma

Prep time: 15 minutes | Cook time: 17 minutes | Serves 4

- 1 pound (454 g) chicken fillet
- ½ teaspoon ground coriander
- ½ teaspoon smoked paprika
- ½ teaspoon dried thyme
- 1 tablespoon tahini sauce
- 1 teaspoon lemon juice
- 1 teaspoon heavy cream
- 1 cup water, for cooking

1. Rub the chicken fillet with ground coriander, smoked paprika, thyme, and wrap in the foil. 2. Then pour water and insert the steamer rack in the instant pot. 3. Place the wrapped chicken in the steamer; close and seal the lid. 4. Cook the chicken on Manual mode (High Pressure) for 17 minutes. Make a quick pressure release. 5. Make the sauce: Mix up heavy cream, lemon juice, and tahini paste. 6. Slice the chicken and sprinkle it with sauce.

Per Serving:

calories: 234 | fat: 10g | protein: 33g | carbs: 1g | net carbs: 1g | fiber: 0g

Chicken Stroganoff

Prep time: 10 minutes | Cook time: 4 hours | Serves 4

- 2 garlic cloves, minced
- 8 ounces mushrooms, chopped
- ¼ teaspoon celery seeds, ground
- 1 cup chicken stock
- 1 cup sour cream
- 1 cup leeks, chopped
- 1 pound chicken breasts
- 1½ teaspoons dried thyme
- 2 tablespoons fresh parsley, chopped
- Salt and black pepper, to taste
- 4 zucchinis, spiralized

1. Place the chicken in a slow cooker. Place in the salt, leeks, sour cream, half of the parsley, celery seeds, garlic, black pepper, mushrooms, stock, and thyme. Cook on high for 4 hours while covered. 2. Uncover the pot and add the rest of the parsley. Heat a pan with water over medium heat, place in some salt, bring to a boil, stir in the zucchini pasta, cook for 1 minute, and drain. 3. Place in serving bowls, top with the chicken mixture, and serve.

Per Serving:

calories: 373 | fat: 18g | protein: 41g | carbs: 14g | net carbs: 10g | fiber: 5g

Chicken Breasts with Spinach & Artichoke

Prep time: 10 minutes | Cook time: 55 minutes | Serves 4

- 4 ounces cream cheese
- 4 chicken breasts
- 8 ounces canned artichoke hearts, chopped
- 1 cup spinach
- ½ cup Pecorino cheese, grated
- 1 tablespoon onion powder
- 1 tablespoon garlic powder
- Salt and ground black pepper, to taste
- 4 ounces Monterrey Jack cheese, shredded

1. Lay the chicken breasts on a lined baking sheet, season with pepper and salt, set in the oven at 350ºF, and bake for 35 minutes. In a bowl, combine the artichokes with onion powder, Pecorino cheese, salt, spinach, cream cheese, garlic powder, and pepper. 2. Remove the chicken from the oven, cut each piece in half, divide artichokes mixture on top, spread with Monterrey cheese, set in the oven at 350ºF, and bake for 20 minutes.

Per Serving:

calories: 518 | fat: 29g | protein: 60g | carbs: 9g | net carbs: 8g | fiber: 2g

Chettinad Chicken

Prep time: 15 minutes | Cook time: 4 to 6 hours | Serves 6

- 1 tablespoon white poppy seeds
- 1 teaspoon coriander seeds
- 2 teaspoons cumin seeds
- 1 teaspoon fennel seeds
- 4 to 5 dried red chiles
- 2-inch piece cinnamon stick
- 6 green cardamom pods
- 4 cloves
- 1½ cups grated coconut
- 4 garlic cloves
- 1 tablespoon freshly grated ginger
- 2 tablespoons coconut oil
- 20 curry leaves
- 3 onions, finely sliced
- 2 star anise
- 4 tomatoes
- 1 teaspoon turmeric
- Sea salt
- 1 teaspoon chili powder
- 12 chicken thighs on the bone, skinned and trimmed
- Juice of 2 or 3 limes
- Handful fresh coriander leaves, chopped

1. In a frying pan, toast the poppy seeds, coriander seeds, cumin seeds, fennel seeds, dried red chiles, cinnamon, green cardamom pods, and cloves until fragrant, about 1 minute. Remove from the pan and set aside to cool. Once cooled, grind to a fine powder in a spice grinder. 2. In the same pan, toast the grated coconut for 3 to 4 minutes until it just starts to turn golden. Remove from the pan and spread on a plate to cool. Once cooled, grind and mix with the ground spices. 3. Crush the garlic and ginger in a mortar and pestle and set aside. 4. Either heat the slow cooker to sauté or use a pan on the stove. Heat the coconut oil and add the curry leaves, when they stop spluttering, add the sliced onions and fry them until they are light brown. Stir in the crushed garlic and ginger, and stir for a minute or two. 5. Add to the slow cooker along with the ground spices and anise. Chop and add the tomatoes, the turmeric, and the salt, and stir in the chili powder. 6. Place the chicken pieces in the cooker, cover and cook on low for 6 hours, or on high for 4 hours, until tender and cooked through. 7. Check the seasoning and adjust if needed, squeeze in the lime juice, and serve topped with fresh coriander leaves.

Per Serving:

calories: 628 | fat: 28g | protein: 79g | carbs: 13g | net carbs: 9g | fiber: 4g

Chicken with Monterey Jack Cheese

Prep time: 15 minutes | Cook time: 35 minutes | Serves 3

- 2 tablespoons butter
- 1 teaspoon garlic, minced
- 1 pound chicken breasts
- 1 teaspoon creole seasoning
- ¼ cup scallions, chopped
- ½ cup tomatoes, chopped
- ½ cup chicken stock
- ¼ cup whipping cream
- ½ cup Monterey Jack cheese, grated
- ¼ cup fresh cilantro, chopped
- Salt and black pepper, to taste
- 4 ounces cream cheese
- 8 eggs
- A pinch of garlic powder

1. Set a pan over medium heat and warm 1 tablespoon butter. Add chicken, season with creole seasoning and cook each side for 2 minutes; remove to a plate. Melt the rest of the butter and stir in garlic and tomatoes; cook for 4 minutes. Return the chicken to the pan and pour in stock; cook for 15 minutes. Place in whipping cream, scallions, salt, Monterey Jack cheese, and pepper; cook for 2 minutes. 2. In a blender, combine the cream cheese with garlic powder, salt, eggs, and pepper, and pulse well. Place the mixture into a lined baking sheet, and then bake for 10 minutes in the oven at 325ºF. Allow the cheese sheet to cool down, place on a cutting board, roll, and slice into medium slices. Split the slices among bowls and top with chicken mixture. Sprinkle with chopped cilantro to serve.

Per Serving:

calories: 571 | fat: 39g | protein: 43g | carbs: 8g | net carbs: 6g | fiber: 1g

Chicken and Mixed Greens Salad

Prep time: 5 minutes | Cook time: 20 minutes | Serves 4

Chicken:
- 2 tablespoons avocado oil
- 1 pound (454 g) chicken breast, cubed
- ½ cup filtered water
- ½ teaspoon ground

turmeric
- ½ teaspoon dried parsley
- ½ teaspoon dried basil
- ½ teaspoon kosher salt
- ½ teaspoon freshly ground black pepper

Salad:
- 1 avocado, mashed
- 1 cup chopped arugula
- 1 cup chopped Swiss chard

- 1 cup chopped kale
- ½ cup chopped spinach
- 2 tablespoons pine nuts, toasted

1. Combine all the chicken ingredients in the Instant Pot. 2. Secure the lid. Select the Manual mode and set the cooking time for 20 minutes at High Pressure. 3. Meanwhile, toss all the salad ingredients in a large salad bowl. 4. Once cooking is complete, do a quick pressure release. Carefully open the lid. 5. Remove the chicken to the salad bowl and serve.

Per Serving:

calories: 378 | fat: 23g | protein: 35g | carbs: 8g | net carbs: 4g | fiber: 4g

Turkey Burgers with Fried Brussels Sprouts

Prep time: 10 minutes | Cook time: 10 minutes | Serves 4

- For the burgers
- 1 pound ground turkey
- 1 free-range egg
- ½ onion, chopped
- 1 teaspoon salt
- ½ teaspoon ground black pepper
- 1 teaspoon dried thyme
- 2 ounces butter

- For the fried Brussels sprouts
- 1½ pounds Brussels sprouts, halved
- 3 ounces butter
- 1 teaspoon salt
- ½ teaspoon ground black pepper

1. Combine the burger ingredients in a mixing bowl. Create patties from the mixture. Set a large pan over medium heat, warm butter, and fry the patties until cooked completely. 2. Place on a plate and cover with aluminium foil to keep warm. Fry brussels sprouts in butter, season to your preference, then set to a bowl. Plate the burgers and brussels sprouts and serve.

Per Serving:

calories: 436 | fat: 31g | protein: 23g | carbs: 20g | net carbs: 14g | fiber: 6g

Blackened Cajun Chicken Tenders

Prep time: 10 minutes | Cook time: 17 minutes | Serves 4

- 2 teaspoons paprika
- 1 teaspoon chili powder
- ½ teaspoon garlic powder
- ½ teaspoon dried thyme
- ¼ teaspoon onion powder
- ⅛ teaspoon ground

cayenne pepper
- 2 tablespoons coconut oil
- 1 pound (454 g) boneless, skinless chicken tenders
- ¼ cup full-fat ranch dressing

1. In a small bowl, combine all seasonings. 2. Drizzle oil over chicken tenders and then generously coat each tender in the spice mixture. Place tenders into the air fryer basket. 3. Adjust the temperature to 375ºF (191ºC) and air fry for 17 minutes. 4. Tenders will be 165ºF (74ºC) internally when fully cooked. Serve with ranch dressing for dipping.

Per Serving:

calories: 287 | fat: 18g | protein: 27g | carbs: 3g | net carbs: 2g | fiber: 1g

Chili Turkey Patties with Cucumber Salsa

Prep time: 10 minutes | Cook time: 6 minutes | Serves 4

- 2 spring onions, thinly sliced
- 1 pound ground turkey
- 1 egg
- 2 garlic cloves, minced
- 1 tablespoon chopped herbs
- 1 small chili pepper, deseeded and diced
- 2 tablespoons ghee
- Cucumber Salsa

- 1 tablespoon apple cider vinegar
- 1 tablespoon chopped dill
- 1 garlic clove, minced
- 2 cucumbers, grated
- 1 cup sour cream
- 1 jalapeño pepper, minced
- 2 tablespoons olive oil

Place all turkey ingredients, except the ghee, in a bowl. Mix to combine. Make patties out of the mixture. 2. Melt the ghee in a skillet over medium heat. Cook the patties for 3 minutes per side. Place all salsa ingredients in a bowl and mix to combine. Serve the patties topped with salsa.

Per Serving:

calories: 520 | fat: 44g | protein: 21g | carbs: 13g | net carbs: 10g | fiber: 3g

Chipotle Dry-Rub Wings

Prep time: 10 minutes | Cook time: 45 minutes | Serves 4

Chipotle Rub:
- 1 tablespoon ground chipotle pepper
- 1 teaspoon paprika
- 1 teaspoon ground cumin
- 1 teaspoon ground mustard
- 1 teaspoon garlic powder
- 1 teaspoon onion powder
- 1 teaspoon pink Himalayan salt
- 2 pounds chicken wings
- 1 teaspoon baking powder

1. Preheat the oven to 250°F and place a wire baking rack inside a rimmed baking sheet. 2. Put the seasonings for the rub in a small bowl and stir with a fork. Divide the spice rub into 2 equal portions. 3. Cut the wings in half, if whole (see Tip), and place in a large zip-top plastic bag. Add the baking powder and half of the spice rub to the bag and shake thoroughly to coat the wings. 4. Lay the wings on the baking rack in a single layer. Bake for 25 minutes. 5. Turn the heat up to 450°F and bake the wings for an additional 20 minutes, until golden brown and crispy. 6. Once the wings are done, place them in a large plastic container with the remaining half of the spice rub and shake to coat. Serve immediately.

Per Serving:

calories: 507 | fat: 36g | protein: 42g | carbs: 3g | net carbs: 3g | fiber: 0g

Turkey Enchilada Bowl

Prep time: 10 minutes | Cook time: 25 minutes | Serves 4

- 2 tablespoons coconut oil
- 1 pound boneless, skinless turkey thighs, cut into pieces
- ¾ cup red enchilada sauce (sugar-free)
- ¼ cup water
- ¼ cup chopped onion
- 3 ounces canned diced
- green chilis
- 1 avocado, diced
- 1 cup shredded mozzarella cheese
- ¼ cup chopped pickled jalapeños
- ½ cup sour cream
- 1 tomato, diced

1. Set a large pan over medium heat. Add coconut oil and warm. Place in the turkey and cook until browned on the outside. Stir in onion, chillis, water, and enchilada sauce, then close with a lid. 2. Allow simmering for 20 minutes until the turkey is cooked through. Spoon the turkey on a serving bowl and top with the sauce, cheese, sour cream, tomato, and avocado.

Per Serving:

calories: 533 | fat: 40g | protein: 32g | carbs: 14g | net carbs: 9g | fiber: 5g

Chicken & Squash Traybake

Prep time: 15 minutes | Cook time: 45 minutes | Serves 4

- 2 pounds chicken thighs
- 1 pound butternut squash, cubed
- ½ cup black olives, pitted
- ¼ cup olive oil
- 5 garlic cloves, sliced
- 1 tablespoon dried oregano
- Salt and black pepper, to taste

1. Set oven to 400°F and grease a baking dish. Place in the chicken with the skin down. Set the garlic, olives and butternut squash around the chicken then drizzle with oil. 2. Spread black pepper, salt, and oregano over the mixture then add into the oven. Cook for 45 minutes.

Per Serving:

calories: 589 | fat: 44g | protein: 44g | carbs: 17g | net carbs: 14g | fiber: 3g

Lazy Lasagna Chicken

Prep time: 10 minutes | Cook time: 28 minutes | Serves 4

- 4 medium boneless, skinless chicken breasts (8 ounces / 227 g each)
- 2 tablespoons butter, melted
- ½ teaspoon sea salt
- ¼ teaspoon black pepper
- ¼ cup ricotta cheese
- 1 large egg
- 2 tablespoons grated Parmesan cheese
- ½ cup marinara sauce, no sugar added
- ½ cup (2 ounces / 57 g) shredded Mozzarella cheese
- 2 tablespoons fresh basil, cut into ribbons

1. Preheat the oven to 375°F (190°C). 2. Place the chicken breasts on a sheet pan at least 1 inch apart. Brush both sides of the chicken with melted butter. Season both sides with sea salt and black pepper. 3. In a small bowl, mix together the ricotta and egg, then stir in the Parmesan. Spread evenly over the chicken breasts. 4. Top each piece of chicken with 2 tablespoons marinara sauce, then sprinkle with 2 tablespoons Mozzarella. 5. Bake for 23 to 28 minutes, until cooked through. Garnish with fresh basil.

Per Serving:

calories: 365 | fat: 16g | protein: 46g | carbs: 3g | net carbs: 3g | fiber: 0g

Cajun Chicken

Prep time: 15 minutes | Cook time: 25 minutes | Serves 4

- 1 teaspoon Cajun seasoning
- ¼ cup apple cider vinegar
- 1 pound (454 g) chicken fillet
- 1 tablespoon sesame oil
- ¼ cup water

1. Put all ingredients in the instant pot. Close and seal the lid. 2. Cook the chicken fillets on Manual mode (High Pressure) for 25 minutes. 3. Allow the natural pressure release for 10 minutes.

Per Serving:

calories: 249 | fat: 12g | protein: 33g | carbs: 0g | net carbs: 0g | fiber: 0g

Baked Chicken with Acorn Squash and Goat's Cheese

Prep time: 15 minutes | Cook time: 45 minutes | Serves 6

- 6 chicken breasts, butterflied
- 1 pound (454 g) acorn squash, cubed
- Salt and black pepper, to taste
- 1 cup goat's cheese, shredded
- 1 tablespoon dried parsley
- 3 tablespoons olive oil

1. Arrange the chicken breasts and squash in a baking dish. Season with salt, black pepper, and parsley. Drizzle with olive oil and pour a cup of water. Cover with aluminium foil and bake in the oven for 30 minutes at 420°F. Discard the foil, scatter goat's cheese, and bake for 15-20 minutes. Remove to a serving plate and enjoy.

Per Serving:

calories: 266 | fat: 18g | protein: 21g | carbs: 5g | net carbs: 5g | fiber: 0g

Chapter 6

Beef, Pork, and Lamb

Sausage and Peppers

Prep time: 7 minutes | Cook time: 35 minutes | Serves 4

- Oil, for spraying
- 2 pounds (907 g) hot or sweet Italian sausage links, cut into thick slices
- 4 large bell peppers of any color, seeded and cut into slices
- 1 onion, thinly sliced
- 1 tablespoon olive oil
- 1 tablespoon chopped fresh parsley
- 1 teaspoon dried oregano
- 1 teaspoon dried basil
- 1 teaspoon balsamic vinegar

1. Line the air fryer basket with parchment and spray lightly with oil. 2. In a large bowl, combine the sausage, bell peppers, and onion. 3. In a small bowl, whisk together the olive oil, parsley, oregano, basil, and balsamic vinegar. Pour the mixture over the sausage and peppers and toss until evenly coated. 4. Using a slotted spoon, transfer the mixture to the prepared basket, taking care to drain out as much excess liquid as possible. 5. Air fry at 350ºF (177ºC) for 20 minutes, stir, and cook for another 15 minutes, or until the sausage is browned and the juices run clear.

Per Serving:

calories: 378 | fat: 23g | protein: 39g | carbs: 6g | net carbs: 4g | fiber: 2g

Sweet Beef Curry

Prep time: 10 minutes | Cook time: 30 minutes | Serves 4

- ½ cup (105 g) coconut oil, or ½ cup (120 ml) avocado oil
- 1 small apple, peeled, cored, and diced
- 1 small yellow onion, sliced
- 2 cloves garlic, minced
- 1 (3-in/7.5-cm) piece fresh ginger root, minced
- 2 tablespoons curry powder
- 2 teaspoons garam masala
- 1 pound (455 g) boneless beef chuck roast, cut into ¾-inch (2-cm) cubes
- 1 small butternut squash (about 1 pound/455 g), cubed
- 1 cup (240 ml) beef bone broth
- 1 tablespoon coconut aminos

1. Heat the oil in a large saucepan over medium heat. Add the apple, onion, garlic, ginger, curry powder, and garam masala and toss to coat. Sauté for 10 minutes, or until fragrant. 2. Add the beef, squash, broth, and coconut aminos. Cover and bring to a boil over high heat. Reduce the heat to medium-low and simmer for 20 minutes, until the squash is fork-tender to soft. 3. Divide the curry among 4 bowls and enjoy.

Per Serving:

calories: 698 | fat: 56g | protein: 32g | carbs: 17g | net carbs: 13g | fiber: 4g

Hot Pork with Dill Pickles

Prep time: 10 minutes | Cook time: 14 minutes | Serves 4

- ¼ cup lime juice
- 4 pork chops
- 1 tablespoon coconut oil, melted
- 2 garlic cloves, minced
- 1 tablespoon chili powder
- 1 teaspoon ground
- cinnamon
- 2 teaspoons cumin
- Salt and black pepper, to taste
- ½ teaspoon hot pepper sauce
- 4 dill pickles, cut into spears and squeezed

1. In a bowl, combine the lime juice with oil, cumin, salt, hot pepper sauce, black pepper, cinnamon, garlic, and chili powder. Place in the pork chops, toss to coat, and refrigerate for 4 hours. 2. Arrange the pork on a preheated grill over medium heat, cook for 7 minutes, turn, add in the dill pickles, and cook for another 7 minutes. Split among serving plates and enjoy.

Per Serving:

calories: 288 | fat: 15g | protein: 29g | carbs: 9g | net carbs: 6g | fiber: 3g

Herby Beef & Veggie Stew

Prep time: 15 minutes | Cook time: 26 minutes | Serves 4

- 1 pound (454 g) ground beef
- 2 tablespoons olive oil
- 1 onion, chopped
- 2 garlic cloves, minced
- 14 ounces (397 g) canned diced tomatoes
- 1 tablespoon dried rosemary
- 1 tablespoon dried sage
- 1 tablespoon dried oregano
- 1 tablespoon dried basil
- 1 tablespoon dried marjoram
- Salt and black pepper, to taste
- 2 carrots, sliced
- 2 celery stalks, chopped
- 1 cup vegetable broth

1. Set a pan over medium heat, add in the olive oil, onion, celery, and garlic, and sauté for 5 minutes. Place in the beef, and cook for 6 minutes. Stir in the tomatoes, carrots, broth, black pepper, oregano, marjoram, basil, rosemary, salt, and sage, and simmer for 15 minutes. Serve and enjoy!

Per Serving:

calories: 250 | fat: 13g | protein: 26g | carbs: 9g | net carbs: 6g | fiber: 3g

North African Lamb

Prep time: 10 minutes | Cook time: 10 minutes | Serves 4

- 2 teaspoons paprika
- 2 garlic cloves, minced
- 2 teaspoons dried oregano
- 2 tablespoons sumac
- 12 lamb cutlets
- ¼ cup sesame oil
- 2 teaspoons cumin
- 4 carrots, sliced
- ¼ cup fresh parsley,
- chopped
- 2 teaspoons harissa paste
- 1 tablespoon red wine vinegar
- Salt and black pepper, to taste
- 2 tablespoons black olives, sliced
- 2 cucumbers, sliced

1. In a bowl, combine the cutlets with the paprika, oregano, black pepper, 2 tablespoons water, half of the oil, sumac, garlic, and salt, and rub well. Add the carrots in a pot, cover with water, bring to a boil over medium heat, cook for 2 minutes then drain before placing them in a salad bowl. 2. Place the cucumbers and olives to the carrots. In another bowl, combine the harissa with the rest of the oil, a splash of water, parsley, vinegar, and cumin. Place this to the carrots mixture, season with pepper and salt, and toss well to coat. 3. Preheat the grill to medium heat and arrange the lamb cutlets on it, grill each side for 3 minutes, and split among separate plates. Serve alongside the carrot salad.

Per Serving:

calories: 354 | fat: 23g | protein: 27g | carbs: 7g | net carbs: 4g | fiber: 3g

Hawaiian Pulled Pork Roast with Cabbage

Prep time: 10 minutes | Cook time: 1 hour 2 minutes minutes | Serves 6

- 1½ tablespoons olive oil
- 3 pounds (1.4 kg) pork shoulder roast, cut into 4 equal-sized pieces
- 3 cloves garlic, minced
- 1 tablespoon liquid smoke
- 2 cups water, divided
- 1 tablespoon sea salt
- 2 cups shredded cabbage

1. Select Sauté mode and add the olive oil to the Instant Pot. Once the oil is hot, add the pork cuts and sear for 5 minutes per side or until browned. Once browned, transfer the pork to a platter and set aside. 2. Add the garlic, liquid smoke, and 1½ cups water to the Instant Pot. Stir to combine. 3. Return the pork to the pot and sprinkle the salt over top. 4. Lock the lid. Select Manual mode and set cooking time for 1 hour on High Pressure. 5. When cooking is complete, allow the pressure to release naturally for 20 minutes, then release any remaining pressure. 6. Open the lid and transfer the pork to a large platter. Using two forks, shred the pork. Set aside. 7. Add the shredded cabbage and remaining water to the liquid in the pot. Stir. 8. Lock the lid. Select Manual mode and set cooking time for 2 minutes on High Pressure. When cooking is complete, quick release the pressure. 9. Transfer the cabbage to the serving platter with the pork. Serve warm.

Per Serving:

calories: 314 | fat: 12g | protein: 47g | carbs: 3g | net carbs: 2g | fiber: 1g

Classic Italian Bolognese Sauce

Prep time: 10 minutes | Cook time: 22 minutes | Serves 5

- 1 pound (454 g) ground beef
- 2 garlic cloves
- 1 onion, chopped
- 1 teaspoon oregano
- 1 teaspoon sage
- 1 teaspoon rosemary
- 7 ounces (198 g) canned chopped tomatoes
- 1 tablespoon olive oil

1. Heat olive oil in a saucepan. Add onion and garlic and cook for 3 minutes. Add beef and cook until browned, about 4-5 minutes. Stir in the herbs and tomatoes. Cook for 15 minutes. Serve with zoodles.

Per Serving:

calories: 216 | fat: 14g | protein: 18g | carbs: 4g | net carbs: 3g | fiber: 1g

Bacon and Cheese Stuffed Pork Chops

Prep time: 10 minutes | Cook time: 12 minutes | Serves 4

- ½ ounce (14 g) plain pork rinds, finely crushed
- ½ cup shredded sharp Cheddar cheese
- 4 slices cooked sugar-
- free bacon, crumbled
- 4 (4-ounce / 113-g) boneless pork chops
- ½ teaspoon salt
- ¼ teaspoon ground black pepper

1. In a small bowl, mix pork rinds, Cheddar, and bacon. 2. Make a 3-inch slit in the side of each pork chop and stuff with ¼ pork rind mixture. Sprinkle each side of pork chops with salt and pepper. 3. Place pork chops into ungreased air fryer basket, stuffed side up. Adjust the temperature to 400ºF (204ºC) and air fry for 12 minutes. Pork chops will be browned and have an internal temperature of at least 145ºF (63ºC) when done. Serve warm.

Per Serving:

calories: 357 | fat: 17g | protein: 39g | carbs: 1g | net carbs: 1g | fiber: 0g

Beef Tenderloin with Red Wine Sauce

Prep time: 30 minutes | Cook time: 10 minutes | Serves 5

- 2 pounds (907 g) beef tenderloin
- Salt and black pepper, to taste
- 2 tablespoons avocado oil
- ½ cup beef broth
- ½ cup dry red wine
- 2 cloves garlic, minced
- 1 teaspoon Worcestershire sauce
- 1½ teaspoons dried rosemary
- ¼ teaspoon xanthan gum
- Chopped fresh rosemary, for garnish (optional)

1. Thirty minutes prior to cooking, take the tenderloin out of the fridge and let it come to room temperature. Crust the outside of the tenderloin in salt and pepper. 2. Turn the pot to Sauté mode and add the avocado oil. Once hot, add the tenderloin and sear on all sides, about 5 minutes. Press Cancel. 3. Add the broth, wine, garlic, Worcestershire sauce, and rosemary to the pot around the beef. 4. Close the lid and seal the vent. Cook on High Pressure for 8 minutes. Quick release the steam. 5. Remove the tenderloin to a platter, tent with aluminum foil, and let it rest for 10 minutes. Press Cancel. 6. Turn the pot to Sauté mode. Once the broth has begun a low boil, add the xanthan gum and whisk until a thin sauce has formed, 2 to 3 minutes. 7. Slice the tenderloin against the grain into thin rounds. Top each slice with the red wine glaze. Garnish with rosemary, if desired.

Per Serving:

calories: 575 | fat: 44g | protein: 33g | carbs: 2g | net carbs: 1g | fiber: 1g

Jalapeño Popper Pork Chops

Prep time: 15 minutes | Cook time: 6 to 8 minutes | Serves 4

- 1¾ pounds (794 g) bone-in, center-cut loin pork chops
- Sea salt and freshly ground black pepper, to taste
- 6 ounces (170 g) cream cheese, at room temperature
- 4 ounces (113 g) sliced bacon, cooked and crumbled
- 4 ounces (113 g) Cheddar cheese, shredded
- 1 jalapeño, seeded and diced
- 1 teaspoon garlic powder

1. Cut a pocket into each pork chop, lengthwise along the side, making sure not to cut it all the way through. Season the outside of the chops with salt and pepper. 2. In a small bowl, combine the cream cheese, bacon, Cheddar cheese, jalapeño, and garlic powder. Divide this mixture among the pork chops, stuffing it into the pocket of each chop. 3.

Set the air fryer to 400ºF (204ºC). Place the pork chops in the air fryer basket in a single layer, working in batches if necessary. Air fry for 3 minutes. Flip the chops and cook for 3 to 5 minutes more, until an instant-read thermometer reads 145ºF (63ºC). 4. Allow the chops to rest for 5 minutes, then serve warm.

Per Serving:

calories: 724 | fat: 51g | protein: 58g | carbs: 5g | net carbs: 4g | fiber: 1g

Paprika Pork Ribs

Prep time: 10 minutes | Cook time: 30 minutes | Serves 4

- 1 pound (454 g) pork ribs
- 1 tablespoon ground paprika
- 1 teaspoon ground
- turmeric
- 3 tablespoons avocado oil
- 1 teaspoon salt
- ½ cup beef broth

1. Rub the pork ribs with ground paprika, turmeric, salt, and avocado oil. 2. Then pour the beef broth in the instant pot. 3. Arrange the pork ribs in the instant pot. Close and seal the lid. 4. Cook the pork ribs for 30 minutes on Manual mode (High Pressure). 5. When the time is finished, make a quick pressure release and chop the ribs into servings.

Per Serving:

calories: 335 | fat: 22g | protein: 31g | carbs: 2g | net carbs: 1g | fiber: 1g

Garlic Balsamic London Broil

Prep time: 30 minutes | Cook time: 8 to 10 minutes | Serves 8

- 2 pounds (907 g) London broil
- 3 large garlic cloves, minced
- 3 tablespoons balsamic vinegar
- 3 tablespoons whole-
- grain mustard
- 2 tablespoons olive oil
- Sea salt and ground black pepper, to taste
- ½ teaspoon dried hot red pepper flakes

1. Score both sides of the cleaned London broil. 2. Thoroughly combine the remaining ingredients; massage this mixture into the meat to coat it on all sides. Let it marinate for at least 3 hours. 3. Set the air fryer to 400ºF (204ºC); Then cook the London broil for 15 minutes. Flip it over and cook another 10 to 12 minutes. Bon appétit!

Per Serving:

calories: 285 | fat: 13g | protein: 37g | carbs: 2g | net carbs: 2g | fiber: 0g

Classic Pork and Cauliflower Keema

Prep time: 15 minutes | Cook time: 8 minutes | Serves 6

- 1 tablespoon sesame oil
- ½ cup yellow onion, chopped
- 1 garlic cloves, minced
- 1 (1-inch) piece fresh ginger, minced
- 1½ pounds (680 g) ground pork
- 1 cup cauliflower, chopped into small florets
- 1 ripe tomatoes, puréed
- 1 jalapeño pepper, seeded and minced
- 4 cloves, whole
- 1 teaspoon garam masala
- ½ teaspoon ground cumin
- ¼ teaspoon turmeric powder
- 1 teaspoon brown mustard seeds
- ½ teaspoon hot paprika
- Sea salt and ground black pepper, to taste
- 1 cup wate

1. Press the Sauté button to heat up the Instant Pot. Heat the sesame oil. Once hot, sauté yellow onion for 3 minutes or until softened. 2. Stir in garlic and ginger; cook for an additional minute. Add the remaining ingredients. 3. Secure the lid. Choose the Manual mode and set cooking time for 5 minutes on High pressure. 4. Once cooking is complete, use a quick pressure release. Carefully remove the lid. 5. Serve immediately.

Per Serving:

calories: 389 | fat: 29g | protein: 30g | carbs: 5g | net carbs: 3g | fiber: 3g

Pork Fried Cauliflower Rice

Prep time: 10 minutes | Cook time: 20 minutes | Serves 4

- 1 pound (454 g) ground pork
- Sea salt and freshly ground black pepper, to taste
- 3 tablespoons toasted sesame oil
- 3 cups thinly sliced cabbage
- 1 cup chopped broccoli
- 1 red bell pepper, cored
- and chopped
- 1 garlic clove, minced
- 1½ cups riced cauliflower
- 1 tablespoon sriracha
- 2 tablespoons liquid aminos or tamari
- 1 teaspoon rice wine vinegar
- 1 teaspoon sesame seeds, for garnish

1. Heat a medium skillet over medium-high heat. Add the pork and sprinkle generously with salt and pepper. Cook, stirring frequently, until browned, about 10 minutes. Remove the meat from the skillet. 2. Reduce the heat to medium and add the sesame oil to the skillet along with the cabbage, broccoli, bell pepper, riced cauliflower, and garlic. Cook for about 5 minutes until slightly softened, then add the sriracha, liquid aminos, and vinegar and mix well. 3. Return the browned pork to the skillet. Simmer together for about 5 minutes more until the cabbage is crisp-tender. Season with salt and pepper, then garnish with the sesame seeds and serve right away.

Per Serving:

calories: 460 | fat: 36g | protein: 23g | carbs: 11g | net carbs: 5g | fiber: 6g

Cheeseburger Casserole

Prep time: 5 minutes | Cook time: 50 minutes | Serves 4

- ¼ pound (113 g) reduced-sodium bacon
- 1 pound (454 g) 85% lean ground beef
- 1 clove garlic, minced
- ¼ teaspoon onion powder
- 4 eggs
- ¼ cup heavy cream
- ¼ cup tomato paste
- 2 tablespoons dill pickle relish
- ¼ teaspoon salt
- ¼ teaspoon freshly ground black pepper
- 1½ cups grated Cheddar cheese, divided

1. Lightly coat a casserole dish that will fit in air fryer, with olive oil and set aside. 2. Arrange the bacon in a single layer in the air fryer basket (it's OK if the bacon sits a bit on the sides). Set the air fryer to 350°F (177°C) and air fry for 10 minutes. Check for crispiness and air fry for 2 to 3 minutes longer if needed. Transfer the bacon to a plate lined with paper towels and let cool. Drain the grease. 3. Set the air fryer to 400°F (204°C). Crumble the beef into a single layer in the air fryer basket. Scatter the garlic on top and sprinkle with the onion powder. Air fry for 15 to 20 minutes until the beef is browned and cooked through. 4. While the beef is baking, in a bowl whisk together the eggs, cream, tomato paste, pickle relish, salt, and pepper. Stir in 1 cup of the cheese. Set aside. 5. When the beef is done, transfer it to the prepared pan. Use the side of a spoon to break up any large pieces of beef. 6. Drain the grease and, when cool enough to handle, wash the air fryer basket. Set the air fryer to 350°F (177°C). 7. Crumble the bacon and add it to the beef, spreading the meats into an even layer. Pour the egg mixture over the beef mixture and top with the remaining ½ cup of cheese. Air fry for 20 to 25 minutes until the eggs are set and the top is golden brown.

Per Serving:

calories: 693 | fat: 57g | protein: 36g | carbs: 6g | net carbs: 4g | fiber: 2g

Lamb Sirloin Masala

Prep time: 10 minutes | Cook time: 25 minutes | Serves 3

- 12 ounces (340 g) lamb sirloin, sliced
- 1 tablespoon garam masala
- 1 tablespoon lemon juice
- 1 tablespoon olive oil
- ¼ cup coconut cream

1. Sprinkle the sliced lamb sirloin with garam masala, lemon juice, olive oil, and coconut cream in a large bowl. Toss to mix well. 2. Transfer the mixture in the Instant Pot. Cook on Sauté mode for 25 minutes. Flip the lamb for every 5 minutes. 3. When cooking is complete, allow to cool for 10 minutes, then serve warm.

Per Serving:
calories: 319 | fat: 20g | protein: 33g | carbs: 1g | net carbs: 1g | fiber: 1g

Better Than Take-Out Beef with Broccoli

Prep time: 10 minutes | Cook time: 20 minutes | Serves 4

Marinade:
- 3 tablespoons coconut aminos (or 2 tablespoons liquid aminos)
- 2 tablespoons coconut oil, melted
- 2 tablespoons toasted sesame oil
- 2 tablespoons fish sauce
- 1 tablespoon coconut

- vinegar or apple cider vinegar
- 1 teaspoon onion powder
- 1 teaspoon garlic powder
- ½ teaspoon ground ginger
- ¼ teaspoon red pepper flakes

Beef and Broccoli:
- 1 pound (454 g) beef sirloin or flank, sliced thinly across the grain
- 2 cups broccoli florets
- 1 tablespoon coconut oil
- 2 garlic cloves, minced

- ½ teaspoon sea salt
- ¼ teaspoon freshly ground black pepper
- 1 tablespoon toasted sesame seeds (optional)

Make the Marinade 1. In a medium bowl, whisk together the coconut aminos, coconut oil, sesame oil, fish sauce, vinegar, onion powder, garlic powder, ginger, and red pepper flakes. Make the Beef and Broccoli 2. In a large plastic bag or medium bowl, pour one-third of the marinade over the beef and let marinate in the refrigerator for a few hours or overnight. Save the rest of the marinade in a small container to use for the sauce. 3. In a large pot, steam the broccoli until just tender. Transfer to a bowl with ice and cold water to

stop the cooking. Drain and set aside. 4. In a large skillet or wok, heat the coconut oil over high heat. Remove the beef from the marinade (discard the marinade) and add the beef to the skillet. Let brown for 2 to 3 minutes. Flip the meat and cook for another 2 to 3 minutes. 5. Add the garlic, salt, and pepper and stir to combine. 6. Add the cooked broccoli florets and the reserved marinade. Stir well and let simmer on medium-low heat for 5 to 10 minutes or until the sauce thickens and the meat is cooked through. Top with sesame seeds (if using).

Per Serving:
calories: 356 | fat: 24g | protein: 29g | carbs: 6g | net carbs: 4g | fiber: 2g

Chicken Fried Steak with Cream Gravy

Prep time: 5 minutes | Cook time: 10 minutes | Serves 4

- 4 small thin cube steaks (about 1 pound / 454 g)
- ½ teaspoon salt
- ½ teaspoon freshly ground black pepper

Cream Gravy:
- ½ cup heavy cream
- 2 ounces (57 g) cream cheese
- ¼ cup bacon grease
- 2 to 3 tablespoons water

- ¼ teaspoon garlic powder
- 1 egg, lightly beaten
- 1 cup crushed pork rinds (about 3 ounces / 85 g)

- 2 to 3 dashes Worcestershire sauce
- Salt and freshly ground black pepper, to taste

1. Preheat the air fryer to 400ºF (204ºC). 2. Working one at a time, place the steak between two sheets of parchment paper and use a meat mallet to pound to an even thickness. 3. In a small bowl, combine the salt, pepper, and garlic power. Season both sides of each steak with the mixture. 4. Place the egg in a small shallow dish and the pork rinds in another small shallow dish. Dip each steak first in the egg wash, followed by the pork rinds, pressing lightly to form an even coating. Working in batches if necessary, arrange the steaks in a single layer in the air fryer basket. Air fry for 10 minutes until crispy and cooked through. 5. To make the cream gravy: In a heavy-bottomed pot, warm the cream, cream cheese, and bacon grease over medium heat, whisking until smooth. Lower the heat if the mixture begins to boil. Continue whisking as you slowly add the water, 1 tablespoon at a time, until the sauce reaches the desired consistency. Season with the Worcestershire sauce and salt and pepper to taste. Serve over the chicken fried steaks.

Per Serving:
calories: 527 | fat: 46g | protein: 28g | carbs: 1g | net carbs: 1g | fiber: 0g

Korean Ground Beef Bowl

Prep time: 5 minutes | Cook time: 10 minutes | Serves 4

- 1 tablespoon sesame oil
- 1½ pounds (680 g) ground sirloin
- 1 teaspoon dried basil
- ½ teaspoon oregano
- Sea salt and ground black pepper, to taste
- ½ cup diced onion
- 1 teaspoon minced garlic
- ¼ teaspoon ground ginger
- 1 teaspoon red pepper flakes
- ¼ teaspoon allspice
- 1 tablespoon coconut aminos
- ½ cup roughly chopped fresh cilantro leaves

1. Press the Sauté button to heat up the Instant Pot. Then, heat the sesame oil until sizzling. 2. Add ground sirloin and cook for a few minutes or until browned. Add the remaining ingredients, except for cilantro. 3. Secure the lid. Choose Manual mode and High Pressure; cook for 5 minutes. Once cooking is complete, use a natural pressure release; carefully remove the lid. 4. Divide among individual bowls and serve garnished with fresh cilantro. Bon appétit!

Per Serving:

calories: 307 | fat: 17g | protein: 34g | carbs: 4g | net carbs: 3g | fiber: 1g

Steak and Egg Bibimbap

Prep time: 10 minutes | Cook time: 15 minutes | Serves 2

- For the Steak
- 1 tablespoon ghee or butter
- 8 ounces skirt steak
- Pink Himalayan salt
- Freshly ground black pepper
- 1 tablespoon soy sauce (or coconut aminos)
- For the Egg and Cauliflower Rice
- 2 tablespoons ghee or butter, divided
- 2 large eggs
- 1 large cucumber, peeled and cut into matchsticks
- 1 tablespoon soy sauce
- 1 cup cauliflower rice
- Pink Himalayan salt
- Freshly ground black pepper

To Make the Steak 1. Over high heat, heat a large skillet. 2. Using a paper towel, pat the steak dry. Season both sides with pink Himalayan salt and pepper. 3. Add the ghee or butter to the skillet. When it melts, put the steak in the skillet. 4. Sear the steak for about 3 minutes on each side for medium-rare. 5. Transfer the steak to a cutting board and let it rest for at least 5 minutes. 6. Slice the skirt steak across the grain and divide it between two bowls. To Make the Egg and Cauliflower Rice 1. In a second large skillet over medium-high heat, heat 1 tablespoon of ghee. When the ghee is very hot, crack the eggs into it. When the whites have cooked through, after 2 to 3 minutes, carefully transfer the eggs to a plate. 2. In a small bowl, marinate the cucumber matchsticks in the soy sauce. 3. Clean out the skillet from the eggs, and add the remaining 1 tablespoon of ghee or butter to the pan over medium-high heat. Add the cauliflower rice, season with pink Himalayan salt and pepper, and stir, cooking for 5 minutes. Turn the heat up to high at the end of the cooking to get a nice crisp on the "rice." 4. Divide the rice between two bowls. 5. Top the rice in each bowl with an egg, the steak, and the marinated cucumber matchsticks and serve.

Per Serving:

calories: 590 | fat: 45g | protein: 39g | carbs: 8g | net carbs: 5g | fiber: g

Cheese Shell Tacos

Prep time: 5 minutes | Cook time: 20 minutes | Serves 6

- Cheese Shells
- (makes 6 large shells)
- 2 cups shredded cheddar cheese
- Taco Filling
- ½ pound ground beef
- 1 tablespoon sugar-free taco seasoning, homemade or store-bought
- ¼ cup water
- Topping Suggestions
- 2 cups shredded lettuce
- 1 medium tomato, diced
- 1 avocado, sliced
- ¾ cup sour cream
- ⅓ cup chopped yellow onions
- Fresh cilantro, for garnish (optional)

1. Preheat the oven to 375°F. Line 2 baking sheets with parchment paper. 2. Arrange the shredded cheese into 6 piles on the parchment-lined baking sheet, leaving several inches between piles so the shells don't run together. Bake for 7 to 10 minutes, until the edges start to brown and the cheese is no longer runny. 3. Meanwhile, prop up a wooden spoon or two kabob skewers, spaced 1 inch apart, with two cups or cans. 4. Remove the melted cheese rounds from the oven and, while the cheese is still flexible, use a spatula to transfer the cheese and drape over a wooden spoon handle or skewers. Prop up the wooden spoon or skewers with 2 cups or cans. The shell will harden as it cools. Repeat this process with the remaining shells. 5. In a medium-sized skillet, brown the ground beef, then drain the fat. Add the taco seasoning and water. Stir well, bring to a simmer, and allow to reduce for 3 to 5 minutes. Remove from the heat. 6. Fill each cheese shell with meat and the toppings of your choice. 7. Garnish with cilantro, if desired.

Per Serving:

calories: 389 | fat: 30g | protein: 28g | carbs: 3g | net carbs: 3g | fiber: 0g

Zucchini Boats with Beef and Pimiento Rojo

Prep time: 10 minutes | Cook time: 25 minutes | Serves 4

- 4 zucchinis
- 2 tablespoons olive oil
- 1½ pounds ground beef
- 1 medium red onion, chopped
- 2 tablespoons chopped
- pimiento
- Pink salt and black pepper to taste
- 1 cup grated yellow cheddar cheese

1. Preheat oven to 350ºF. 2. Lay the zucchinis on a flat surface, trim off the ends and cut in half lengthwise. Scoop out the pulp from each half with a spoon to make shells. Chop the pulp. 3. Heat oil in a skillet; add the ground beef, red onion, pimiento, and zucchini pulp, and season with salt and black pepper. Cook for 6 minutes while stirring to break up lumps until beef is no longer pink. Turn the heat off. Spoon the beef into the boats and sprinkle with cheddar cheese. 4. Place on a greased baking sheet and cook to melt the cheese for 15 minutes until zucchini boats are tender. Take out, cool for 2 minutes, and serve warm with a mixed green salad.

Per Serving:

calories: 508 | fat: 38g | protein: 33g | carbs: 9g | net carbs: 7g | fiber: 2g

Kheema Meatloaf

Prep time: 10 minutes | Cook time: 15 minutes | Serves 4

- 1 pound (454 g) 85% lean ground beef
- 2 large eggs, lightly beaten
- 1 cup diced yellow onion
- ¼ cup chopped fresh cilantro
- 1 tablespoon minced fresh ginger
- 1 tablespoon minced garlic
- 2 teaspoons garam masala
- 1 teaspoon kosher salt
- 1 teaspoon ground turmeric
- 1 teaspoon cayenne pepper
- ½ teaspoon ground cinnamon
- ⅛ teaspoon ground cardamom

1. In a large bowl, gently mix the ground beef, eggs, onion, cilantro, ginger, garlic, garam masala, salt, turmeric, cayenne, cinnamon, and cardamom until thoroughly combined. 2. Place the seasoned meat in a baking pan. Place the pan in the air fryer basket. Set the air fryer to 350ºF (177ºC) for 15 minutes. Use a meat thermometer to ensure the meat loaf has reached an internal temperature of 160ºF /

71ºC (medium). 3. Drain the fat and liquid from the pan and let stand for 5 minutes before slicing. 4. Slice and serve hot.

Per Serving:

calories: 359 | fat: 24g | protein: 29g | carbs: 8g | net carbs: 6g | fiber: 2g

Russian Beef Gratin

Prep time: 10 minutes | Cook time: 25 minutes | Serves 5

- 2 teaspoons onion flakes
- 2 pounds ground beef
- 2 garlic cloves, minced
- Salt and black pepper, to taste
- 1 cup mozzarella cheese, shredded
- 2 cups fontina cheese,
- shredded
- 1 cup Russian dressing
- 2 tablespoons sesame seeds, toasted
- 20 dill pickle slices
- 1 iceberg lettuce head, torn

1. Set a pan over medium heat, place in beef, garlic, salt, onion flakes, and pepper, and cook for 5 minutes. Remove to a baking dish, stir in Russian dressing, mozzarella, and spread 1 cup of the fontina cheese. 2. Lay the pickle slices on top, spread over the remaining fontina cheese and sesame seeds, place in the oven at 350ºF, and bake for 20 minutes. Arrange the lettuce on a serving platter and top with the gratin.

Per Serving:

calories: 735 | fat: 56g | protein: 53g | carbs: 6g | net carbs: 5g | fiber: 1g

Apple and Pumpkin Ham

Prep time: 10 minutes | Cook time: 10 minutes | Serves 6

- 1 cup apple cider vinegar
- 1 pound (454 g) ham, cooked
- 2 tablespoons erythritol
- 1 tablespoon avocado oil
- 2 tablespoons butter
- ½ teaspoon pumpkin pie spices

1. Pour apple cider vinegar in the Instant Pot and insert the trivet. 2. Rub the ham with erythritol avocado oil,, butter, and pumpkin pie spices. 3. Put the ham on the trivet. Close the lid. 4. Select Manual mode and set cooking time for 10 minutes on High Pressure. 5. When timer beeps, use a natural pressure release for 5 minutes, then release any remaining pressure and open the lid. 6. Slice the ham and serve.

Per Serving:

calories: 134 | fat: 5g | protein: 17g | carbs: 7g | net carbs: 7g | fiber: 0g

Easy Zucchini Beef Lasagna

Prep time: 10 minutes | Cook time: 45 minutes | Serves 4

- 1 pound ground beef
- 2 large zucchinis, sliced lengthwise
- 3 cloves garlic
- 1 medium white onion, finely chopped
- 3 tomatoes, chopped
- Salt and black pepper to taste
- 2 teaspoons sweet paprika
- 1 teaspoon dried thyme
- 1 teaspoon dried basil
- 1 cup shredded mozzarella cheese
- 1 tablespoon olive oil
- Cooking spray

1. Preheat the oven to 370°F and lightly grease a baking dish with cooking spray. 2. Heat the olive oil in a skillet and cook the beef for 4 minutes while breaking any lumps as you stir. Top with onion, garlic, tomatoes, salt, paprika, and pepper. Stir and continue cooking for 5 minutes. 3. Then, lay ⅓ of the zucchini slices in the baking dish. Top with ⅓ of the beef mixture and repeat the layering process two more times with the same quantities. Season with basil and thyme. 4. Finally, sprinkle the mozzarella cheese on top and tuck the baking dish in the oven. Bake for 35 minutes. Remove the lasagna and let it rest for 10 minutes before serving.

Per Serving:

calories: 396 | fat: 27g | protein: 27g | carbs: 12g | net carbs: 9g | fiber: 3g

Pork Larb Lettuce Wraps

Prep time: 8 minutes | Cook time: 20 minutes | Serves 2

- 1 pound (454 g) ground pork
- ¼ medium onion, finely chopped
- 1 fresh long red chile, thinly sliced
- 2 garlic cloves, minced
- Juice of 1 lime
- 2 tablespoons chopped fresh basil
- 1 tablespoon chopped fresh cilantro or dried coriander
- 1 tablespoon fish sauce
- 1 teaspoon granulated erythritol
- 1 teaspoon dried mint
- 1 tablespoon extra-virgin olive oil
- Pink Himalayan sea salt
- Freshly ground black pepper
- 4 large, firm leaves of iceberg or butterhead lettuce
- 4 lime wedges, for garnish

1. In a large bowl, combine the pork, onion, chile, and garlic. 2. In a small bowl, combine the lime juice, basil, cilantro, fish sauce, erythritol, and mint. 3. In a large sauté pan or skillet, heat the olive oil over medium-high heat. Add the pork mixture and cook for 8 to 10 minutes, until no pink remains. 4. Add the sauce and cook for 5 to 8 minutes more, until most of the sauce is reduced. Season with salt and pepper. 5. Divide the meat mixture among the 4 lettuce leaves, fold into wraps, and serve with a wedge of lime.

Per Serving:

calories: 675 | fat: 55g | protein: 39g | carbs: 5g | net carbs: 5g | fiber: 0g

Sesame Pork and Green Beans

Prep time: 5 minutes | Cook time: 10 minutes | Serves 2

- 2 boneless pork chops
- Pink Himalayan salt
- Freshly ground black pepper
- 2 tablespoons toasted
- sesame oil, divided
- 2 tablespoons soy sauce
- 1 teaspoon Sriracha sauce
- 1 cup fresh green beans

1. On a cutting board, pat the pork chops dry with a paper towel. Slice the chops into strips, and season with pink Himalayan salt and pepper. 2. In a large skillet over medium heat, heat 1 tablespoon of sesame oil. 3. Add the pork strips and cook them for 7 minutes, stirring occasionally. 4. In a small bowl, mix to combine the remaining 1 tablespoon of sesame oil, the soy sauce, and the Sriracha sauce. Pour into the skillet with the pork. 5. Add the green beans to the skillet, reduce the heat to medium-low, and simmer for 3 to 5 minutes. 6. Divide the pork, green beans, and sauce between two wide, shallow bowls and serve.

Per Serving:

calories: 366 | fat: 24g | protein: 33g | carbs: 5g | net carbs: 3g | fiber: 2g

Pork and Mushroom Bake

Prep time: 5 minutes | Cook time: 45 minutes | Serves 6

- 1 onion, chopped
- 2(10.5 ounces) cans mushroom soup
- 6 pork chops
- ½ cup sliced mushrooms
- Salt and ground pepper, to taste

1. Preheat the oven to 370°F. 2. Season the pork chops with salt and black pepper, and place in a baking dish. Combine the mushroom soup, mushrooms, and onion, in a bowl. Pour this mixture over the pork chops. Bake for 45 minutes.

Per Serving:

calories: 302 | fat: 10g | protein: 42g | carbs: 9g | net carbs: 8g | fiber: 1g

Italian Beef Burgers

Prep time: 10 minutes | Cook time: 12 minutes | Serves 4

- 1 pound 75% lean ground beef
- ¼ cup ground almonds
- 2 tablespoons chopped fresh basil
- 1 teaspoon minced garlic
- ¼ teaspoon sea salt
- 1 tablespoon olive oil
- 1 tomato, cut into 4 thick slices
- ¼ sweet onion, sliced thinly

1. In a medium bowl, mix together the ground beef, ground almonds, basil, garlic, and salt until well mixed. 2. Form the beef mixture into four equal patties and flatten them to about ½ inch thick. 3. Place a large skillet on medium-high heat and add the olive oil. 4. Panfry the burgers until cooked through, flipping them once, about 12 minutes in total. 5. Pat away any excess grease with paper towels and serve the burgers with a slice of tomato and onion.

Per Serving:

calories: 441 | fat: 37g | protein: 22g | carbs: 4g | net carbs: 3g | fiber: 1g

Grilled Skirt Steak with Jalapeño Compound Butter

Prep time: 10 minutes | Cook time: 10 minutes | Serves 4

- ¼ cup unsalted grass-fed butter, at room temperature
- ½ jalapeño pepper, seeded and minced very finely
- Zest and juice of ½ lime
- ½ teaspoon sea salt
- 4 (4-ounce) skirt steaks
- 1 tablespoon olive oil
- Sea salt, for seasoning
- Freshly ground black pepper, for seasoning

1. Make the compound butter. In a medium bowl, stir together the butter, jalapeño pepper, lime zest, lime juice, and salt until everything is well combined. Lay a piece of plastic wrap on a clean work surface and spoon the butter mixture into the middle. Form the butter into a log about 1 inch thick by folding the plastic wrap over the butter and twisting the two ends in opposite directions. Roll the butter log on the counter to smooth the edges and put it in the freezer until it's very firm, about 4 hours. 2. Grill the steak. Preheat the grill to high heat. Lightly oil the steaks with the olive oil and season them lightly with salt and pepper. Grill the steaks for about 5 minutes per side for medium (140°F internal temperature) or until they're done the way you like them. 3. Rest and serve. Let the steaks rest for 10 minutes and serve them sliced across the grain, topped with a thick slice of the compound butter.

Per Serving:

calories: 404 | fat: 32g | protein: 29g | carbs: 0g | net carbs: 0g | fiber: 0g

Lemon Pork Chops with Buttered Brussels Sprouts

Prep time: 10 minutes | Cook time: 22 minutes | Serves 6

- 3 tablespoons lemon juice
- 3 cloves garlic, pureed
- 1 tablespoon olive oil
- 6 pork loin chops
- 1 tablespoon butter
- 1 pound brussels sprouts, trimmed and halved
- 2 tablespoons white wine
- Salt and black pepper to taste

1. Preheat broiler to 400°F and mix the lemon juice, garlic, salt, black pepper, and oil in a bowl. 2. Brush the pork with the mixture, place in a baking sheet, and cook for 6 minutes on each side until browned. Share into 6 plates and make the side dish. 3. Melt butter in a small wok or pan and cook in brussels sprouts for 5 minutes until tender. Drizzle with white wine, sprinkle with salt and black pepper and cook for another 5 minutes. Ladle brussels sprouts to the side of the chops and serve with a hot sauce.

Per Serving:

calories: 300 | fat: 11g | protein: 42g | carbs: 7g | net carbs: 4g | fiber: 3g

Peppercorn-Crusted Beef Tenderloin

Prep time: 10 minutes | Cook time: 25 minutes | Serves 6

- 2 tablespoons salted butter, melted
- 2 teaspoons minced roasted garlic
- 3 tablespoons ground
- 4-peppercorn blend
- 1 (2 pounds / 907 g) beef tenderloin, trimmed of visible fat

1. In a small bowl, mix the butter and roasted garlic. Brush it over the beef tenderloin. 2. Place the ground peppercorns onto a plate and roll the tenderloin through them, creating a crust. Place tenderloin into the air fryer basket. 3. Adjust the temperature to 400°F (204°C) and roast for 25 minutes. 4. Turn the tenderloin halfway through the cooking time. 5. Allow meat to rest 10 minutes before slicing.

Per Serving:

calories: 352 | fat: 19g | protein: 41g | carbs: 2g | net carbs: 2g | fiber: 0g

Pork Chops with Pecan Crust

Prep time: 10 minutes | Cook time: 25 minutes | Serves 4

- ➤ 2 eggs, lightly beaten
- ➤ 2 tablespoons coconut milk
- ➤ 1½ cups finely chopped pecans
- ➤ ¼ cup Parmesan cheese
- ➤ 4 (4-ounce) pork loin chops, about ½ inch thick
- ➤ Sea salt, for seasoning
- ➤ Freshly ground black pepper, for seasoning
- ➤ 2 tablespoons good-quality olive oil

1. Prepare the pork chops. Stir together the eggs and coconut milk in a small bowl. On a small plate, mix the pecans and Parmesan together and set the plate beside the egg mixture. Pat the pork chops dry and season them lightly with salt and pepper. Dip the pork chops first in the egg mixture, letting the excess run off, then roll them through the pecan mixture so they're coated. Set them aside on a plate. 2. Fry the pork. In a large skillet over medium heat, warm the olive oil. Fry the pork chops in a single layer, turning them several times, until they're cooked through and golden, 10 to 12 minutes per side. 3. Serve. Divide the pork chops between four plates and serve them immediately.

Per Serving:

calories: 567 | fat: 48g | protein: 33g | carbs: 6g | net carbs: 2g | fiber: 4g

Beef Burger

Prep time: 20 minutes | Cook time: 12 minutes | Serves 4

- ➤ 1¼ pounds (567 g) lean ground beef
- ➤ 1 tablespoon coconut aminos
- ➤ 1 teaspoon Dijon mustard
- ➤ A few dashes of liquid smoke
- ➤ 1 teaspoon shallot powder
- ➤ 1 clove garlic, minced
- ➤ ½ teaspoon cumin powder
- ➤ ¼ cup scallions, minced
- ➤ ⅓ teaspoon sea salt flakes
- ➤ ⅓ teaspoon freshly cracked mixed peppercorns
- ➤ 1 teaspoon celery seeds
- ➤ 1 teaspoon parsley flakes

1. Mix all of the above ingredients in a bowl; knead until everything is well incorporated. 2. Shape the mixture into four patties. Next, make a shallow dip in the center of each patty to prevent them puffing up during air frying. 3. Spritz the patties on all sides using nonstick cooking spray. Cook approximately 12 minutes at 360ºF (182ºC). 4. Check for doneness, an instant-read thermometer should read 160ºF (71ºC). Bon appétit!

Per Serving:

calories: 307 | fat: 19g | protein: 27g | carbs: 3g | net carbs: 2g | fiber: 1g

Parmesan Pork Chops and Roasted Asparagus

Prep time: 10 minutes | Cook time: 25 minutes | Serves 2

- ➤ ¼ cup grated Parmesan cheese
- ➤ ¼ cup crushed pork rinds
- ➤ 1 teaspoon garlic powder
- ➤ 2 boneless pork chops
- ➤ Pink Himalayan salt
- ➤ Freshly ground black pepper
- ➤ Olive oil, for drizzling
- ➤ ½ pound asparagus spears, tough ends snapped off

1. Preheat the oven to 350°F. Line a baking sheet with aluminum foil or a silicone baking mat. 2. In a medium bowl, mix to combine the Parmesan cheese, pork rinds, and garlic powder. 3. Pat the pork chops dry with a paper towel, and season with pink Himalayan salt and pepper. 4. Place a pork chop in the bowl with the Parmesan–pork rind mixture, and press the "breading" to the pork chop so it sticks. Place the coated pork chop on the prepared baking sheet. Repeat for the second pork chop. 5. Drizzle a small amount of olive oil over each pork chop. 6. Place the asparagus on the baking sheet around the pork chops. Drizzle with olive oil, and season with pink Himalayan salt and pepper. Sprinkle any leftover Parmesan cheese–pork rind mixture over the asparagus. 7. Bake for 20 to 25 minutes. Thinner pork chops will cook faster than thicker ones. 8. Serve hot.

Per Serving:

calories: 370 | fat: 21g | protein: 40g | carbs: 6g | net carbs: 4g | fiber: 3g

Fajita Meatball Lettuce Wraps

Prep time: 10 minutes | Cook time: 10 minutes | Serves 4

- 1 pound (454 g) ground beef (85% lean)
- ½ cup salsa, plus more for serving if desired
- ¼ cup chopped onions
- ¼ cup diced green or red bell peppers
- 1 large egg, beaten

- 1 teaspoon fine sea salt
- ½ teaspoon chili powder
- ½ teaspoon ground cumin
- 1 clove garlic, minced

For Serving (Optional):

- 8 leaves Boston lettuce
- Pico de gallo or salsa

- Lime slices

1. Spray the air fryer basket with avocado oil. Preheat the air fryer to 350°F (177°C). 2. In a large bowl, mix together all the ingredients until well combined. 3. Shape the meat mixture into eight 1-inch balls. Place the meatballs in the air fryer basket, leaving a little space between them. Air fry for 10 minutes, or until cooked through and no longer pink inside and the internal temperature reaches 145°F (63°C). 4. Serve each meatball on a lettuce leaf, topped with pico de gallo or salsa, if desired. Serve with lime slices if desired. 5. Store leftovers in an airtight container in the fridge for 3 days or in the freezer for up to a month. Reheat in a preheated 350°F (177°C) air fryer for 4 minutes, or until heated through.

Per Serving:

calories: 277 | fat: 18g | protein: 21g | carbs: 6g | net carbs: 4g | fiber: 2g

Chapter 7

Snacks and Appetizers

Salami Chips with Pesto

Prep time: 10 minutes | Cook time: 12 minutes | Serves 6

Chips:
- ➤ 6 ounces sliced Genoa salami

Pesto:
- ➤ 1 cup fresh basil leaves
- ➤ 3 cloves garlic
- ➤ ¼ cup grated Parmesan cheese
- ➤ ¼ cup raw walnuts
- ➤ ¼ teaspoon pink
- Himalayan salt
- ➤ ¼ teaspoon ground black pepper
- ➤ ½ cup extra-virgin olive oil

1. Make the chips: Preheat the oven to 375°F and line 2 rimmed baking sheets with parchment paper. 2. Arrange the salami in a single layer on the lined baking sheets. Bake for 10 to 12 minutes, until crisp. Transfer to a paper towel–lined plate to absorb the excess oil. Allow to cool and crisp up further. 3. Make the pesto: Put all the pesto ingredients, except for the olive oil, in a food processor and pulse until everything is roughly chopped and a coarse paste has formed. 4. With the food processor running, slowly pour in the olive oil. Process until all of the oil has been added and the ingredients are fully incorporated. Taste and season with additional salt and pepper, if desired. 5. Pour the pesto into a small serving bowl and serve the salami chips alongside. Store leftover pesto in a sealed container in the refrigerator for up to 2 weeks; store the chips in a zip-top plastic bag in the refrigerator for up to 5 days.

Per Serving:

calories: 202 | fat: 9g | protein: 8g | carbs: 1g | net carbs: 1g | fiber: 0g

Red Wine Mushrooms

Prep time: 5 minutes | Cook time: 15 minutes | Serves 2

- ➤ 8 ounces (227 g) sliced mushrooms
- ➤ ¼ cup dry red wine
- ➤ 2 tablespoons beef broth
- ➤ ½ teaspoon garlic powder
- ➤ ¼ teaspoon Worcestershire sauce
- ➤ Pinch of salt
- ➤ Pinch of black pepper
- ➤ ¼ teaspoon xanthan gum

1. Add the mushrooms, wine, broth, garlic powder, Worcestershire sauce, salt, and pepper to the pot. 2. Close the lid and seal the vent. Cook on High Pressure for 13 minutes. Quick release the steam. Press Cancel. 3. Turn the pot to Sauté mode. Add the xanthan gum and whisk until the juices have thickened, 1 to 2 minutes.

Per Serving:

calories: 94 | fat: 1g | protein: 4g | carbs: 8g | net carbs: 6g | fiber: 2g

Keto Taco Shells

Prep time: 5 minutes | Cook time: 20 minutes | Serves 4

- ➤ 6 ounces (170 g) shredded cheese

1. Preheat the oven to 350°F (180°C). 2. Line a baking sheet with a silicone baking mat or parchment paper. 3. Separate the cheese into 4 (1½-ounce / 43-g) portions and make small circular piles a few inches apart (they will spread a bit in the oven). Pat the cheese down so all the piles are equally thick. Bake for 10 to 12 minutes or until the edges begin to brown. Cool for just a couple of minutes. 4. Lay a wooden spoon or spatula across two overturned glasses. Repeat to make a second setup, and carefully transfer a baked cheese circle to drape over the length of each spoon or spatula. Let them cool into the shape of a taco shell. 5. Fill with your choice of protein and top with chopped lettuce, avocado, salsa, sour cream, or whatever else you like on your tacos. These taco shells will keep refrigerated in an airtight container for a few days, but they are best freshly made and still a little warm.

Per Serving:

1 taco shell: calories: 168 | fat: 14g | protein: 11g | carbs: 1g | net carbs: 1g | fiber: 0g

Taste of the Mediterranean Fat Bombs

Prep time: 15 minutes | Cook time: 0 minutes | Makes 6 fat bombs

- ➤ 1 cup crumbled goat cheese
- ➤ 4 tablespoons jarred pesto
- ➤ 12 pitted Kalamata
- olives, finely chopped
- ➤ ½ cup finely chopped walnuts
- ➤ 1 tablespoon chopped fresh rosemary

1. In a medium bowl, combine the goat cheese, pesto, and olives and mix well using a fork. Place in the refrigerator for at least 4 hours to harden. 2. Using your hands, form the mixture into 6 balls, about ¾-inch diameter. The mixture will be sticky. 3. In a small bowl, place the walnuts and rosemary and roll the goat cheese balls in the nut mixture to coat. 4. Store the fat bombs in the refrigerator for up to 1 week or in the freezer for up to 1 month.

Per Serving:

1 fat bomb: calories: 220 | fat: 20g | protein: 7g | carbs: 4g | net carbs: 3g | fiber: 1g

Chocolate Soft-Serve Ice Cream

Prep time: 10 minutes | Cook time: 0 minutes | Serves 4

- 1 (13½ ounces/400 ml) can full-fat coconut milk
- ¼ cup (40 g) collagen peptides or protein powder (optional)
- ¼ cup (25 g) unflavored MCT oil powder (optional)
- 2 tablespoons smooth
- unsweetened almond butter
- 2 tablespoons cocoa powder
- 3 drops liquid stevia, or 1 tablespoon erythritol
- 1 teaspoon vanilla extract

1. Place all the ingredients in a blender or food processor. Blend until smooth and fully incorporated. 2. Divide the mixture among 4 freezer-safe serving bowls and place in the freezer for 30 minutes. At the 30 minutes mark, remove from the freezer and mash with a fork until the ice cream is smooth. If it's still too runny and doesn't develop the consistency of soft-serve as you mash it, freeze for another 15 minutes, then mash with a fork again. 3. Enjoy immediately.

Per Serving:

calories: 478 | fat: 47g | protein: 6g | carbs: 9g | net carbs: 4g | fiber: 5g

Cool Ranch Dorito Crackers

Prep time: 15 minutes | Cook time: 37 minutes | Serves 7

- 2 cups riced cauliflower, uncooked
- 1½ cups grated Parmesan cheese
- 2 teaspoons ranch seasoning powder
- ⅛ teaspoon salt
- ⅛ teaspoon black pepper

1. Preheat oven to 375°F. 2. In a medium microwave-safe bowl, microwave riced cauliflower 1 minute. Stir and microwave 1 more minute. 3. Let cool and scoop cauliflower onto a clean dish towel. Squeeze out excess water. 4. Return to bowl and add Parmesan, ranch seasoning, salt, and pepper. Mix thoroughly until moist dough is formed. 5. Place the dough on a large piece of parchment paper. Then place a second piece of parchment paper on top of the dough. Use a rolling pin to flatten the dough to the thickness of a Dorito. 6. After the dough is rolled to the desired thickness, remove the top piece of parchment paper and use a pizza cutter to cut the dough into triangle shapes that are roughly the size of Doritos. 7. Transfer the parchment paper with the cut crackers to a baking sheet. Leave enough space between each cracker so they cook evenly and won't stick to nearby crackers during baking. 8. Bake 25 to 35 minutes until

golden brown. 9. Let cool and serve.

Per Serving:

calories: 119 | fat: 8g | protein: 11g | carbs: 4g | net carbs: 3g | fiber: 1g

Buttered Cabbage

Prep time: 5 minutes | Cook time: 5 minutes | Serves 4

- 1 medium head white cabbage, sliced into strips
- 4 tablespoons butter
- ½ teaspoon salt
- ¼ teaspoon pepper
- 1 cup water

1. Place cabbage in 7-cup glass bowl with butter, salt, and pepper. 2. Pour water into Instant Pot and place steam rack on bottom. Place bowl on steam rack. Click lid closed. Press the Manual button and adjust time for 5 minutes. When timer beeps, quick-release the pressure.

Per Serving:

calories: 158 | fat: 10g | protein: 3g | carbs: 13g | net carbs: 8g | fiber: 5g

Cheese Chips and Guacamole

Prep time: 10 minutes | Cook time: 10 minutes | Serves 2

For The Cheese Chips:
- 1 cup shredded cheese (I use Mexican blend)

For The Guacamole:
- 1 avocado, mashed
- Juice of ½ lime
- 1 teaspoon diced jalapeño
- 2 tablespoons chopped
- fresh cilantro leaves
- Pink Himalayan salt
- Freshly ground black pepper

To Make The Cheese Chips: 1. Preheat the oven to 350°F. Line a baking sheet with parchment paper or a silicone baking mat. 2. Add ¼-cup mounds of shredded cheese to the pan, leaving plenty of space between them, and bake until the edges are brown and the middles have fully melted, about 7 minutes. 3. Set the pan on a cooling rack, and let the cheese chips cool for 5 minutes. The chips will be floppy when they first come out of the oven but will crisp as they cool. To Make The Guacamole: 1. In a medium bowl, mix together the avocado, lime juice, jalapeño, and cilantro, and season with pink Himalayan salt and pepper. 2. Top the cheese chips with the guacamole, and serve.

Per Serving:

calories: 323 | fat: 27g | protein: 15g | carbs: 8g | net carbs: 3g | fiber: 5g

Keto Crackers-Two Ways

Prep time: 15 minutes | Cook time: 6 minutes | Serves 2

- Simple Keto Crackers
- ½ cup shredded mozzarella cheese
- ⅓ cup blanched almond flour
- ⅛ teaspoon garlic powder
- Dash of salt
- 1 large egg yolk
- Keto Cheddar Cheese

- Crackers
- ½ cup shredded cheddar cheese
- ⅓ cup blanched almond flour
- ⅛ teaspoon garlic powder
- Dash of salt
- 1 large egg yolk

1. Preheat the oven to 425°F. 2. In a microwave-safe bowl, combine the cheese, almond flour, garlic powder, and salt. Microwave for 30 seconds. 3. Use your hands to knead the dough until fully mixed. Add the egg yolk and knead until it's blended into the dough. 4. Lay a piece of parchment paper on a flat surface, place the dough on top, and place another piece of parchment on top of the dough. Press down and spread the dough (with your hands or a rolling pin) into a very thin, even rectangle. 5. Using a fork, gently poke holes in the dough to prevent it from bubbling while baking. (Don't skip this step!) 6. Use a knife to cut the dough into 1-inch squares. 7. Line a baking sheet with parchment paper and lay the squares on the parchment with a bit of space between them. Bake for 5 to 6 minutes, until golden brown. 8. For extra-crunchy crackers, flip them over and bake for an additional 2 to 4 minutes, watching closely to ensure that they don't burn!

Per Serving:

calories: 234 | fat: 20g | protein: 12g | carbs: 5g | net carbs: 3g | fiber: 2g

Bacon-Pepper Fat Bombs

Prep time: 10 minutes | Cook time: 0 minutes | Makes 12 fat bombs

- 2 ounces goat cheese, at room temperature
- 2 ounces cream cheese, at room temperature
- ¼ cup butter, at room

- temperature
- 8 bacon slices, cooked and chopped
- Pinch freshly ground black pepper

1. Line a small baking sheet with parchment paper and set aside. 2. In a medium bowl, stir together the goat cheese, cream cheese, butter, bacon, and pepper until well combined. 3. Use a tablespoon to drop mounds of the bomb mixture on the baking sheet and place the sheet in the freezer until the

fat bombs are very firm but not frozen, about 1 hour. 4. Store the fat bombs in a sealed container in the refrigerator for up to 2 weeks.

Per Serving:

1 fat bomb: calories: 89 | fat: 8g | protein: 3g | carbs: 0g | net carbs: 0g | fiber: 0g

Almond Sesame Crackers

Prep time: 15 minutes | Cook time: 15 minutes | Makes about 36 (1-inch-square) crackers

- 1½ cups almond flour
- 1 egg
- 3 tablespoons sesame

- seeds, divided
- Salt and freshly ground black pepper, to taste

1. Preheat the oven to 350ºF (180ºC). 2. Line a baking sheet with parchment paper. 3. In a large bowl, mix together the almond flour, egg, and 1½ tablespoons of sesame seeds. Transfer the dough to a sheet of parchment and pat it out flat with your clean hands. Cover with another piece of parchment paper and roll it into a large square, at least 10 inches wide. 4. Remove the top piece of parchment and use a pizza cutter or sharp knife to cut the dough into small squares, about 1 inch wide. Season with salt and pepper and sprinkle with the remaining 1½ tablespoons of sesame seeds. 5. Remove the crackers from the parchment and place them on the prepared baking sheet. Bake for about 15 minutes or until the crackers begin to brown. Cool before serving, and store any leftovers in an airtight bag or container on your counter for up to 2 weeks.

Per Serving:

10 crackers: calories: 108 | fat: 9g | protein: 5g | carbs: 3g | net carbs: 1g | fiber: 2g

Warm Herbed Olives

Prep time: 5 minutes | Cook time: 4 minutes | Serves 4

- ¼ cup good-quality olive oil
- 4 ounces green olives
- 4 ounces Kalamata

- olives
- ½ teaspoon dried thyme
- ¼ teaspoon fennel seeds
- Pinch red pepper flakes

1. Sauté the olives. In a large skillet over medium heat, warm the olive oil. Sauté the olives, thyme, fennel seeds, and red pepper flakes until the olives start to brown, 3 to 4 minutes. 2. Serve. Put the olives into a bowl and serve them warm.

Per Serving:

calories: 165 | fat: 17g | protein: 1g | carbs: 3g | net carbs: 2g | fiber: 1g

Smoked Salmon Cream Cheese Rollups with Arugula and Truffle Oil Drizzle

Prep time: 10 minutes | Cook time: 0 minutes | Serves 4

- ½ cup cream cheese
- ¼ cup plain Greek-style yogurt
- 2 teaspoons chopped fresh dill
- 12 slices (½ pound) smoked salmon
- ¾ cup arugula
- Truffle oil, for garnish

1. Mix the filling. In a small bowl, blend together the cream cheese, yogurt, and dill until the mixture is smooth. 2. Make the rollups. Spread the cream cheese mixture onto the smoked salmon slices, dividing it evenly. Place several arugula leaves at one end of each slice and roll them up. Secure them with a toothpick if they're starting to unroll. 3. Serve. Drizzle the rolls with truffle oil and place three rolls on each of four plates.

Per Serving:

calories: 234 | fat: 20g | protein: 13g | carbs: 2g | net carbs: 2g | fiber: 0g

Cheesy Spinach Puffs

Prep time: 10 minutes | Cook time: 10 minutes | Serves 8

- 16 ounces (454 g) frozen spinach, thawed, drained, and squeezed of as much excess liquid as possible
- 1 cup almond flour
- 4 tablespoons butter, melted, plus more for the baking sheet
- 2 eggs
- ¼ cup grated Parmesan
- cheese
- ¼ cup cream cheese
- 3 tablespoons heavy (whipping) cream
- 1 tablespoon onion powder
- 1 teaspoon garlic powder
- Salt and freshly ground black pepper, to taste

1. In a food processor, combine the spinach, almond flour, butter, eggs, Parmesan, cream cheese, cream, onion powder, and garlic powder. Season with salt and pepper. Blend until smooth. Transfer to the refrigerator and chill for 10 to 15 minutes. 2. Preheat the oven to 350ºF (180ºC). 3. Grease a baking sheet with butter. 4. Scoop the spinach mixture in heaping tablespoons and roll into balls. Place on the prepared baking sheet and bake for about 10 minutes until set. When tapped with your finger, they should not still be soft. Enjoy warm (best!) or cold. Refrigerate in an airtight container for up to 4 days.

Per Serving:

calories: 159 | fat: 14g | protein: 6g | carbs: 3g | net carbs:
1g | fiber: 2g

Crab Salad–Stuffed Avocado

Prep time: 20 minutes | Cook time: 0 minutes | Serves 2

- 1 avocado, peeled, halved lengthwise, and pitted
- ½ teaspoon freshly squeezed lemon juice
- 4½ ounces Dungeness crabmeat
- ½ cup cream cheese
- ¼ cup chopped red bell
- pepper
- ¼ cup chopped, peeled English cucumber
- ½ scallion, chopped
- 1 teaspoon chopped cilantro
- Pinch sea salt
- Freshly ground black pepper

1. Brush the cut edges of the avocado with the lemon juice and set the halves aside on a plate. 2. In a medium bowl, stir together the crabmeat, cream cheese, red pepper, cucumber, scallion, cilantro, salt, and pepper until well mixed. 3. Divide the crab mixture between the avocado halves and store them, covered with plastic wrap, in the refrigerator until you want to serve them, up to 2 days.

Per Serving:

calories: 389 | fat: 31g | protein: 19g | carbs: 10g | net carbs: 5g | fiber: 5g

Peanut Butter Keto Fudge

Prep time: 5 minutes | Cook time: 10 minutes | Serves 12

- ½ cup (1 stick) butter
- 8 ounces (227 g) cream cheese
- 1 cup unsweetened peanut butter
- 1 teaspoon vanilla extract (or the seeds from 1 vanilla bean)
- 1 teaspoon liquid stevia (optional)

1. Line an 8 or 9-inch square or 9-by-13-inch rectangular baking dish with parchment paper. Set aside. 2. In a saucepan over medium heat, melt the butter and cream cheese together, stirring frequently, for about 5 minutes. 3. Add the peanut butter and continue to stir until smooth. Remove from the heat. 4. Stir in the vanilla and stevia (if using). Pour the mixture into the prepared dish and spread into an even layer. Refrigerate for about 1 hour until thickened and set enough to cut and handle. Cut into small squares and enjoy! Refrigerate, covered, for up to 1 week.

Per Serving:

1 fudge square: calories: 261 | fat: 24g | protein: 8g | carbs: 5g | net carbs: 4g | fiber: 1g

Avocado Salsa

Prep time: 10 minutes | Cook time: 0 minutes | Serves 4

- 2 or 3 avocados, peeled, pitted, and diced
- ¼ red onion, diced
- 1 garlic clove, minced
- Zest of ½ lime
- Juice of 1 lime
- ¼ cup olive oil
- Salt and freshly ground black pepper, to taste
- ¼ cup chopped fresh cilantro

1. In a large bowl, gently toss together the diced avocados, onion, garlic, lime zest and juice, and olive oil. Season with salt and pepper. Cover and refrigerate in an airtight container for up to 4 days. Top with the cilantro before serving.

Per Serving:

calories: 450 | fat: 42g | protein: 3g | carbs: 15g | net carbs: 5g | fiber: 10g

Mac Fatties

Prep time: 10 minutes | Cook time: 0 minutes | Makes 20 fat cups

- 1¾ cups (280 g) roasted and salted macadamia nuts
- ⅓ cup (70 g) coconut oil

Rosemary Lemon Flavor:
- 1 teaspoon finely chopped fresh rosemary
- ¼ teaspoon lemon juice

Spicy Cumin Flavor:
- ½ teaspoon ground cumin
- ¼ teaspoon cayenne pepper

Turmeric Flavor:
- ½ teaspoon turmeric powder
- ¼ teaspoon ginger powder

Garlic Herb Flavor:
- 1¼ teaspoons dried oregano leaves
- ½ teaspoon paprika
- ½ teaspoon garlic powder

1. Place the macadamia nuts and oil in a blender or food processor. Blend until smooth, or as close to smooth as you can get it with the equipment you're using. 2. Divide the mixture among 4 small bowls, placing ¼ cup (87 g) in each bowl. 3. To the first bowl, add the rosemary and lemon juice and stir to combine. 4. To the second bowl, add the cumin and cayenne and stir to combine. 5. To the third bowl, add the turmeric and ginger and stir to combine. 6. To the fourth bowl, add the oregano, paprika, and garlic powder and stir to combine. 7. Set a 24-well silicone or metal mini muffin pan on the counter. If using a metal pan, line 20 of the wells with mini foil liners. (Do not use paper; it would soak up all the fat.) Spoon the mixtures into the wells, using about 1 tablespoon per well. 8. Place in the freezer for 1 hour, or until firm. Enjoy directly from the freezer.

Per Serving:

calories: 139 | fat: 14g | protein: 1g | carbs: 2g | net carbs: 1g | fiber: 1g

Italian Tomatillos

Prep time: 10 minutes | Cook time: 10 minutes | Serves 4

- 1 tablespoon Italian seasoning
- 4 tomatillos, sliced
- 4 teaspoons olive oil
- 4 tablespoons water

1. Sprinkle the tomatillos with Italian seasoning. 2. Then pour the olive oil in the instant pot and heat it up on Sauté mode for 1 minute. 3. Put the tomatillos in the instant pot in one layer and cook them for 2 minutes from each side. 4. Then add water and close the lid. 5. Sauté the vegetables for 3 minutes more.

Per Serving:

calories: 51 | fat: 5g | protein: 0g | carbs: 2g | net carbs: 1g | fiber: 1g

The Best Deviled Eggs

Prep time: 15 minutes | Cook time: 0 minutes | Serves 4

- 1 tablespoon mayonnaise
- 1 tablespoon extra-virgin olive oil
- 1 teaspoon Dijon mustard
- 1 teaspoon anchovy paste
- ¼ teaspoon freshly ground black pepper
- 4 large hard-boiled eggs, shelled
- 8 pitted green olives, chopped
- 1 tablespoon red onion, minced
- 1 tablespoon fresh parsley, minced

1. In a small bowl, whisk together the mayonnaise, olive oil, mustard, anchovy paste, and pepper. Set aside. 2. Slice the hard-boiled eggs in half lengthwise, remove the yolks, and place the yolks in a medium bowl. Reserve the egg white halves and set aside. 3. Smash the yolks well with a fork and stir in the mayonnaise mixture. Add the olives, onion, and parsley and stir to combine. 4. Spoon the filling into each egg white half. Cover and chill for 30 minutes or up to 24 hours before serving cold.

Per Serving:

calories: 137 | fat: 12g | protein: 7g | carbs: 1g | net carbs: 1g | fiber: 0g

Devilish Eggs

Prep time: 10 minutes | Cook time: 9 minutes | Serves 6

- 6 large eggs
- 3 tablespoons full-fat mayonnaise
- 1 teaspoon plain white vinegar
- 1 teaspoon spicy mustard
- ⅛ teaspoon salt
- ⅛ teaspoon black pepper
- ⅛ teaspoon ground cayenne
- ⅛ teaspoon paprika

1. Preferred Method: Hard-boil eggs using a steamer basket in the Instant Pot® on high pressure for 9 minutes. Release pressure and remove eggs. 2. Alternate Method: Place eggs in a large pot. Cover with water by 1". Cover with a lid and place the pot over high heat until it reaches a boil. Turn off heat, leave covered, and let it sit for 13 minutes. Then, remove the eggs from the pan, place them in an ice water bath, and let them cool 5 minutes. 3. When cooled, peel eggs and slice in half lengthwise. Place yolks in a medium bowl. 4. Mash and mix yolks with mayonnaise, vinegar, mustard, salt, and black pepper. 5. Scrape mixture into a sandwich-sized plastic bag and snip off one corner, making a hole about the width of a pencil. Use makeshift pastry bag to fill egg white halves with yolk mixture. 6. Garnish Devilish Eggs with cayenne and paprika (mostly for color) and serve.

Per Serving:

calories: 125| fat: 9g | protein: 6g | carbs: 1g | net carbs: 1g | fiber: 0g

Creamed Onion Spinach

Prep time: 3 minutes | Cook time: 5 minutes | Serves 6

- 4 tablespoons butter
- ¼ cup diced onion
- 8 ounces (227 g) cream cheese
- 1 (12 ounces / 340 g) bag
- frozen spinach
- ½ cup chicken broth
- 1 cup shredded whole-milk Mozzarella cheese

1. Press the Sauté button and add butter. Once butter is melted, add onion to Instant Pot and sauté for 2 minutes or until onion begins to turn translucent. 2. Break cream cheese into pieces and add to Instant Pot. Press the Cancel button. Add frozen spinach and broth. Click lid closed. Press the Manual button and adjust time for 5 minutes. When timer beeps, quick-release the pressure and stir in shredded Mozzarella. If mixture is too watery, press the Sauté button and reduce for additional 5 minutes, stirring constantly.

Per Serving:

calories: 273 | fat: 24g | protein: 9g | carbs: 5g | net carbs:

3g | fiber: 2g

Cheddar Chips

Prep time: 10 minutes | Cook time: 5 minutes | Serves 4

- 1 cup shredded Cheddar cheese
- 1 tablespoon almond flour

1. Mix up Cheddar cheese and almond flour. 2. Then preheat the instant pot on Sauté mode. 3. Line the instant pot bowl with baking paper. 4. After this, make the small rounds from the cheese in the instant pot (on the baking paper) and close the lid. 5. Cook them for 5 minutes on Sauté mode or until the cheese is melted. 6. Then switch off the instant pot and remove the baking paper with cheese rounds from it. 7. Cool the chips well and remove them from the baking paper.

Per Serving:

calories: 154 | fat: 13g | protein: 9g | carbs: 2g | net carbs: 1g | fiber: 1g

Broccoli with Garlic-Herb Cheese Sauce

Prep time: 5 minutes | Cook time: 3 minutes | Serves 4

- ½ cup water
- 1 pound (454 g) broccoli (frozen or fresh)
- ½ cup heavy cream
- 1 tablespoon butter
- ½ cup shredded Cheddar
- cheese
- 3 tablespoons garlic and herb cheese spread
- Pinch of salt
- Pinch of black pepper

1. Add the water to the pot and place the trivet inside. 2. Put the steamer basket on top of the trivet. Place the broccoli in the basket. 3. Close the lid and seal the vent. Cook on Low Pressure for 1 minute. Quick release the steam. Press Cancel. 4. Carefully remove the steamer basket from the pot and drain the water. If you steamed a full bunch of broccoli, pull the florets off the stem. (Chop the stem into bite-size pieces, it's surprisingly creamy.) 5. Turn the pot to Sauté mode. Add the cream and butter. Stir continuously while the butter melts and the cream warms up. 6. When the cream begins to bubble on the edges, add the Cheddar cheese, cheese spread, salt, and pepper. Whisk continuously until the cheeses are melted and a sauce consistency is reached, 1 to 2 minutes. 7. Top one-fourth of the broccoli with 2 tablespoons cheese sauce.

Per Serving:

calories: 134 | fat: 12g | protein:4 g | carbs: 5g | net carbs: 3g | fiber: 2g

Rosemary Chicken Wings

Prep time: 10 minutes | Cook time: 16 minutes | Serves 4

- 4 boneless chicken wings
- 1 tablespoon olive oil
- 1 teaspoon dried rosemary
- ½ teaspoon garlic powder
- ¼ teaspoon salt

1. In the mixing bowl, mix up olive oil, dried rosemary, garlic powder, and salt. 2. Then rub the chicken wings with the rosemary mixture and leave for 10 minutes to marinate. 3. After this, put the chicken wings in the instant pot, add the remaining rosemary marinade and cook them on Sauté mode for 8 minutes from each side.

Per Serving:

calories: 222 | fat: 11g | protein: 27g | carbs: 2g | net carbs: 2g | fiber: 0g

Fresh Rosemary Keto Bread

Prep time: 1 hour 45 minutes | Cook time: 55 minutes | serves 6

- 1½ cups warm water, divided, plus up to ¼ cup more if needed
- 1 (¼-ounce) packet active dry yeast
- 1 teaspoon cane sugar
- 1 cup coconut flour
- 3 tablespoons ground psyllium husk
- 1 rosemary sprig
- ¾ cup tahini
- Sea salt

1. In a small bowl, whisk together ½ cup of warm water with the yeast and sugar. Set aside for 10 minutes to allow the yeast to activate and foam. 2. In a separate small mixing bowl, whisk together the coconut flour, psyllium, and rosemary. 3. In a large mixing bowl, stir together the yeast mixture, tahini, and the remaining 1 cup of warm water. 4. Stir the dry ingredients into the wet ingredients, making sure there are no clumps or dry crumbles. If the dough is crumbly or not well combined, add up to ¼ cup of warm water, 1 tablespoon at a time, until the dough comes together. 5. Line a bread pan with parchment paper and press the dough into the pan. If you don't have parchment paper, use a greased pan. Set the dough to rise in a cool, dark place for 90 minutes. It should rise and expand to double its original size. 6. Preheat the oven to 350°F. 7. Bake the bread for 50 to 55 minutes, or until the crust is firm to the touch. 8. While the bread is still warm, remove it from the pan. Let it cool completely before slicing and serving.

Per Serving:

calories: 278 | fat: 18g | protein: 8g | carbs: 24g | net carbs: 10g | fiber: 14g

Cauliflower Popcorn

Prep time: 5 minutes | Cook time: 40 minutes | Serves 2 to 3

Nonstick avocado oil cooking spray, for greasing
1 small to medium head cauliflower, florets with stems chopped into bite-size pieces
- ½ cup avocado oil
- ½ cup neutral-flavored grass-fed collagen protein powder (optional)

Popcorn seasonings of choice: salt, freshly ground black pepper, garlic powder, onion powder, dried oregano, dried sage, and/or nutritional yeast

1. Preheat the oven to 400ºF (205ºC). Coat a broiling pan with nonstick avocado oil spray. (If you have an air fryer, you can make your Cauliflower Popcorn in there instead; just coat the fryer basket with nonstick spray.) 2. Put the cauliflower in a mixing bowl. Pour the avocado oil over the top and sprinkle in the protein powder. Add the seasonings of your choice to the bowl. Stir all together to evenly coat the cauliflower. 3. Spread the cauliflower in an even layer on the prepared pan and place in the oven (or pour into your air fryer). Cook for roughly 40 minutes, checking periodically and stirring every 10 minutes or so (same goes for the air fryer, if using). 4. Remove from the oven (or air fryer) and serve.

Per Serving:

calories: 389 | fat: 37g | protein: 4g | carbs: 10g | net carbs: 5g | fiber: 5g

Salmon-Stuffed Cucumbers

Prep time: 10 minutes | Cook time: 0 minutes | Serves 4

- 2 large cucumbers, peeled
- 1 (4 ounces / 113 g) can red salmon
- 1 medium very ripe avocado, peeled, pitted, and mashed
- 1 tablespoon extra-virgin
- olive oil
- Zest and juice of 1 lime
- 3 tablespoons chopped fresh cilantro
- ½ teaspoon salt
- ¼ teaspoon freshly ground black pepper

1. Slice the cucumber into 1-inch-thick segments and using a spoon, scrape seeds out of center of each segment and stand up on a plate. 2. In a medium bowl, combine the salmon, avocado, olive oil, lime zest and juice, cilantro, salt, and pepper and mix until creamy. 3. Spoon the salmon mixture into the center of each cucumber segment and serve chilled.

Per Serving:

calories: 174 | fat: 12g | protein: 10g | carbs: 9g | net carbs: 6g | fiber: 3g

Bacon Avocado Mousse Cups

Prep time: 10 minutes | Cook time: 20 minutes | Serves 6

- 12 bacon slices
- 2 or 3 ripe avocados, halved and pitted
- ½ cup plain Greek
- yogurt
- Juice of ½ lime
- Salt and freshly ground black pepper, to taste

1. Preheat the oven to 425ºF (220ºC). 2. Wrap each piece of bacon around the sides and bottom of the wells of a mini muffin tin to create little bacon cups. Bake for 15 to 20 minutes or until the bacon is cooked through and crisp. 3. While the bacon cooks, in a medium bowl, combine the avocado flesh, yogurt, and lime juice. Mix well until combined and smooth. Season with salt and pepper and transfer to a piping bag (or a plastic bag with the tip cut off). 4. Remove the bacon from the oven and cool slightly. Pipe each bacon cup full of avocado mousse. Serve immediately.

Per Serving:

2 filled cups: calories: 530 | fat: 38g | protein: 31g | carbs: 16g | net carbs: 9g | fiber: 7g

Cheese Almond Crackers

Prep time: 10 minutes | Cook time: 20 minutes | Serves 4

- Olive oil cooking spray
- 1 cup almond flour
- ½ cup finely shredded Cheddar cheese
- 1 tablespoon nutritional yeast
- ¼ teaspoon baking soda
- ¼ teaspoon garlic powder
- ¼ teaspoon sea salt
- 1 egg
- 2 teaspoons good-quality olive oil

1. Preheat the oven. Set the oven temperature to 350°F. Line a baking sheet with parchment paper and set it aside. Lightly grease two sheets of parchment paper with olive oil cooking spray and set them aside. 2. Mix the dry ingredients. In a large bowl, stir together the almond flour, Cheddar, nutritional yeast, baking soda, garlic powder, and salt until everything is well blended. 3. Mix the wet ingredients. In a small bowl, whisk together the egg and olive oil. Using a wooden spoon, mix the wet ingredients into the dry until the dough sticks together to form a ball. Gather the ball together using your hands, and knead it firmly a few times. 4. Roll out the dough. Place the ball on one of the lightly greased parchment paper pieces and press it down to form a disk. Place the other piece of greased parchment paper on top and use a rolling pin to roll the dough into a 9-by-12-inch rectangle about ⅛ inch thick. 5. Cut the dough. Use a pizza cutter and a ruler to cut the edges of the dough into an even

rectangle and cut the dough into 1½-by-1½-inch columns and rows. Transfer the crackers to the baking sheet. 6. Bake. Bake the crackers for 15 to 20 minutes until they're crisp. Transfer them to a wire rack and let them cool completely. 7. Serve. Eat the crackers immediately or store them in an airtight container in the refrigerator for up to one week.

Per Serving:

calories: 146 | fat: 12g | protein: 7g | carbs: 1g | net carbs: 0g | fiber: 1g

Zucchini and Cheese Tots

Prep time: 15 minutes | Cook time: 10 minutes | Serves 6

- 4 ounces (113 g) Parmesan, grated
- 4 ounces (113 g) Cheddar cheese, grated
- 1 zucchini, grated
- 1 egg, beaten
- 1 teaspoon dried oregano
- 1 tablespoon coconut oil

1. In the mixing bowl, mix up Parmesan, Cheddar cheese, zucchini, egg, and dried oregano. 2. Make the small tots with the help of the fingertips. 3. Then melt the coconut oil in the instant pot on Sauté mode. 4. Put the prepared zucchini tots in the hot coconut oil and cook them for 3 minutes from each side or until they are light brown. Cool the zucchini tots for 5 minutes.

Per Serving:

calories: 173 | fat: 13g | protein: 12g | carbs: 2g | net carbs: 2g | fiber: 0g

Bacon-Wrapped Avocados

Prep time: 10 minutes | Cook time: 15 minutes | Serves 4

- 8 bacon slices
- 1 ripe avocado, peeled and cut into 8 wedges
- Salt and freshly ground
- black pepper, to taste
- 1 or 2 lime wedges
- Ground cayenne pepper

1. Wrap 1 bacon slice around each avocado wedge. If needed, use a toothpick to secure them. 2. Heat a nonstick skillet over medium-high heat. Evenly space the bacon-wrapped wedges around the skillet. If you aren't using a toothpick, place the loose end of the bacon facing down to create a seal as it cooks. Cook for 6 to 8 minutes, turning every couple of minutes until the bacon is cooked. 3. Remove from the heat and finish with a sprinkle of salt, pepper, lime juice, and cayenne. Serve warm.

Per Serving:

calories: 314 | fat: 26g | protein: 15g | carbs: 5g | net carbs: 2g | fiber: 3g

Marinated Cheese

Prep time: 10 minutes | Cook time: 0 minutes | Serves 8

- ½ cup olive oil
- ½ cup white wine vinegar
- 2 or 3 garlic cloves, minced
- 4 scallions, green parts only, thinly sliced
- 3 tablespoons chopped fresh parsley leaves
- 1 (2-ounce / 57-g) jar diced pimientos, drained
- Salt and freshly ground
- black pepper, to taste
- 1 (8-ounce / 227-g) block sharp Cheddar cheese, halved lengthwise and cut widthwise into ½-inch squares
- 1 (8-ounce / 227-g) block cream cheese halved lengthwise and cut widthwise into ½-inch squares

1. In a small bowl, whisk together the olive oil, vinegar, garlic, scallions, parsley, pimientos, and season with some salt and pepper. 2. In a container with a lid, assemble the cheese (we like to alternate pieces of Cheddar and cream cheese for a prettier presentation) and cover with the marinade. Cover and refrigerate for at least 8 hours. 3. Remove from the refrigerator 15 to 20 minutes before serving, and transfer the cheese to a serving platter, pouring the marinade over the top. Refrigerate leftovers in an airtight container for up to 1 week.

Per Serving:
calories: 336 | fat: 32g | protein: 10g | carbs: 2g | net carbs: 1g | fiber: 1g

Road Trip Red Pepper Edamame

Prep time: 1 minutes | Cook time: 18 minutes | Serves 4

- 2 cups frozen raw edamame in the shell
- 1 tablespoon peanut oil
- 2 cloves garlic, peeled
- and minced
- ⅛ teaspoon salt
- ½ teaspoon red pepper flakes

1. In a medium microwave-safe bowl with ½ cup water, microwave edamame 4–5 minutes. 2. In a medium saucepan over medium heat, add peanut oil. Add minced garlic and salt. Stir 3–5 minutes to soften garlic. 3. Add edamame and stir 2–3 minutes until well heated and coated. Turn off heat and cover saucepan to steam edamame for 5 additional minutes. 4. Remove lid. Add red pepper flakes and toss to coat. 5. Serve immediately for best results.

Per Serving:
calories: 128 | fat: 7g | protein: 10g | carbs: 8g | net carbs: 4g | fiber: 4g

Bacon-Wrapped Jalapeños

Prep time: 10 minutes | Cook time: 20 minutes | Serves 4

- 10 jalapeños
- 8 ounces cream cheese, at room temperature
- 1 pound bacon (you will use about half a slice per popper)

1. Preheat the oven to 450°F. Line a baking sheet with aluminum foil or a silicone baking mat. 2. Halve the jalapeños lengthwise, and remove the seeds and membranes (if you like the extra heat, leave them in). Place them on the prepared pan cut-side up. 3. Spread some of the cream cheese inside each jalapeño half. 4. Wrap a jalapeño half with a slice of bacon (depending on the size of the jalapeño, use a whole slice of bacon, or half). 5. Secure the bacon around each jalapeño with 1 to 2 toothpicks so it stays put while baking. 6. Bake for 20 minutes, until the bacon is done and crispy. 7. Serve hot or at room temperature. Either way, they are delicious!

Per Serving:
calories: 164 | fat: 13g | protein: 9g | carbs: 1g | net carbs: 1g | fiber: 0g

Bacon-Studded Pimento Cheese

Prep time: 10 minutes | Cook time: 5 minutes | Serves 6

- 2 ounces (57 g) bacon (about 4 thick slices)
- 4 ounces (113 g) cream cheese, room temperature
- ¼ cup mayonnaise
- ¼ teaspoon onion powder
- ¼ teaspoon cayenne pepper (optional)
- 1 cup thick-shredded extra-sharp Cheddar cheese
- 2 ounces (57 g) jarred diced pimentos, drained

1. Chop the raw bacon into ½-inch-thick pieces. Cook in a small skillet over medium heat until crispy, 3 to 4 minutes. Use a slotted spoon to transfer the bacon onto a layer of paper towels. Reserve the rendered fat. 2. In a large bowl, combine the cream cheese, mayonnaise, onion powder, and cayenne (if using), and beat with an electric mixer or by hand until smooth and creamy. 3. Add the rendered bacon fat, Cheddar cheese, and pimentos and mix until well combined. 4. Refrigerate for at least 30 minutes before serving to allow flavors to blend. Serve cold with raw veggies.

Per Serving:
calories: 216 | fat: 20g | protein: 8g | carbs: 2g | net carbs: 0g | fiber: 2

Dairy-Free Queso

Prep time: 10 minutes | Cook time: 10 minutes | Serves 5

- 1 cup (130 g) raw cashews
- ½ cup (120 ml) nondairy milk
- ¼ cup (17 g) nutritional yeast
- ½ teaspoon finely ground sea salt
- ¼ cup (60 ml) avocado oil
- 1 medium yellow onion, sliced
- 2 cloves garlic, roughly chopped
- 1 tablespoon chili

- powder
- 1 teaspoon ground cumin
- ¾ teaspoon garlic powder
- ¼ teaspoon onion powder
- ½ teaspoon dried oregano leaves
- ⅛ teaspoon paprika
- ⅛ teaspoon cayenne pepper
- 3½ ounces (100 g) pork rinds, or 2 medium zucchinis, cut into sticks, for serving (optional)

1. Place the cashews in a 12-ounce (350-ml) or larger sealable container. Cover with water. Seal and place in the fridge to soak for 12 hours. 2. After 12 hours, drain and rinse the cashews, then place them in a food processor or blender along with the milk, nutritional yeast, and salt. Set aside. 3. Heat the oil in a medium-sized frying pan over medium-low heat until shimmering. Add the onion, garlic, and spices and toss to coat the onion with the seasonings. Stir the mixture every couple of minutes until the onion begins to soften, about 10 minutes. 4. Transfer the onion mixture to the food processor or blender. Cover and blend until smooth. 5. Enjoy the queso with pork rinds or zucchini sticks, if desired.

Per Serving:
calories: 300 | fat: 24g | protein: 7g | carbs: 14g | net carbs: 11g | fiber: 3g

Prosciutto-Wrapped Asparagus

Prep time: 5 minutes | Cook time: 12 minutes | Serves 6

- 18 asparagus spears, ends trimmed
- 2 tablespoons coconut

- oil, melted
- 6 slices prosciutto
- 1 teaspoon garlic powder

1. Preheat the oven to 400°F. Line a rimmed baking sheet with parchment paper. 2. Place the asparagus and coconut oil in a large zip-top plastic bag. Seal and toss until the asparagus is evenly coated. 3. Wrap a slice of prosciutto around 3 grouped asparagus spears. Repeat with the remaining prosciutto and asparagus, making a total of 6 bundles. Arrange the bundles in a single layer on the lined baking sheet. Sprinkle the garlic powder over the bundles. 4. Bake for 8 to 12 minutes, until the asparagus is tender.

Per Serving:
calories: 122 | fat: 10g | protein: 8g | carbs: 3g | net carbs: 2g | fiber: 1g

English Cucumber Tea Sandwiches

Prep time: 10 minutes | Cook time: 0 minutes | Makes 12 snacks

- 1 large cucumber, peeled (approximately 10 ounces / 283 g)
- 4 ounces (113 g) cream cheese, softened

- 2 tablespoons finely chopped fresh dill
- Freshly ground black pepper, to taste

1. Slice the cucumbers into 24 rounds approximately ¼ inch (6 mm) thick. Place in a single layer between two kitchen towels. Put a cutting board on top. Allow to sit about 5 minutes. 2. Mix the cream cheese and dill. 3. Spread 2 teaspoons cream cheese on half the cucumber slices. Grind black pepper over the cheese. Place another slice of cucumber on top of each and secure with a toothpick, if desired.

Per Serving:
calories: 96 | fat: 8g | protein: 3g | carbs: 3g | net carbs: 1g | fiber: 2g

Keto Trail Mix

Prep time: 5 minutes | Cook time: 0 minutes | Serves 4

- ¼ cup pumpkin seeds
- ¼ cup salted almonds
- ¼ cup salted macadamia nuts
- ¼ cup salted walnuts

- 1 cup crunchy cheese snack
- ¼ cup sugar-free chocolate chips

1. In a resealable 1-quart plastic bag, combine the pumpkin seeds, almonds, macadamia nuts, walnuts, cheese snack, and chocolate chips. Seal the bag and shake to mix.

Per Serving:
calories: 253 | fat: 23g | protein: 7g | carbs: 5g | net carbs: 2g | fiber: 3g

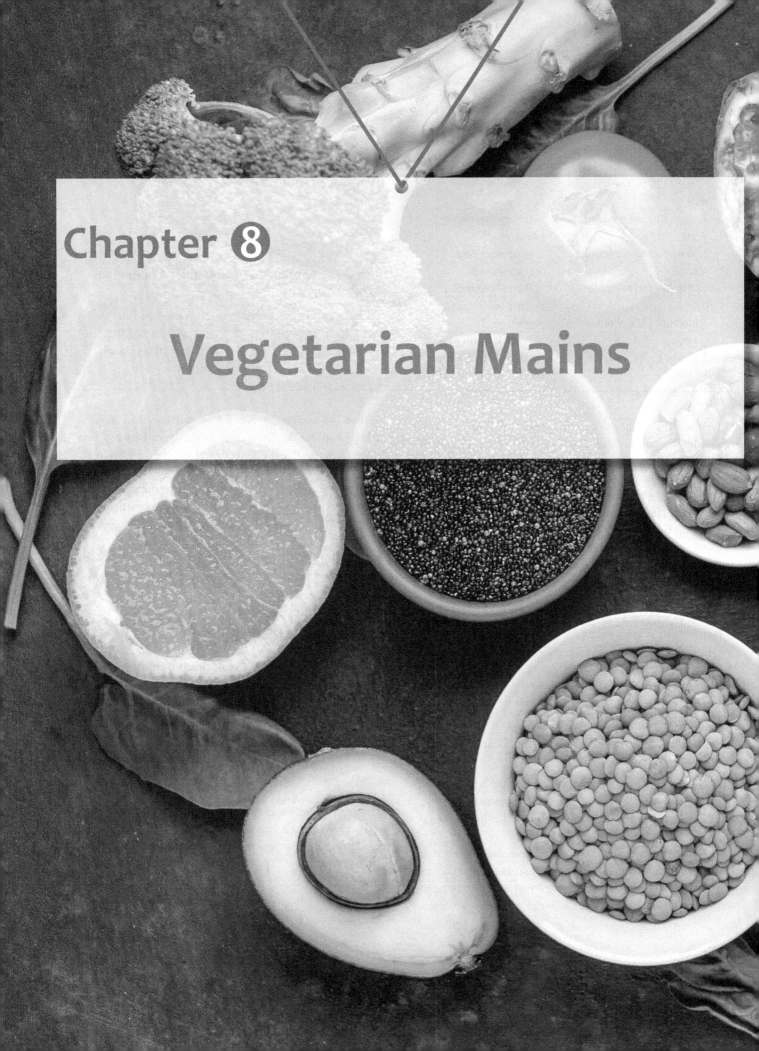

Chapter 8

Vegetarian Mains

Broccoli-Cheese Fritters

Prep time: 5 minutes | Cook time: 20 to 25 minutes | Serves 4

- 1 cup broccoli florets
- 1 cup shredded Mozzarella cheese
- ¾ cup almond flour
- ½ cup flaxseed meal, divided
- 2 teaspoons baking powder
- 1 teaspoon garlic powder
- Salt and freshly ground black pepper, to taste
- 2 eggs, lightly beaten
- ½ cup ranch dressing

1. Preheat the air fryer to 400°F (204°C). 2. In a food processor fitted with a metal blade, pulse the broccoli until very finely chopped. 3. Transfer the broccoli to a large bowl and add the Mozzarella, almond flour, ¼ cup of the flaxseed meal, baking powder, and garlic powder. Stir until thoroughly combined. Season to taste with salt and black pepper. Add the eggs and stir again to form a sticky dough. Shape the dough into 1¼-inch fritters. 4. Place the remaining ¼ cup flaxseed meal in a shallow bowl and roll the fritters in the meal to form an even coating. 5. Working in batches if necessary, arrange the fritters in a single layer in the basket of the air fryer and spray generously with olive oil. Pausing halfway through the cooking time to shake the basket, air fry for 20 to 25 minutes until the fritters are golden brown and crispy. Serve with the ranch dressing for dipping.

Per Serving:

calories: 638 | fat: 54g | protein: 28g | carbs: 16g | net carbs: 9g | fiber: 7g

Zucchini Lasagna

Prep time: 15 minutes | Cook time: 1 hour | Serves 8

- ½ cup extra-virgin olive oil, divided
- 4 to 5 medium zucchini squash
- 1 teaspoon salt
- 8 ounces (227 g) frozen spinach, thawed and well drained (about 1 cup)
- 2 cups whole-milk ricotta cheese
- ¼ cup chopped fresh basil or 2 teaspoons dried basil
- 1 teaspoon garlic powder
- ½ teaspoon freshly ground black pepper
- 2 cups shredded fresh whole-milk mozzarella cheese
- 1¾ cups shredded Parmesan cheese
- ½ (24 ounces / 680 g) jar low-sugar marinara sauce (less than 5 grams sugar)

1. Preheat the oven to 425°F (220°C). 2. Line two baking sheets with parchment paper or aluminum foil and drizzle each with 2 tablespoons olive oil, spreading evenly. 3. Slice the zucchini lengthwise into ¼-inch-thick long slices and place on the prepared baking sheet in a single layer. Sprinkle with ½ teaspoon salt per sheet. Bake until softened, but not mushy, 15 to 18 minutes. Remove from the oven and allow to cool slightly before assembling the lasagna. 4. Reduce the oven temperature to 375°F (190°C). 5. While the zucchini cooks, prep the filling. In a large bowl, combine the spinach, ricotta, basil, garlic powder, and pepper. In a small bowl, mix together the mozzarella and Parmesan cheeses. In a medium bowl, combine the marinara sauce and remaining ¼ cup olive oil and stir to fully incorporate the oil into sauce. 6. To assemble the lasagna, spoon a third of the marinara sauce mixture into the bottom of a 9-by-13-inch glass baking dish and spread evenly. Place 1 layer of softened zucchini slices to fully cover the sauce, then add a third of the ricotta-spinach mixture and spread evenly on top of the zucchini. Sprinkle a third of the mozzarella-Parmesan mixture on top of the ricotta. Repeat with 2 more cycles of these layers: marinara, zucchini, ricotta-spinach, then cheese blend. 7. Bake until the cheese is bubbly and melted, 30 to 35 minutes. Turn the broiler to low and broil until the top is golden brown, about 5 minutes. Remove from the oven and allow to cool slightly before slicing.

Per Serving:

calories: 520 | fat: 43g | protein: 26g | carbs: 10g | net carbs: 7g | fiber: 3g

Broccoli with Garlic Sauce

Prep time: 19 minutes | Cook time: 15 minutes | Serves 4

- 2 tablespoons olive oil
- Kosher salt and freshly ground black pepper, to taste
- 1 pound (454 g) broccoli florets

Dipping Sauce:
- 2 teaspoons dried rosemary, crushed
- 3 garlic cloves, minced
- ⅓ teaspoon dried marjoram, crushed
- ¼ cup sour cream
- ⅓ cup mayonnaise

1. Lightly grease your broccoli with a thin layer of olive oil. Season with salt and ground black pepper. 2. Arrange the seasoned broccoli in the air fryer basket. Bake at 395°F (202°C) for 15 minutes, shaking once or twice. In the meantime, prepare the dipping sauce by mixing all the sauce ingredients. Serve warm broccoli with the dipping sauce and enjoy!

Per Serving:

calories: 250 | fat: 23g | protein: 3g | carbs: 10g | net carbs: 9g | fiber: 1g

Loaded Cauliflower Steak

Prep time: 5 minutes | Cook time: 7 minutes | Serves 4

- 1 medium head cauliflower
- ¼ cup hot sauce
- 2 tablespoons salted butter, melted
- ¼ cup blue cheese crumbles
- ¼ cup full-fat ranch dressing

1. Remove cauliflower leaves. Slice the head in ½-inch-thick slices. 2. In a small bowl, mix hot sauce and butter. Brush the mixture over the cauliflower. 3. Place each cauliflower steak into the air fryer, working in batches if necessary. 4. Adjust the temperature to 400°F (204°C) and air fry for 7 minutes. 5. When cooked, edges will begin turning dark and caramelized. 6. To serve, sprinkle steaks with crumbled blue cheese. Drizzle with ranch dressing.

Per Serving:
calories: 140 | fat: 12g | protein: 5g | carbs: 6g | net carbs: 5g | fiber: 1g

Zucchini Roll Manicotti

Prep time: 15 minutes | Cook time: 30 minutes | Serves 4

- Olive oil cooking spray
- 4 zucchini
- 2 tablespoons good-quality olive oil
- 1 red bell pepper, diced
- ½ onion, minced
- 2 teaspoons minced garlic
- 1 cup goat cheese
- 1 cup shredded
- mozzarella cheese
- 1 tablespoon chopped fresh oregano
- Sea salt, for seasoning
- Freshly ground black pepper, for seasoning
- 2 cups low-carb marinara sauce, divided
- ½ cup grated Parmesan cheese

1. Preheat the oven. Set the oven temperature to 375°F. Lightly grease a 9-by-13-inch baking dish with olive oil cooking spray. 2. Prepare the zucchini. Cut the zucchini lengthwise into ⅛-inch-thick slices and set them aside. 3. Make the filling. In a medium skillet over medium-high heat, warm the olive oil. Add the red bell pepper, onion, and garlic and sauté until they've softened, about 4 minutes. Remove the skillet from the heat and transfer the vegetables to a medium bowl. Stir the goat cheese, mozzarella, and oregano into the vegetables. Season it all with salt and pepper. 4. Assemble the manicotti. Spread 1 cup of the marinara sauce in the bottom of the baking dish. Lay a zucchini slice on a clean cutting board and place a couple tablespoons of filling at one end. Roll the slice up and place it in the baking dish,

seam-side down. Repeat with the remaining zucchini slices. Spoon the remaining sauce over the rolls and top with the Parmesan. 5. Bake. Bake the rolls for 30 to 35 minutes until the zucchini is tender and the cheese is golden. 6. Serve. Spoon the rolls onto four plates and serve them hot.

Per Serving:
calories: 342 | fat: 24g | protein: 20g | carbs: 14g | net carbs: 11g | fiber: 3g

Eggplant and Zucchini Bites

Prep time: 30 minutes | Cook time: 30 minutes | Serves 8

- 2 teaspoons fresh mint leaves, chopped
- 1½ teaspoons red pepper chili flakes
- 2 tablespoons melted butter
- 1 pound (454 g)
- eggplant, peeled and cubed
- 1 pound (454 g) zucchini, peeled and cubed
- 3 tablespoons olive oil

1. Toss all the above ingredients in a large-sized mixing dish. 2. Roast the eggplant and zucchini bites for 30 minutes at 325°F (163°C) in your air fryer, turning once or twice. 3. Serve with a homemade dipping sauce.

Per Serving:
calories: 140 | fat: 12g | protein: 2g | carbs: 8g | net carbs: 6g | fiber: 2g

Quiche-Stuffed Peppers

Prep time: 5 minutes | Cook time: 15 minutes | Serves 2

- 2 medium green bell peppers
- 3 large eggs
- ¼ cup full-fat ricotta cheese
- ¼ cup diced yellow onion
- ½ cup chopped broccoli
- ½ cup shredded medium Cheddar cheese

1. Cut the tops off of the peppers and remove the seeds and white membranes with a small knife. 2. In a medium bowl, whisk eggs and ricotta. 3. Add onion and broccoli. Pour the egg and vegetable mixture evenly into each pepper. Top with Cheddar. Place peppers into a 4-cup round baking dish and place into the air fryer basket. 4. Adjust the temperature to 350°F (177°C) and bake for 15 minutes. 5. Eggs will be mostly firm and peppers tender when fully cooked. Serve immediately.

Per Serving:
calories: 382 | fat: 27g | protein: 24g | carbs: 11g | net carbs: 7g | fiber: 4g

Crispy Eggplant Rounds

Prep time: 15 minutes | Cook time: 10 minutes | Serves 4

- 1 large eggplant, ends trimmed, cut into ½-inch slices
- ½ teaspoon salt
- 2 ounces (57 g) Parmesan 100% cheese
- crisps, finely ground
- ½ teaspoon paprika
- ¼ teaspoon garlic powder
- 1 large egg

1. Sprinkle eggplant rounds with salt. Place rounds on a kitchen towel for 30 minutes to draw out excess water. Pat rounds dry. 2. In a medium bowl, mix cheese crisps, paprika, and garlic powder. In a separate medium bowl, whisk egg. Dip each eggplant round in egg, then gently press into cheese crisps to coat both sides. 3. Place eggplant rounds into ungreased air fryer basket. Adjust the temperature to 400ºF (204ºC) and air fry for 10 minutes, turning rounds halfway through cooking. Eggplant will be golden and crispy when done. Serve warm.

Per Serving:

calories: 133 | fat: 8g | protein: 10g | carbs: 6g | net carbs: 4g | fiber: 3g

Cauliflower Steak with Gremolata

Prep time: 15 minutes | Cook time: 25 minutes | Serves 4

- 2 tablespoons olive oil
- 1 tablespoon Italian seasoning
- 1 large head cauliflower, outer leaves removed and sliced lengthwise

Gremolata:
- 1 bunch Italian parsley (about 1 cup packed)
- 2 cloves garlic
- Zest of 1 small lemon,
- through the core into thick "steaks"
- Salt and freshly ground black pepper, to taste
- ¼ cup Parmesan cheese

- plus 1 to 2 teaspoons lemon juice
- ½ cup olive oil
- Salt and pepper, to taste

1. Preheat the air fryer to 400ºF (204ºC). 2. In a small bowl, combine the olive oil and Italian seasoning. Brush both sides of each cauliflower "steak" generously with the oil. Season to taste with salt and black pepper. 3. Working in batches if necessary, arrange the cauliflower in a single layer in the air fryer basket. Pausing halfway through the cooking time to turn the "steaks," air fry for 15 to 20 minutes until the cauliflower is tender and the edges begin to brown. Sprinkle with the Parmesan and air fry for 5 minutes longer. 4. To make the gremolata: In a food processor fitted with a metal blade, combine the parsley, garlic, and lemon zest and juice. With the motor running, add the olive oil in a steady stream until the mixture forms a bright green sauce. Season to taste with salt and black pepper. Serve the cauliflower steaks with the gremolata spooned over the top.

Per Serving:

calories: 257 | fat: 23g | protein: 6g | carbs: 9g | net carbs: 7g | fiber: 4g

Roasted Spaghetti Squash

Prep time: 10 minutes | Cook time: 45 minutes | Serves 6

- 1 (4 pounds / 1.8 kg) spaghetti squash, halved and seeded
- 2 tablespoons coconut oil
- 4 tablespoons salted butter, melted
- 1 teaspoon garlic powder
- 2 teaspoons dried parsley

1. Brush shell of spaghetti squash with coconut oil. Brush inside with butter. Sprinkle inside with garlic powder and parsley. 2. Place squash skin side down into ungreased air fryer basket, working in batches if needed. Adjust the temperature to 350ºF (177ºC) and set the timer for 30 minutes. When the timer beeps, flip squash and cook an additional 15 minutes until fork-tender. 3. Use a fork to remove spaghetti strands from shell and serve warm.

Per Serving:

calories: 210 | fat: 19g | protein: 2g | carbs: 11g | net carbs: 8g | fiber: 3g

Roasted Veggie Bowl

Prep time: 10 minutes | Cook time: 15 minutes | Serves 2

- 1 cup broccoli florets
- 1 cup quartered Brussels sprouts
- ½ cup cauliflower florets
- ¼ medium white onion, peeled and sliced ¼ inch thick
- ½ medium green bell
- pepper, seeded and sliced ¼ inch thick
- 1 tablespoon coconut oil
- 2 teaspoons chili powder
- ½ teaspoon garlic powder
- ½ teaspoon cumin

1. Toss all ingredients together in a large bowl until vegetables are fully coated with oil and seasoning. 2. Pour vegetables into the air fryer basket. 3. Adjust the temperature to 360ºF (182ºC) and roast for 15 minutes. 4. Shake two or three times during cooking. Serve warm.

Per Serving:

calories: 168 | fat: 11g | protein: 4g | carbs: 15g | net carbs: 9g | fiber: 6g

Vegetarian Chili with Avocado and Sour Cream

Prep time: 10 minutes | Cook time: 25 minutes | Serves 8

- 2 tablespoons good-quality olive oil
- ½ onion, finely chopped
- 1 red bell pepper, diced
- 2 jalapeño peppers, chopped
- 1 tablespoon minced garlic
- 2 tablespoons chili

- powder
- 1 teaspoon ground cumin
- 4 cups canned diced tomatoes
- 2 cups pecans, chopped
- 1 cup sour cream
- 1 avocado, diced
- 2 tablespoons chopped fresh cilantro

1. Sauté the vegetables. In a large pot over medium-high heat, warm the olive oil. Add the onion, red bell pepper, jalapeño peppers, and garlic and sauté until they've softened, about 4 minutes. Stir in the chili powder and cumin, stirring to coat the vegetables with the spices. 2. Cook the chili. Stir in the tomatoes and pecans and bring the chili to a boil, then reduce the heat to low and simmer until the vegetables are soft and the flavors mellow, about 20 minutes. 3. Serve. Ladle the chili into bowls and serve it with the sour cream, avocado, and cilantro.

Per Serving:

calories: 332 | fat: 32g | protein: 5g | carbs: 11g | net carbs: 5g | fiber: 6g

Cheesy Broccoli Casserole

Prep time: 10 minutes | Cook time: 35 minutes | Serves 4

- 2 tablespoons butter
- ¼ white onion, diced
- 1 garlic clove, minced
- 1 pound (454 g) broccoli florets, roughly chopped
- Salt, to taste
- Freshly ground black pepper, to taste

- 4 ounces (113 g) cream cheese, at room temperature
- 1 cup shredded Cheddar cheese, divided
- ½ cup heavy (whipping) cream
- 2 eggs

1. Preheat the oven to 350ºF (180ºC). 2. In a large skillet over medium heat, melt the butter. 3. Add the onion and garlic. Sauté for 5 to 7 minutes until the onion is softened and translucent. 4. Add the broccoli. Season with salt and pepper. Cook for 4 to 5 minutes until just softened. Transfer to a 7-by-11-inch baking dish. 5. In a medium bowl, stir together the cream cheese, ½ cup of Cheddar, the cream, and eggs. Pour over the broccoli. Season with more salt and pepper, and top with the remaining ½ cup of Cheddar. Bake

for 20 minutes. Refrigerate leftovers in an airtight container for up to 1 week.

Per Serving:

calories: 440 | fat: 39g | protein: 16g | carbs: 11g | net carbs: 8g | fiber: 3g

Sweet Pepper Nachos

Prep time: 10 minutes | Cook time: 5 minutes | Serves 2

- 6 mini sweet peppers, seeded and sliced in half
- ¾ cup shredded Colby jack cheese
- ¼ cup sliced pickled

- jalapeños
- ½ medium avocado, peeled, pitted, and diced
- 2 tablespoons sour cream

1. Place peppers into an ungreased round nonstick baking dish. Sprinkle with Colby and top with jalapeños. 2. Place dish into air fryer basket. Adjust the temperature to 350ºF (177ºC) and bake for 5 minutes. Cheese will be melted and bubbly when done. 3. Remove dish from air fryer and top with avocado. Drizzle with sour cream. Serve warm.

Per Serving:

calories: 255 | fat: 21g | protein: 11g | carbs: 9g | net carbs: 5g | fiber: 4g

Herbed Ricotta–Stuffed Mushrooms

Prep time: 10 minutes | Cook time: 30 minutes | Serves 4

- 6 tablespoons extra-virgin olive oil, divided
- 4 portobello mushroom caps, cleaned and gills removed
- 1 cup whole-milk ricotta cheese
- ⅓ cup chopped fresh

- herbs (such as basil, parsley, rosemary, oregano, or thyme)
- 2 garlic cloves, finely minced
- ½ teaspoon salt
- ¼ teaspoon freshly ground black pepper

1. Preheat the oven to 400ºF (205ºC). 2. Line a baking sheet with parchment or foil and drizzle with 2 tablespoons olive oil, spreading evenly. Place the mushroom caps on the baking sheet, gill-side up. 3. In a medium bowl, mix together the ricotta, herbs, 2 tablespoons olive oil, garlic, salt, and pepper. Stuff each mushroom cap with one-quarter of the cheese mixture, pressing down if needed. Drizzle with remaining 2 tablespoons olive oil and bake until golden brown and the mushrooms are soft, 30 to 35 minutes, depending on the size of the mushrooms.

Per Serving:

calories: 400 | fat: 36g | protein: 12g | carbs: 7g | net carbs: 6g | fiber: 1g

Eggplant Parmesan

Prep time: 15 minutes | Cook time: 17 minutes | Serves 4

- 1 medium eggplant, ends trimmed, sliced into ½-inch rounds
- ¼ teaspoon salt
- 2 tablespoons coconut oil
- ½ cup grated Parmesan cheese
- 1 ounce (28 g) 100% cheese crisps, finely crushed
- ½ cup low-carb marinara sauce
- ½ cup shredded Mozzarella cheese

1. Sprinkle eggplant rounds with salt on both sides and wrap in a kitchen towel for 30 minutes. Press to remove excess water, then drizzle rounds with coconut oil on both sides. 2. In a medium bowl, mix Parmesan and cheese crisps. Press each eggplant slice into mixture to coat both sides. 3. Place rounds into ungreased air fryer basket. Adjust the temperature to 350ºF (177ºC) and air fry for 15 minutes, turning rounds halfway through cooking. They will be crispy around the edges when done. 4. Spoon marinara over rounds and sprinkle with Mozzarella. Continue cooking an additional 2 minutes at 350ºF (177ºC) until cheese is melted. Serve warm.

Per Serving:

calories: 330 | fat: 24g | protein: 18g | carbs: 13g | net carbs: 9g | fiber: 4g

Broccoli Crust Pizza

Prep time: 15 minutes | Cook time: 12 minutes | Serves 4

- 3 cups riced broccoli, steamed and drained well
- 1 large egg
- ½ cup grated vegetarian Parmesan cheese
- 3 tablespoons low-carb Alfredo sauce
- ½ cup shredded Mozzarella cheese

1. In a large bowl, mix broccoli, egg, and Parmesan. 2. Cut a piece of parchment to fit your air fryer basket. Press out the pizza mixture to fit on the parchment, working in two batches if necessary. Place into the air fryer basket. 3. Adjust the temperature to 370ºF (188ºC) and air fry for 5 minutes. 4. The crust should be firm enough to flip. If not, add 2 additional minutes. Flip crust. 5. Top with Alfredo sauce and Mozzarella. Return to the air fryer basket and cook an additional 7 minutes or until cheese is golden and bubbling. Serve warm.

Per Serving:

calories: 178 | fat: 11g | protein: 15g | carbs: 10g | net carbs: 4g | fiber: 6g

Crustless Spinach Cheese Pie

Prep time: 10 minutes | Cook time: 20 minutes | Serves 4

- 6 large eggs
- ¼ cup heavy whipping cream
- 1 cup frozen chopped spinach, drained
- 1 cup shredded sharp Cheddar cheese
- ¼ cup diced yellow onion

1. In a medium bowl, whisk eggs and add cream. Add remaining ingredients to bowl. 2. Pour into a round baking dish. Place into the air fryer basket. 3. Adjust the temperature to 320ºF (160ºC) and bake for 20 minutes. 4. Eggs will be firm and slightly browned when cooked. Serve immediately.

Per Serving:

calories: 317 | fat: 24g | protein: 21g | carbs: 4g | net carbs: 3g | fiber: 1g

Cheesy Garden Veggie Crustless Quiche

Prep time: 5 minutes | Cook time: 25 minutes | Serves 4

- 1 tablespoon grass-fed butter, divided
- 6 eggs
- ¾ cup heavy (whipping) cream
- 3 ounces goat cheese, divided
- ½ cup sliced mushrooms, chopped
- 1 scallion, white and green parts, chopped
- 1 cup shredded fresh spinach
- 10 cherry tomatoes, cut in half

1. Preheat the oven. Set the oven temperature to 350°F. Grease a 9-inch pie plate with ½ teaspoon of the butter and set it aside. 2. Mix the quiche base. In a medium bowl, whisk the eggs, cream, and 2 ounces of the cheese until it's all well blended. Set it aside. 3. Sauté the vegetables. In a small skillet over medium-high heat, melt the remaining butter. Add the mushrooms and scallion and sauté them until they've softened, about 2 minutes. Add the spinach and sauté until it's wilted, about 2 minutes. 4. Assemble and bake. Spread the vegetable mixture in the bottom of the pie plate and pour the egg-and-cream mixture over the vegetables. Scatter the cherry tomatoes and the remaining 1 ounce of goat cheese on top. Bake for 20 to 25 minutes until the quiche is cooked through, puffed, and lightly browned. 5. Serve. Cut the quiche into wedges and divide it between four plates. Serve it warm or cold.

Per Serving:

calories: 355 | fat: 30g | protein: 18g | carbs: 5g | net carbs: 4g | fiber: 1g

Cauliflower Rice-Stuffed Peppers

Prep time: 10 minutes | Cook time: 15 minutes | Serves 4

- 2 cups uncooked cauliflower rice
- ¾ cup drained canned petite diced tomatoes
- 2 tablespoons olive oil
- 1 cup shredded Mozzarella cheese
- ¼ teaspoon salt
- ¼ teaspoon ground black pepper
- 4 medium green bell peppers, tops removed, seeded

1. In a large bowl, mix all ingredients except bell peppers. Scoop mixture evenly into peppers. 2. Place peppers into ungreased air fryer basket. Adjust the temperature to 350°F (177°C) and air fry for 15 minutes. Peppers will be tender and cheese will be melted when done. Serve warm.

Per Serving:
calories: 309 | fat: 23g | protein: 16g | carbs: 11g | net carbs: 7g | fiber: 4g

Crustless Spanakopita

Prep time: 15 minutes | Cook time: 45 minutes | Serves 6

- 12 tablespoons extra-virgin olive oil, divided
- 1 small yellow onion, diced
- 1 (32-ounce / 907-g) bag frozen chopped spinach, thawed, fully drained, and patted dry (about 4 cups)
- 4 garlic cloves, minced
- ½ teaspoon salt
- ½ teaspoon freshly ground black pepper
- 1 cup whole-milk ricotta cheese
- 4 large eggs
- ¾ cup crumbled traditional feta cheese
- ¼ cup pine nuts

1. Preheat the oven to 375°F (190°C). 2. In a large skillet, heat 4 tablespoons olive oil over medium-high heat. Add the onion and sauté until softened, 6 to 8 minutes. 3. Add the spinach, garlic, salt, and pepper and sauté another 5 minutes. Remove from the heat and allow to cool slightly. 4. In a medium bowl, whisk together the ricotta and eggs. Add to the cooled spinach and stir to combine. 5. Pour 4 tablespoons olive oil in the bottom of a 9-by-13-inch glass baking dish and swirl to coat the bottom and sides. Add the spinach-ricotta mixture and spread into an even layer. 6. Bake for 20 minutes or until the mixture begins to set. Remove from the oven and crumble the feta evenly across the top of the spinach. Add the pine nuts and drizzle with the remaining 4 tablespoons olive oil. Return to the oven and bake for an additional 15 to 20 minutes, or until the spinach is fully set and the top is starting to turn golden brown. Allow to cool slightly before cutting to serve.

Per Serving:
calories: 440 | fat: 38g | protein: 17g | carbs: 9g | net carbs: 8g | fiber: 1g

Spinach Cheese Casserole

Prep time: 15 minutes | Cook time: 15 minutes | Serves 4

- 1 tablespoon salted butter, melted
- ¼ cup diced yellow onion
- 8 ounces (227 g) full-fat cream cheese, softened
- ⅓ cup full-fat mayonnaise
- ⅓ cup full-fat sour cream
- ¼ cup chopped pickled jalapeños
- 2 cups fresh spinach, chopped
- 2 cups cauliflower florets, chopped
- 1 cup artichoke hearts, chopped

1. In a large bowl, mix butter, onion, cream cheese, mayonnaise, and sour cream. Fold in jalapeños, spinach, cauliflower, and artichokes. 2. Pour the mixture into a round baking dish. Cover with foil and place into the air fryer basket. 3. Adjust the temperature to 370°F (188°C) and set the timer for 15 minutes. In the last 2 minutes of cooking, remove the foil to brown the top. Serve warm.

Per Serving:
calories: 490 | fat: 46g | protein: 9g | carbs: 12g | net carbs: 8g | fiber: 4g

Cheese Stuffed Peppers

Prep time: 20 minutes | Cook time: 15 minutes | Serves 2

- 1 red bell pepper, top and seeds removed
- 1 yellow bell pepper, top and seeds removed
- Salt and pepper, to taste
- 1 cup Cottage cheese
- 4 tablespoons mayonnaise
- 2 pickles, chopped

1. Arrange the peppers in the lightly greased air fryer basket. Cook in the preheated air fryer at 400°F (204°C) for 15 minutes, turning them over halfway through the cooking time. 2. Season with salt and pepper. Then, in a mixing bowl, combine the cream cheese with the mayonnaise and chopped pickles. Stuff the pepper with the cream cheese mixture and serve. Enjoy!

Per Serving:
calories: 250 | fat: 20g | protein: 11g | carbs: 8g | net carbs: 6g | fiber: 2g

Vegetable Burgers

Prep time: 10 minutes | Cook time: 12 minutes | Serves 4

- 8 ounces (227 g) cremini mushrooms
- 2 large egg yolks
- ½ medium zucchini, trimmed and chopped
- ¼ cup peeled and
- chopped yellow onion
- 1 clove garlic, peeled and finely minced
- ½ teaspoon salt
- ¼ teaspoon ground black pepper

1. Place all ingredients into a food processor and pulse twenty times until finely chopped and combined. 2. Separate mixture into four equal sections and press each into a burger shape. Place burgers into ungreased air fryer basket. Adjust the temperature to 375ºF (191ºC) and air fry for 12 minutes, turning burgers halfway through cooking. Burgers will be browned and firm when done. 3. Place burgers on a large plate and let cool 5 minutes before serving.

Per Serving:

calories: 62 | fat: 3g | protein: 3g | carbs: 6g | net carbs: 4g | fiber: 2g

Greek Vegetable Briam

Prep time: 10 minutes | Cook time: 30 minutes | Serves 4

- ⅓ cup good-quality olive oil, divided
- 1 onion, thinly sliced
- 1 tablespoon minced garlic
- ¾ small eggplant, diced
- 2 zucchini, diced
- 2 cups chopped cauliflower
- 1 red bell pepper, diced
- 2 cups diced tomatoes
- 2 tablespoons chopped fresh parsley
- 2 tablespoons chopped fresh oregano
- Sea salt, for seasoning
- Freshly ground black pepper, for seasoning
- 1½ cups crumbled feta cheese
- ¼ cup pumpkin seeds

1. Preheat the oven. Set the oven to broil and lightly grease a 9-by-13-inch casserole dish with olive oil. 2. Sauté the aromatics. In a medium stockpot over medium heat, warm 3 tablespoons of the olive oil. Add the onion and garlic and sauté until they've softened, about 3 minutes. 3. Sauté the vegetables. Stir in the eggplant and cook for 5 minutes, stirring occasionally. Add the zucchini, cauliflower, and red bell pepper and cook for 5 minutes. Stir in the tomatoes, parsley, and oregano and cook, giving it a stir from time to time, until the vegetables are tender, about 10 minutes. Season it with salt and pepper. 4. Broil. Transfer the vegetable mixture to the casserole dish and top with the crumbled feta. Broil for about 4 minutes until the cheese is golden. 5. Serve. Divide the casserole between four plates and top it with the pumpkin seeds. Drizzle with the remaining olive oil.

Per Serving:

calories: 356 | fat: 28g | protein: 11g | carbs: 18g | net carbs: 11g | fiber: 7g

Mediterranean Pan Pizza

Prep time: 5 minutes | Cook time: 8 minutes | Serves 2

- 1 cup shredded Mozzarella cheese
- ¼ medium red bell pepper, seeded and chopped
- ½ cup chopped fresh
- spinach leaves
- 2 tablespoons chopped black olives
- 2 tablespoons crumbled feta cheese

1. Sprinkle Mozzarella into an ungreased round nonstick baking dish in an even layer. Add remaining ingredients on top. 2. Place dish into air fryer basket. Adjust the temperature to 350ºF (177ºC) and bake for 8 minutes, checking halfway through to avoid burning. Top of pizza will be golden brown and the cheese melted when done. 3. Remove dish from fryer and let cool 5 minutes before slicing and serving.

Per Serving:

calories: 239 | fat: 17g | protein: 17g | carbs: 6g | net carbs: 5g | fiber: 1g

Parmesan Artichokes

Prep time: 10 minutes | Cook time: 10 minutes | Serves 4

- 2 medium artichokes, trimmed and quartered, center removed
- 2 tablespoons coconut oil
- 1 large egg, beaten
- ½ cup grated vegetarian
- Parmesan cheese
- ¼ cup blanched finely ground almond flour
- ½ teaspoon crushed red pepper flakes

1. In a large bowl, toss artichokes in coconut oil and then dip each piece into the egg. 2. Mix the Parmesan and almond flour in a large bowl. Add artichoke pieces and toss to cover as completely as possible, sprinkle with pepper flakes. Place into the air fryer basket. 3. Adjust the temperature to 400ºF (204ºC) and air fry for 10 minutes. 4. Toss the basket two times during cooking. Serve warm.

Per Serving:

calories: 220 | fat: 18g | protein: 10g | carbs: 9g | net carbs: 4g | fiber: 5g

Stuffed Portobellos

Prep time: 10 minutes | Cook time: 8 minutes | Serves 4

- 3 ounces (85 g) cream cheese, softened
- ½ medium zucchini, trimmed and chopped
- ¼ cup seeded and chopped red bell pepper
- 1½ cups chopped fresh

- spinach leaves
- 4 large portobello mushrooms, stems removed
- 2 tablespoons coconut oil, melted
- ½ teaspoon salt

1. In a medium bowl, mix cream cheese, zucchini, pepper, and spinach. 2. Drizzle mushrooms with coconut oil and sprinkle with salt. Scoop ¼ zucchini mixture into each mushroom. 3. Place mushrooms into ungreased air fryer basket. Adjust the temperature to 400ºF (204ºC) and air fry for 8 minutes. Portobellos will be tender and tops will be browned when done. Serve warm.

Per Serving:

calories: 157 | fat: 14g | protein: 4g | carbs: 5g | net carbs: 3g | fiber: 2g

Zucchini and Spinach Croquettes

Prep time: 9 minutes | Cook time: 7 minutes | Serves 6

- 4 eggs, slightly beaten
- ½ cup almond flour
- ½ cup goat cheese, crumbled
- 1 teaspoon fine sea salt
- 4 garlic cloves, minced
- 1 cup baby spinach
- ½ cup Parmesan cheese,

- grated
- ⅓ teaspoon red pepper flakes
- 1 pound (454 g) zucchini, peeled and grated
- ⅓ teaspoon dried dill weed

1. Thoroughly combine all ingredients in a bowl. Now, roll the mixture to form small croquettes. 2. Air fry at 340ºF (171ºC) for 7 minutes or until golden. Tate, adjust for seasonings and serve warm.

Per Serving:

calories: 179 | fat: 12g | protein: 11g | carbs: 6g | net carbs: 3g | fiber: 3g

Basic Spaghetti Squash

Prep time: 10 minutes | Cook time: 45 minutes | Serves 2

- ½ large spaghetti squash
- 1 tablespoon coconut oil
- 2 tablespoons salted butter, melted

- ½ teaspoon garlic powder
- 1 teaspoon dried parsley

1. Brush shell of spaghetti squash with coconut oil. Place the skin side down and brush the inside with butter. Sprinkle with garlic powder and parsley. 2. Place squash with the skin side down into the air fryer basket. 3. Adjust the temperature to 350ºF (177ºC) and air fry for 30 minutes. 4. Flip the squash so skin side is up and cook an additional 15 minutes or until fork tender. Serve warm.

Per Serving:

calories: 180 | fat: 17g | protein: 1g | carbs: 8g | net carbs: 5g | fiber: 3g

Whole Roasted Lemon Cauliflower

Prep time: 5 minutes | Cook time: 15 minutes | Serves 4

- 1 medium head cauliflower
- 2 tablespoons salted butter, melted

- 1 medium lemon
- ½ teaspoon garlic powder
- 1 teaspoon dried parsley

1. Remove the leaves from the head of cauliflower and brush it with melted butter. Cut the lemon in half and zest one half onto the cauliflower. Squeeze the juice of the zested lemon half and pour it over the cauliflower. 2. Sprinkle with garlic powder and parsley. Place cauliflower head into the air fryer basket. 3. Adjust the temperature to 350ºF (177ºC) and air fry for 15 minutes. 4. Check cauliflower every 5 minutes to avoid overcooking. It should be fork tender. 5. To serve, squeeze juice from other lemon half over cauliflower. Serve immediately.

Per Serving:

calories: 90 | fat: 7g | protein: 3g | carbs: 6g | net carbs: 4g | fiber: 2g

Caprese Eggplant Stacks

Prep time: 5 minutes | Cook time: 12 minutes | Serves 4

- ➢ 1 medium eggplant, cut into ¼-inch slices
- ➢ 2 large tomatoes, cut into ¼-inch slices
- ➢ 4 ounces (113 g) fresh Mozzarella, cut into ½-ounce /
- 14-g slices
- ➢ 2 tablespoons olive oil
- ➢ ¼ cup fresh basil, sliced

1. In a baking dish, place four slices of eggplant on the bottom. Place a slice of tomato on top of each eggplant round, then Mozzarella, then eggplant. Repeat as necessary. 2. Drizzle with olive oil. Cover dish with foil and place dish into the air fryer basket. 3. Adjust the temperature to 350ºF (177ºC) and bake for 12 minutes. 4. When done, eggplant will be tender. Garnish with fresh basil to serve.

Per Serving:

calories: 203 | fat: 16g | protein: 8g | carbs: 10g | net carbs: 7g | fiber: 3g

Cheesy Cauliflower Pizza Crust

Prep time: 15 minutes | Cook time: 11 minutes | Serves 2

- ➢ 1 (12 ounces / 340 g) steamer bag cauliflower
- ➢ ½ cup shredded sharp Cheddar cheese
- ➢ 1 large egg
- ➢ 2 tablespoons blanched finely ground almond flour
- ➢ 1 teaspoon Italian blend seasoning

1. Cook cauliflower according to package instructions. Remove from bag and place into cheesecloth or paper towel to remove excess water. Place cauliflower into a large bowl. 2. Add cheese, egg, almond flour, and Italian seasoning to the bowl and mix well. 3. Cut a piece of parchment to fit your air fryer basket. Press cauliflower into 6-inch round circle. Place into the air fryer basket. 4. Adjust the temperature to 360ºF (182ºC) and air fry for 11 minutes. 5. After 7 minutes, flip the pizza crust. 6. Add preferred toppings to pizza. Place back into air fryer basket and cook an additional 4 minutes or until fully cooked and golden. Serve immediately.

Per Serving:

calories: 248 | fat: 18g | protein: 16g | carbs: 8g | net carbs: 4g | fiber: 4g

Chapter **9**

Desserts

Strawberry Panna Cotta

Prep time: 10 minutes | Cook time: 10 minutes | Serves 4

- 2 tablespoons warm water
- 2 teaspoons gelatin powder
- 2 cups heavy cream
- 1 cup sliced strawberries, plus more for garnish
- 1 to 2 tablespoons sugar-free sweetener of choice (optional)
- 1½ teaspoons pure vanilla extract
- 4 to 6 fresh mint leaves, for garnish (optional)

1. Pour the warm water into a small bowl. Sprinkle the gelatin over the water and stir well to dissolve. Allow the mixture to sit for 10 minutes. 2. In a blender or a large bowl, if using an immersion blender, combine the cream, strawberries, sweetener (if using), and vanilla. Blend until the mixture is smooth and the strawberries are well puréed. 3. Transfer the mixture to a saucepan and heat over medium-low heat until just below a simmer. Remove from the heat and cool for 5 minutes. 4. Whisking constantly, add in the gelatin mixture until smooth. Divide the custard between ramekins or small glass bowls, cover and refrigerate until set, 4 to 6 hours. 5. Serve chilled, garnishing with additional sliced strawberries or mint leaves (if using).

Per Serving:

calories: 540 | fat: 57g | protein: 6g | carbs: 8g | net carbs: 7g | fiber: 1g

Lush Chocolate Cake

Prep time: 10 minutes | Cook time: 35 minutes | Serves 8

For Cake:
- 2 cups almond flour
- ⅓ cup unsweetened cocoa powder
- 1½ teaspoons baking powder
- 1 cup granulated erythritol
- Pinch of salt
- 4 eggs
- 1 teaspoon vanilla extract
- ½ cup butter, melted and cooled
- 6 tablespoons strong coffee, cooled
- ½ cup water

For Frosting:
- 4 ounces (113 g) cream cheese, softened
- ½ cup butter, softened
- ¼ teaspoon vanilla extract
- 2½ tablespoons powdered erythritol
- 2 tablespoons unsweetened cocoa powder

1. To make the cake: In a large bowl, whisk together the almond flour, cocoa powder, baking powder, granulated erythritol, and salt. Whisk well to remove any lumps. 2. Add the eggs and vanilla and mix with a hand mixer until combined. 3. With the mixer still on low speed, slowly add the melted butter and mix until well combined. 4. Add the coffee and mix on low speed until the batter is thoroughly combined. Scrape the sides and bottom of the bowl to make sure everything is well mixed. 5. Spray the cake pan with cooking spray. Pour the batter into the pan. Cover tightly with aluminum foil. 6. Add the water to the pot. Place the cake pan on the trivet and carefully lower then pan into the pot. 7. Close the lid. Select Manual mode and set cooking time for 35 minutes on High Pressure. 8. When timer beeps, use a quick pressure release and open the lid. 9. Carefully remove the cake pan from the pot and place on a wire rack to cool. Flip the cake onto a plate once it is cool enough to touch. Cool completely before frosting. 10. To make the frosting: In a medium bowl, use the mixer to whip the cream cheese, butter, and vanilla until light and fluffy, 1 to 2 minutes. With the mixer running, slowly add the powdered erythritol and cocoa powder. Mix until everything is well combined. 11. Once the cake is completely cooled, spread the frosting on the top and down the sides.

Per Serving:

calories: 475 | fat: 44g | protein: 11g | carbs: 9g | net carbs: 4g | fiber: 4g

Electrolyte Gummies

Prep time: 5 minutes | Cook time: 0 minutes | Makes 10 gummies

- 1 cup cold water
- 2 tablespoons unflavored gelatin
- 2 packets/scoops flavored electrolyte powder

Stovetop Directions 1. In a small saucepan, whisk together the water and gelatin until dissolved. Heat over medium heat for about 5 minutes until it just begins to simmer. Add your flavoring of choice and whisk until well combined. 2. Pour the mixture into silicone molds and refrigerate for 30 to 40 minutes or until set. 3. Pop the gummies out of the molds and enjoy! Microwave Directions 1. Pour the water into a small microwavable bowl or measuring cup (preferably with a spout). 2. Whisk in the gelatin until dissolved and then microwave for 2 minutes or until just starting to bubble. 3. Add your flavoring of choice and whisk until well combined. 4. Pour the mixture into silicone molds and refrigerate for 30 to 40 minutes or until set. 5. Pop the gummies out of the molds and enjoy! Store in an airtight container in the refrigerator for up to 3 weeks.

Per Serving:

1 gummy: calories: 4 | fat: 0g | protein: 1g | carbs: 0g | net carbs: 0g | fiber: 0g

Jelly Pie Jars

Prep time: 20 minutes | Cook time: 15 minutes | Serves 8

- Coconut oil, for the jars

Pie Base:
- 1 cup (110 g) blanched almond flour
- 1 tablespoon plus 1½ teaspoons whisked egg (about ½ large egg)
- 1 tablespoon lard
- 2 drops liquid stevia
- ¼ teaspoon ground cinnamon
- Pinch of finely ground gray sea salt

Jam Filling:
- 1½ heaping cups (260 g) fresh blackberries
- ⅓ cup (80 ml) water
- 1½ teaspoons vanilla extract
- 3 drops liquid stevia
- ¼ cup (38 g) chia seeds
- 1½ teaspoons balsamic vinegar

Almond Butter Topping:
- ¾ cup (210 g) unsweetened smooth almond butter
- ¼ cup (60 ml) melted coconut oil or ghee (if tolerated)
- 1 teaspoon ground cinnamon
- 2 to 4 drops liquid stevia

For Garnish (Optional):
- 16 to 24 fresh blackberries

1. Preheat the oven to 325°F (163°C). Grease eight 4-ounce (120-ml) mason jars with a dab of coconut oil and set on a rimmed baking sheet. 2. To prepare the base, place the ingredients for the base in a large bowl and mix with a fork until fully combined. 3. Divide the dough evenly among the jars, pressing it in firmly and evening it out with your fingers. Place the jars back on the baking sheet and bake for 15 to 17 minutes, until the tops are golden. Remove from the oven and allow to cool completely, at least 30 minutes. Meanwhile, make the filling. 4. To prepare the jam filling, place the blackberries, water, vanilla, and stevia in a medium-sized saucepan. Cook, covered, over medium heat for 5 minutes. 5. Reduce the heat to low and add the chia seeds and balsamic vinegar. Cook, uncovered, for another 3 to 4 minutes, stirring frequently, until the mixture has thickened. Transfer the mixture to a heat-safe bowl and set aside to cool to room temperature, at least 30 minutes. 6. To prepare the almond butter topping, place the topping ingredients in a small bowl and whisk to combine. 7. To assemble, divide the cooled jam filling among the jars, being sure to keep the layer as flat as possible. Then add the almond butter topping, pouring it in slowly to avoid spillover. Transfer the assembled jars to the fridge to cool for 30 minutes. 8. Before serving, top each jar with 2 or 3 blackberries, if desired. Enjoy!

Per Serving:
calories: 388 | fat: 32g | protein: 11g | carbs: 13g | net carbs: 4g | fiber: 9g

Whipped Cream

Prep time: 5 minutes | Cook time: 0 minutes | Makes 2 cups

- 1 cup heavy whipping cream
- 2 tablespoons granular
- erythritol
- 1 teaspoon vanilla extract

1. Place the ingredients in a large mixing bowl. Use a hand mixer or stand mixer to blend until stiff peaks form. Whipped cream is best if used the same day it's made, but leftovers can be stored in an airtight container in the refrigerator for up to 3 days.

Per Serving:
calories: 220 | fat: 22g | protein: 1g | carbs: 1g | net carbs: 1g | fiber: 0g

Chocolate Macadamia Bark

Prep time: 5 minutes | Cook time: 20 minutes | Serves 20

- 16 ounces (454 g) raw dark chocolate
- 3 tablespoons raw coconut butter
- 2 tablespoons coconut oil
- 2 cups chopped
- macadamia nuts
- 1 tablespoon almond butter
- ½ teaspoon salt
- ⅓ cup Swerve, or more to taste

1. In a large bowl, mix together the chocolate, coconut butter, coconut oil, macadamia nuts, almond butter, salt, and Swerve. Combine them very thoroughly, until a perfectly even mixture is obtained. 2. Pour 1 cup of filtered water into the Instant Pot, and insert the trivet. Transfer the mixture from the bowl into a well-greased, Instant Pot-friendly dish. 3. Place the dish onto the trivet, and cover loosely with aluminum foil. Close the lid, set the pressure release to Sealing, and select Manual. Set the Instant Pot to 20 minutes on High Pressure, and let cook. 4. Once cooked, let the pressure naturally disperse from the Instant Pot for about 10 minutes, then carefully switch the pressure release to Venting. 5. Open the Instant Pot and remove the dish. Cool in the refrigerator until set. Break into pieces, serve, and enjoy! Store remaining bark in the refrigerator or freezer.

Per Serving:
calories: 258 | fat: 22g | protein: 2g | carbs: 15g | net carbs: 12g | fiber: 3g

Cheesecake

Prep time: 10 minutes | Cook time: 40 minutes | Serves 4

Crust:
- ⅔ cup almond flour
- 2 teaspoons granulated erythritol
- ¼ teaspoon psyllium husk powder
- ⅛ teaspoon ground

cinnamon
- 2 tablespoons butter, melted
- 1½ teaspoons heavy (whipping) cream

Filling:
- 8 ounces (227 g) full-fat cream cheese, at room temperature
- 1 large egg
- 2 tablespoons granulated erythritol

- 2 tablespoons sour cream
- ¼ teaspoon freshly squeezed lemon juice
- ½ teaspoon liquid stevia
- Pinch of pink Himalayan sea salt

1. Preheat the oven to 325ºF (163ºC). 2. To make the crust: In a small bowl, combine the almond flour, erythritol, psyllium husk powder, and cinnamon. 3. Add the butter and cream and combine with a fork. 4. Transfer the mixture to a 7-inch springform pan. 5. Using a fork or your hands, pack the mixture against the bottom of the pan to form a crust. Do not put crust up the sides. 6. To make the filling: In a large mixing bowl, using a whisk or hand mixer on medium-high speed, combine the cream cheese, egg, erythritol, sour cream, lemon juice, stevia, and salt. 7. Pour the filling directly over the crust. 8. Bake for 38 to 40 minutes, until the very edges have a hint of brown. 9. Remove cheesecake from the oven and let cool for 1 hour. Release the springform pan and transfer the cheesecake to the refrigerator to chill for at least 1 hour. 10. Cut the cheesecake into 4 pieces and serve.

Per Serving:

calories: 373 | fat: 36g | protein: 9g | carbs: 6g | net carbs: 4g | fiber: 2g

Sweetened Condensed Coconut Milk

Prep time: 10 minutes | Cook time: 35 minutes | Serves 12

- 1 (13½ ounces/400 ml) can full-fat coconut milk
- 2 tablespoons

confectioners'-style erythritol

1. Place all the ingredients in a small saucepan and bring to a rapid boil over medium-high heat. Reduce the heat and simmer lightly for 32 to 35 minutes, until the milk has thickened and reduced by about half. Use immediately in a recipe that calls for it, or let it cool and store in the fridge for later use.

Per Serving:

calories: 68 | fat: 7g | protein: 1g | carbs: 1g | net carbs: 1g | fiber: 0g

Olive Oil Cake

Prep time: 10 minutes | Cook time: 30 minutes | Serves 8

- 2 cups blanched finely ground almond flour
- 5 large eggs, whisked
- ¾ cup extra-virgin olive oil

- ⅓ cup granular erythritol
- 1 teaspoon vanilla extract
- 1 teaspoon baking powder

1. In a large bowl, mix all ingredients. Pour batter into an ungreased round nonstick baking dish. 2. Place dish into air fryer basket. Adjust the temperature to 300ºF (149ºC) and bake for 30 minutes. The cake will be golden on top and firm in the center when done. 3. Let cake cool in dish 30 minutes before slicing and serving.

Per Serving:

calories: 363 | fat: 35g | protein: 9g | carbs: 6g | net carbs: 3g | fiber: 3g

Hazelnut Butter Cookies

Prep time: 30 minutes | Cook time: 20 minutes | Serves 10

- 4 tablespoons liquid monk fruit
- ½ cup hazelnuts, ground
- 1 stick butter, room temperature
- 2 cups almond flour

- 1 cup coconut flour
- 2 ounces (57 g) granulated Swerve
- 2 teaspoons ground cinnamon

1. Firstly, cream liquid monk fruit with butter until the mixture becomes fluffy. Sift in both types of flour. 2. Now, stir in the hazelnuts. Now, knead the mixture to form a dough; place in the refrigerator for about 35 minutes. 3. To finish, shape the prepared dough into the bite-sized balls; arrange them on a baking dish; flatten the balls using the back of a spoon. 4. Mix granulated Swerve with ground cinnamon. Press your cookies in the cinnamon mixture until they are completely covered. 5. Bake the cookies for 20 minutes at 310ºF (154ºC). 6. Leave them to cool for about 10 minutes before transferring them to a wire rack. Bon appétit!

Per Serving:

calories: 244 | fat: 24g | protein: 5g | carbs: 6g | net carbs: 2g | fiber: 4g

Cholesterol Caring Nut Clusters

Prep time: 5 minutes | Cook time: 20 minutes | Makes 18 mini clusters

Cluster Base:
- 1 cup macadamia nuts
- 1 cup pecan halves
- ½ cup pistachios
- ¼ cup tahini or coconut butter (although tahini is preferable)
- 1 large egg
- 1 teaspoon vanilla powder
- 2 teaspoons cinnamon

Topping:
- 2 ounces (57 g) dark chocolate
- 1 tablespoon virgin coconut oil or cacao butter
- Pinch of flaked salt

1. Preheat the oven to 285°F (140°C) fan assisted or 320°F (160°C) conventional. 2. Make the cluster base: Roughly chop the nuts or place in a food processor and pulse until chopped but still chunky. Add the remaining base ingredients. Press the "dough" into 18 mini muffin cups and bake for 15 to 20 minutes, until crispy. Remove from the oven and allow to cool completely. Just before adding the chocolate topping, place them in the freezer for 5 to 10 minutes. 3. Meanwhile, make the topping: Melt the dark chocolate and coconut oil in a double boiler, or use a heatproof bowl placed over a small saucepan filled with 1 cup of water, placed over medium heat. Let cool to room temperature. Alternatively, use a microwave and melt in short 10- to 15-second bursts until melted, stirring in between. 4. Top the cooled clusters with the melted dark chocolate and flaked salt. Store in a sealed container in the fridge for up to 2 weeks or freeze for up to 3 months.

Per Serving:
calories: 149 | fat: 14g | protein: 3g | carbs: 5g | net carbs: 3g | fiber: 2g

Iced Tea Lemonade Gummies

Prep time: 10 minutes | Cook time: 5 minutes | Serves 4

- ¾ cup (180 ml) boiling water
- 3 tea bags
- ¼ cup (40 g) unflavored gelatin
- ¾ cup (180 ml) fresh lemon juice
- 2 tablespoons confectioners'-style erythritol or granulated xylitol

Special Equipment:
- Silicone mold(s) with 36 (½ ounce/15 ml) cavities

1. Set the silicone mold(s) on a rimmed baking sheet. 2. Place the boiling water in a heat-safe mug and steep the tea according to type, following the suggested steep time on the package. Once complete, remove the tea bags and wring out as much liquid from the bags as possible. Sprinkle the gelatin over the tea and set aside. 3. Pour the lemon juice into a small saucepan. Add the erythritol and bring to a light simmer over medium heat, about 5 minutes. 4. Once at a light simmer, remove the pan from the heat. Whisk the tea mixture until the gelatin dissolves, then pour it into the hot lemon juice mixture. Whisk to combine. 5. Pour the hot mixture into the mold(s) and transfer the baking sheet to the fridge to set for at least 1 hour. Once firm, remove the gummies from the mold(s) and enjoy!

Per Serving:
calories: 48 | fat: 0g | protein: 10g | carbs: 1g | net carbs: 1g | fiber: 0g

Pumpkin Cookie with Cream Cheese Frosting

Prep time: 10 minutes | Cook time: 7 minutes | Serves 6

- ½ cup blanched finely ground almond flour
- ½ cup powdered erythritol, divided
- 2 tablespoons butter, softened
- 1 large egg
- ½ teaspoon unflavored gelatin
- ½ teaspoon baking powder
- ½ teaspoon vanilla extract
- ½ teaspoon pumpkin pie spice
- 2 tablespoons pure pumpkin purée
- ½ teaspoon ground cinnamon, divided
- ¼ cup low-carb, sugar-free chocolate chips
- 3 ounces (85 g) full-fat cream cheese, softened

1. In a large bowl, mix almond flour and ¼ cup erythritol. Stir in butter, egg, and gelatin until combined. 2. Stir in baking powder, vanilla, pumpkin pie spice, pumpkin purée, and ¼ teaspoon cinnamon, then fold in chocolate chips. 3. Pour batter into a round baking pan. Place pan into the air fryer basket. 4. Adjust the temperature to 300°F (149°C) and bake for 7 minutes. 5. When fully cooked, the top will be golden brown and a toothpick inserted in center will come out clean. Let cool at least 20 minutes. 6. To make the frosting: mix cream cheese, remaining ¼ teaspoon cinnamon, and remaining ¼ cup erythritol in a large bowl. Using an electric mixer, beat until it becomes fluffy. Spread onto the cooled cookie. Garnish with additional cinnamon if desired.

Per Serving:
calories: 186 | fat: 16g | protein: 4g | carbs: 5g | net carbs: 4g | fiber: 2g

Chocolate Chip Almond Cookies

Prep time: 15 minutes | Cook time: 10 minutes | Makes 20 cookies

- 1 cup grass-fed butter, at room temperature
- ¾ cup monk fruit sweetener, granulated form
- 2 eggs
- 1 tablespoon vanilla extract
- 3½ cups almond flour
- 1 teaspoon baking soda
- ½ teaspoon sea salt
- 1½ cups keto-friendly chocolate chips, like Lily's Dark Chocolate Chips

1. Preheat the oven. Set the oven temperature to 350°F. Line a baking sheet with parchment paper and set it aside. 2. Mix the wet ingredients. In a large bowl, cream the butter and sweetener until the mixture is very fluffy, either by hand or with a hand mixer. Add the eggs and vanilla and beat until everything is well blended. 3. Mix the dry ingredients. In a medium bowl, stir together the almond flour, baking soda, and salt until they're well mixed together. 4. Add the dry to the wet ingredients. Stir the dry ingredients into the wet ingredients and mix until everything is well combined. Stir in the chocolate chips. 5. Bake. Drop the batter by tablespoons onto the baking sheet about 2 inches apart and flatten them down slightly. Bake the cookies for 10 minutes, or until they're golden. Repeat with any remaining dough. Transfer the cookies to a wire rack and let them cool. 6. Store. Store the cookies in a sealed container in the refrigerator for up to five days, or in the freezer for up to one month.

Per Serving:

calories: 226 | fat: 27g | protein: 3g | carbs: 1g | net carbs: 0g | fiber: 1g

Baked Cheesecake

Prep time: 30 minutes | Cook time: 35 minutes | Serves 6

- ½ cup almond flour
- 1½ tablespoons unsalted butter, melted
- 2 tablespoons erythritol
- 1 (8 ounces / 227 g) package cream cheese,

softened
- ¼ cup powdered erythritol
- ½ teaspoon vanilla paste
- 1 egg, at room temperature

Topping:
- 1½ cups sour cream
- 3 tablespoons powdered erythritol
- 1 teaspoon vanilla extract

1. Thoroughly combine the almond flour, butter, and 2 tablespoons of erythritol in a mixing bowl. Press the mixture into the bottom of lightly greased custard cups. 2. Then, mix the cream cheese, ¼ cup of powdered erythritol, vanilla, and egg using an electric mixer on low speed. Pour the batter into the pan, covering the crust. 3. Bake in the preheated air fryer at 330°F (166°C) for 35 minutes until edges are puffed and the surface is firm. 4. Mix the sour cream, 3 tablespoons of powdered erythritol, and vanilla for the topping; spread over the crust and allow it to cool to room temperature. 5. Transfer to your refrigerator for 6 to 8 hours. Serve well chilled.

Per Serving:

calories: 290 | fat: 27g | protein: 6g | carbs: 7g | net carbs: 4g | fiber: 3g

Fudge Pops

Prep time: 5 minutes | Cook time: 0 minutes | serves 4

- 1 (14-ounce) can full-fat coconut cream
- 3 avocados, peeled, pitted, and chopped
- ⅓ cup cacao powder
- 5 or 6 drops liquid stevia
- ⅓ cup freshly grated orange zest
- Sea salt

1. In a high-powered blender, combine the coconut cream with the avocados, cacao powder, and stevia. 2. Whip the mixture in the blender for 5 minutes until it becomes airy. 3. Stir in the orange zest and salt and pour the mixture into popsicle molds. 4. Place the molds in the freezer overnight to set. 5. To serve, run warm water over the popsicle molds to loosen the fudge pops.

Per Serving:

calories: 434 | fat: 40g | protein: 4g | carbs: 21g | net carbs: 9g | fiber: 12g

Coffee Fat Bombs

Prep time: 5 minutes | Cook time: 0 minutes | Serves 6

- 1½ cups mascarpone cheese
- ½ cup melted butter
- 3 tablespoons unsweetened cocoa

powder
- ¼ cup erythritol
- 6 tablespoons brewed coffee, room temperature

1. Whisk the mascarpone cheese, butter, cocoa powder, erythritol, and coffee with a hand mixer until creamy and fluffy, for 1 minute. Fill into muffin tins and freeze for 3 hours until firm.

Per Serving:

calories: 505 | fat: 52g | protein: 6g | carbs: 6g | net carbs: 3g | fiber: 3g

Candied Mixed Nuts

Prep time: 5 minutes | Cook time: 15 minutes | Serves 8

- 1 cup pecan halves
- 1 cup chopped walnuts
- ⅓ cup Swerve, or more to taste
- ⅓ cup grass-fed butter
- 1 teaspoon ground cinnamon

1. Preheat your oven to 350ºF (180ºC), and line a baking sheet with aluminum foil. 2. While your oven is warming, pour ½ cup of filtered water into the inner pot of the Instant Pot, followed by the pecans, walnuts, Swerve, butter, and cinnamon. Stir nut mixture, close the lid, and then set the pressure valve to Sealing. Use the Manual mode to cook at High Pressure, for 5 minutes. 3. Once cooked, perform a quick release by carefully switching the pressure valve to Venting, and strain the nuts. Pour the nuts onto the baking sheet, spreading them out in an even layer. Place in the oven for 5 to 10 minutes (or until crisp, being careful not to overcook). Cool before serving. Store leftovers in the refrigerator or freezer.

Per Serving:

calories: 122 | fat: 12g | protein: 4g | carbs: 3g | net carbs: 1g | fiber: 2g

Cinnamon Churros

Prep time: 25 minutes | Cook time: 30 minutes | Serves 12

- Churros
- ⅔ cup unblanched almond flour
- ¼ cup coconut flour
- 1 tablespoon flaxseed meal
- 1 teaspoon xanthan gum
- 1 cup water
- ¼ cup unsalted butter
- 2 tablespoons 0g net carb sweetener
- ¼ teaspoon salt
- 2 large eggs, lightly beaten
- 1 teaspoon pure vanilla extract
- Garnish
- 1 tablespoon unsalted butter, melted
- 2 teaspoons ground cinnamon
- ¼ cup 0g net carb sweetener

1. Preheat oven to 350°F. Line a large baking sheet with parchment paper. 2. In a medium bowl, whisk together almond flour, coconut flour, flaxseed meal, and xanthan gum. 3. In a medium pot over medium heat, heat water almost to a boil and mix in ¼ cup butter, 2 tablespoons sweetener, and ¼ teaspoon salt until butter is melted and well blended. Add flour mix and keep stirring until a ball is formed. 4. Return dough to bowl and let cool for 5 minutes. Mix eggs and vanilla in with dough. 5. Let dough cool to room temperature, 10–15 minutes. Transfer dough into a pastry piping bag with star tip. Make twelve churros and place on baking sheet. 6. Bake 15–20 minutes until deep golden. 7. Remove from oven and brush with butter. Garnish with cinnamon and sweetener. Serve warm.

Per Serving:

calories: 100 | fat: 9g | protein: 3g | carbs: 6g | net carbs: 2g | fiber: 4g

Appendix ❶
Conversion Chart

VOLUME EQUIVALENTS(DRY)

US STANDARD	METRIC (APPROXIMATE)
1/8 teaspoon	0.5 mL
1/4 teaspoon	1 mL
1/2 teaspoon	2 mL
3/4 teaspoon	4 mL
1 teaspoon	5 mL
1 tablespoon	15 mL
1/4 cup	59 mL
1/2 cup	118 mL
3/4 cup	177 mL
1 cup	235 mL
2 cups	475 mL
3 cups	700 mL
4 cups	1 L

VOLUME EQUIVALENTS(LIQUID)

US STANDARD	US STANDARD (OUNCES)	METRIC (APPROXIMATE)
2 tablespoons	1 fl.oz.	30 mL
1/4 cup	2 fl.oz.	60 mL
1/2 cup	4 fl.oz.	120 mL
1 cup	8 fl.oz.	240 mL
1 1/2 cup	12 fl.oz.	355 mL
2 cups or 1 pint	16 fl.oz.	475 mL
4 cups or 1 quart	32 fl.oz.	1 L
1 gallon	128 fl.oz.	4 L

TEMPERATURES EQUIVALENTS

FAHRENHEIT(F)	CELSIUS(C) (APPROXIMATE)
225 °F	107 °C
250 °F	120 °C
275 °F	135 °C
300 °F	150 °C
325 °F	160 °C
350 °F	180 °C
375 °F	190 °C
400 °F	205 °C
425 °F	220 °C
450 °F	235 °C
475 °F	245 °C
500 °F	260 °C

WEIGHT EQUIVALENTS

US STANDARD	METRIC (APPROXIMATE)
1 ounce	28 g
2 ounces	57 g
5 ounces	142 g
10 ounces	284 g
15 ounces	425 g
16 ounces (1 pound)	455 g
1.5 pounds	680 g
2 pounds	907 g

Appendix ❷

The Dirty Dozen and Clean Fifteen

The Environmental Working Group (EWG) is a nonprofit, nonpartisan organization dedicated to protecting human health and the environment Its mission is to empower people to live healthier lives in a healthier environment. This organization publishes an annual list of the twelve kinds of produce, in sequence, that have the highest amount of pesticide residue-the Dirty Dozen-as well as a list of the fifteen kinds ofproduce that have the least amount of pesticide residue-the Clean Fifteen.

THE DIRTY DOZEN	THE CLEAN FIFTEEN
• The 2016 Dirty Dozen includes the following produce. These are considered among the year's most important produce to buy organic:	• The least critical to buy organically are the Clean Fifteen list. The following are on the 2016 list:

THE DIRTY DOZEN

Strawberries	Spinach
Apples	Tomatoes
Nectarines	Bell peppers
Peaches	Cherry tomatoes
Celery	Cucumbers
Grapes	Kale/collard greens
Cherries	Hot peppers

• *The Dirty Dozen list contains two additional itemskale/collard greens and hot peppers-because they tend to contain trace levels of highly hazardous pesticides.*

THE CLEAN FIFTEEN

Avocados	Papayas
Corn	Kiw
Pineapples	Eggplant
Cabbage	Honeydew
Sweet peas	Grapefruit
Onions	Cantaloupe
Asparagus	Cauliflower
Mangos	

• *Some of the sweet corn sold in the United States are made from genetically engineered (GE) seedstock. Buy organic varieties of these crops to avoid GE produce.*

Appendix ❸

Recipe Index

T

V

W

Z

Made in the USA
Coppell, TX
11 November 2024

40019263R00057